'This skilfully written devotiona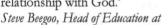
all set in the context of biblical
to those who recognise their
relationship with God.'
Steve Beegoo, Head of Education at

'In Isaiah, God's people are li
fletcher, but being so remote from those days the beauty of the
metaphor is easily missed by us. Jenny carefully and biblically takes us
through each "fletching" stage, showing how it relates to our daily
walk with God into His glorious purposes. I heartily recommend it.'
John Peel, former prison governor; retired pastor, teacher; Plymouth

'It's time for followers of Jesus to step up and press in. We're living
in a period of cultural turmoil that is desperately crying out for
relevance and authenticity. There's no higher calling than becoming
one of God's "polished arrows" – ready, willing and obedient to His
call. Jenny unpacks the process of how God makes His arrows ready
to fulfil His purposes. Will you be one of them?'
*Simon Guillebaud, evangelist, author, speaker, founder of Great Lakes Outreach,
Burundi*

'This book is a challenging call to action for every Christian in a world
which seems to be falling apart and spiralling downwards into chaos
with a lack of accepted morals and culture. It is life changing and
brings home the reality of the spiritual battle we are facing.'
Alan Evans OBE, Church of England Licensed Lay Minister

'In these post-Covid and uncertain times, the biblical metaphor of the
Christian life being like that of a polished arrow in God's hands is
both refreshing and true. Jenny Sanders is an accomplished storyteller.
She naturally retells familiar Bible stories and uses relevant anecdotes
from life. If you want a reset on identity and what really matters in
your relationship with God, then this is a great starting point.'
Phil Moon, school founder, teacher and course director, Christian Schools Trust

'Jenny has wonderfully articulated the growth and preparation of a
Jesus follower in an intimate and practical way by using the symbolic
process of making and preparing an arrow. She gently exposes
religiosity and explains kingdom life truthfully and beautifully while

bringing fresh understanding to the fundamental aspects of the Christian faith that are necessary for maturity. Using the penetrating personal questions at the end of each chapter will help disarm and strip us of religious thinking and practices.

'Jenny is quiet, observant and a meticulous thinker with deep prophetic perception. She is a polished arrow, which makes this book authentic. It is not written from word only, but from deed, clearly accomplished in her through Jesus Christ.

'I highly recommend *Polished Arrows* as a must read.'
John Boerstra, pioneer, Apostolic Mission, Africa

'Jenny has a very accessible writing style, weaving biblical truths to help us understand how God wants to equip and shape us for life. This book is full of truth about the reality of how God enables us to overcome. It's great Bible study material for personal or group use.'
Avril McIntyre MBE DL, Lifeline Church, Barking and Dagenham; Convener of BDCollective Executive Director, Community Resources

'Jenny Sanders has written a very helpful book, carefully outlining the foundational truths of our faith. The metaphor of an arrow being made and polished ready to be sent to its target stops this being simply a set of static beliefs. The Christian is called to a purposeful life, sent out to accomplish what the Lord has intended for us to do. So this book helps not only to establish the believer but also to motivate and energise us to engage with His mission. May this book not only inform but also move you to action!'
Wendy Virgo, author and speaker

'This book is a prophetic call for us to be ready to influence our disintegrating culture. Jenny skilfully takes the reader on a journey, weaving a captivating narrative through the stages and processes of transforming an unspectacular branch into a beautiful, unassuming but deadly polished arrow. In the hands of the skilled archer, such a weapon is able to hit its mark with incredible accuracy and impact.

'Jenny cleverly applies these processes to show how God shapes us into *Polished Arrows* who will cut through the fog and confusion that engulfs our world. This is beautifully undergirded by stories of biblical characters that illustrate each part of the transformation. Please read this book. Come to it with an open and an attentive heart, willing to be persuaded, hearing God's gracious call to be transformed from one degree of glory to another.'

Ian Rowlands, church planting innovator, international speaker, mentor and coach; podcast host: 'Hope in a Mad World'

'As Christians, how do we have maximum impact in a world that needs to see that God is alive and well? In *Polished Arrows*, Jenny Sanders takes us on a journey using the analogy of arrow making. Bit by bit the craftsman transforms a stick into a lethal weapon. Under the hand of an expert arrow maker, a God who loves us, wants the best for us and has so much grace available for us, we too can become as polished arrows in His quiver (Isaiah 49:2).

'Jenny's book is deep, thought provoking, challenging, grounded in Scripture, but needed. It is a call to spiritual maturity, a reminder that we are called, not only to be different, but also to represent God and His truth and to advance His kingdom. If you look at society and wonder how you can make a difference, how you can be most effective for God, then this book is for you.'

Joy Margetts, author of The Healing *series and* Christ Illuminated

'Having known Jenny Sanders for more than fifteen years, it brought so much warmth to my heart to read her powerful book that not only explains what we should aim to become as Christ's followers, but also depicts her life. The unfamiliar territory and blurring of moral boundaries are worsening by the day. Here in Zimbabwe, the free-fall, as Jenny correctly describes, has left a lot of people fleeing to other countries or simply retreating into their shells, as the prospect of being an audible voice of reason in society seems overwhelming and even dangerous. The debate of the role of the children of God in all of this has become a household conversation, with the solutions seeming more and more confusing by the day.

'*Polished Arrows* perfectly captures the frustrating and frightening position that most of us find ourselves in, but proceeds to answer the questions that we have, while giving the ultimate solution for our fears and doubts: to become an arrow for God, resting safely in His quiver but ready for firing. This book is an urgent tool that must not only be available on all the bookshelves around the world, but also that all Christians should use as a guide when discussing the role of an effective church in a world gone wild.'

Pastor Andrew Simba, Glad Tidings, Harare, Zimbabwe

'Jenny uses this less-familiar biblical metaphor, along with Scriptures from the Old and New Testaments, to creatively encourage and inspire readers to purposefully pursue Jesus, readying themselves for His purposes. As with every metaphor regarding discipleship, each section overlaps other sections. I love her use of Scripture, rooting the call to be honed by God which resurfaces throughout the Bible, and not just in the metaphor of creating an arrow. Jenny clearly reminds us that discipleship is about joining God's purposes and being used and useful to God rather than simply being a better person.'
Mark Madavan, senior pastor, Fishponds Baptist Church, Bristol

'I love this book! Jenny masterfully employs the metaphor of how an arrow is made to mirror our development as Christians in our Master's hands. It would make a great gift for a person new to faith (owing to it covering vital aspects of daily discipleship), and is also a rich resource for those who have walked with God for many years. I particularly love how no subject is off limits – such as suffering and how it is a vital part of the process. It was also great to read the biblical examples provided in each chapter, as well as anecdotes from Jenny's own life. The questions at the end of chapters allow readers to really think about and apply the principles to their own lives.

'This is a fantastic resource – do get hold of a copy for yourself, and another to gift to someone else!'
Claire Musters, author, speaker, editor and host of the Woman Alive *Book Club*

'*Polished Arrows* is a delightful and timely read; and wonderfully biblical and practical. It is punctuated with compelling illustrations and winsome wit, which progressively draws the reader into the wonder and sovereignty of God's shaping work in ordinary people. Jenny slowly and skilfully draws her audience into the "little by little" agenda of a Saviour who accepts us as we are, yet will not leave us as we are. The choice of a polished arrow as allegorical to our formation and ultimate commissioning is a brilliant reminder that although we can feel hidden for a season in God's quiver, we are destined for His bow.

'I think this book would be super helpful for small group journeys and for all who are hungry for a fresh encounter with a good Father who longs to include us in His global purposes.'
Rigby Wallace, serving and overseeing the Common Ground family of churches in Cape Town, South Africa

Polished Arrows

Jenny Sanders

instant apostle

First published in Great Britain in 2024

Instant Apostle
The Barn
1 Watford House Lane
Watford
Herts
WD17 1BJ

British Library Cataloguing-in-Publication Data

A catalogue record for this book is available from the British Library.

This book and all other Instant Apostle books are available from Instant Apostle:

Website: www.instantapostle.com

Email: info@instantapostle.com

ISBN 978-1-912726-78-3

Printed in Great Britain.

Dedication, acknowledgements and thanks

For all the warriors I've been privileged to share the Jesus
journey with
for more than half a century, some of whom are now partying
in heaven.
You've inspired me, championed me, sharpened me,
and joined me in pressing on and pressing in to know more of
the abundant life of Jesus.
Thank you for your faithfulness, your laughter and your
determination
to stay on course and finish well.

Thank you:
to those who used the basis of this material many years ago;
your feedback has been invaluable.

to Gail MacDonald: it has been such a pleasure to connect
with you;
I feel I've known you for almost forty years.
Your encouragement and wisdom have been very precious.

to everyone who has taken time to read, review and endorse
Polished Arrows; I am grateful to you all.

to those who have joined the treasure-seeking task of hunting
down sources and quotes;
your willingness and tenacity have been outstanding.

to the wonderful 'Priceless Ladies' for your ongoing support.
I love being on the bus with you all.

to the team at Instant Apostle who, once again, have helped
me
navigate the path to publishing and
given so generously of their time and expertise.

to my patient, prayerful, adventuring, warrior husband,
who continues to make time and space for me to write
while pioneering, pushing onwards and focusing on the
God-given horizon.

And thank you Father God for your living, relevant, powerful
word
and for the Word made flesh:
Jesus Himself.

Also by Jenny Sanders

Spiritual Feasting (Instant Apostle, 2020)

Are you spiritually satisfied or hungering for more?

Psalm 23 pictures the Father preparing a table where we can feast in intimacy with Him, victorious in the presence of our enemies. An innovative guide, *Spiritual Feasting* encourages us to take our assigned places, to enjoy spiritual nourishment and to engage with the Holy Spirit as we eat. The 'menu' may not always be to our taste, but the exquisite privilege of dining with Jesus can turn even a bitter 'dish' into a feast.

So if you recognise that Jesus never promised a trouble-free life, but want to experience the reality of living life to the full with Him, then pick up your spiritual knife and fork and tuck in – it's time to stop snacking and to start feasting!

> 'Inspired, accessible and immediately draws you in. Deeply moving at times, it is challenging and thought-provoking in equal measure. It's also the sort of book you want to come back to regularly, for digesting alone or chewing over within church groups.'
> *Dr David Simmons, Cinnamon Network*

Listen to me, you islands;
hear this, you distant nations:
before I was born the LORD called me;
from my mother's womb he has spoken my name.
He made my mouth like a sharpened sword,
in the shadow of his hand he hid me;
he made me into a polished arrow
and concealed me in his quiver.
Isaiah 49:1-2

You uncovered your bow,
you called for many arrows.
Habakkuk 3:9

Contents

Foreword
Steve Petch

As teenagers my brothers and I used to make 'arrows'. We'd take a bamboo cane, add cardboard flights, insert a nail into the front to balance the weight, and then launch them using a length of string like a slingshot. Getting a good distance with one of those 'arrows' depended on more than the power of your throw; it depended on the quality of the flights, how well the weight was balanced and how straight and true the cane was. With the right combination we could get them to fly all the way across the field.

Teenagers grow up and find different things to do with their time, but growing older is not the same as growing in maturity. Like the shaping of an arrow, our lives need to be shaped by God if we're going to go the distance and hit the targets He has for our lives.

This book is all about God's shaping process; a process that is often surprising and sometimes painful.

My wife and I met Jenny when we were first married, living in a new town and attending a new church that Jenny and her husband were pastoring. For some reason, they saw something in us and decided to invest in our lives, which meant we were regularly invited round to 'drink tea and chat'. While I wasn't initially a fan of Jenny's Earl Grey tea, I soon learned to love it. What really impacted us was the nature of the conversations we had, which were often challenging. We'd never encountered real discipleship before, but we soon learned to love that too.

Those evenings were our introduction to the process of God shaping our lives like 'arrows' for his future calling. Over time, some of the rough parts of our character were sanded down. We were slowly being shaped and given a new sense of purpose that has impacted the rest of our lives. We longed to have kingdom impact, but we needed a lot of shaping – and that process of shaping is what this book is all about.

This is really a handbook. It describes some of the ways God shapes our character and prepares us for His calling on our lives. I'd recommend it both to new Christians and to Christians of longstanding – after all, God's shaping process is lifelong. If you also long to have kingdom impact and you're up for the process of shaping, or even if you just want to grow to be more like Jesus, this is for you.

I'd recommend reading it thoughtfully, making time for God to speak as you do. You will discover how God does His work in us and what His aim is for each of us. Every chapter has questions for reflection and a worked biblical example of the process in action.

I've been in pastoral leadership now for more than twenty years. I love seeing God take the raw material of someone's messy life and transform it into something beautiful and purposeful. He takes rough, often unlikely looking 'branches' and turns them into well-crafted 'arrows', ready to fly from His bow to the target.

This book is a great resource for anyone serious about engaging with that process and becoming the person God created them to be; and that has to be worth pursuing.

Steve Petch, lead pastor, Welcome Church, Woking, UK

Introduction

We're in a season of enormous global shift. Things are moving fast.

Any one of us can look up from our everyday tasks and find ourselves in frighteningly unfamiliar territory, on a regular basis. Some nations appear to be in freefall; many are grappling with the grim realities and consequences of climate change, civil wars and the challenges of simply putting food on the table. Meanwhile, Western economies are floundering; artificial intelligence has gone from far-fetched fiction to immediate fact; objective, scientific realities around gender are being dismissed as bigoted and outmoded. Our moral boundaries have been blurred and battered to a pulp, yet arms are opened to embrace ideologies and lifestyles from which our grandparents would have recoiled; debate is frequently closed down, and our collective mental health is in parlous shape.

Presented as progressive, there are days when it feels more probable that we are actually regressing rapidly, as the divides between humanity – male and female, rich and poor, East and West – split further and further apart, opening the door to emotional, verbal and physical violence on an individual, corporate and national level.

If you spend any time at all reading, listening to or watching national news programmes, or scrolling through your social media feeds, then you are familiar with all of this. But what, if anything, can we do about it? It can all feel horribly negative.

What can I do?

Is there anything we can do about it? Do you feel like the rabbit caught in the headlights – simultaneously paralysed and terrified – a victim of things way out of your control? Are we simply on a downward spiral of hopelessness and destruction? How should we react and live, as the people of God, in circumstances that might all too easily send us running for cover?

When things are out of our control and outside our personal responsibility, when the world has become a frightening place, how appealing it is to retreat from it all, to immerse ourselves in familiar and comfortable bubbles of work, family or church activities; to nurture the small space over which we do have influence, and hope that somehow things beyond that will simply get better.

Our reflex responses may be on constant alert. When circumstances threaten us, we react in one of four ways: fight, flight, freeze or fold. Sometimes we do all four in the space of a day. And, make no mistake, many people do feel threatened and scared; perhaps you are one of them.

It's not overly dramatic to note that Brexit threw some of us off kilter; Covid unravelled us; the Russian invasion of Ukraine shook many of us to the core as war in Europe raised its ugly head again. Long-term unrest in the Middle East has recently turned into something darker and more brutal than we could have imagined. There was a period not so long ago when the UK had three different prime ministers in the space of two months; even the death of Her Majesty the Queen launched us into a new era of less certainty and more insecurity. The ground is still shifting beneath our feet as gender ideology and cancel culture take up more of the spotlight wherever we look.

Where was God in some of those moments? Where is God now, and where do we fit?

The answer is that He's alive and well and working through His body on earth, the Church, just as He has been for hundreds of years. His Bride, though full of people who are far from perfect, and made up from a spectrum of traditions and cultures around the globe, are those who, in His wisdom, God has decided to have represent Him.

God's people were never designed to be passive observers of the world around us. We could be like the ostrich, who puts its head in the sand when circumstances look threatening, and simply pretends it's not there. We could catastrophise everything and assume that there are no solutions; this must surely be the end of everything – though that's quite a leap. Nevertheless, over the past few months, countless anxious people have asked me, 'Are these the last days?' My honest, but simple reply: 'I've no idea; but I do know that they're the only days we've got.'

In many ways, it's an irrelevant question, because would that really make a difference to how we live? When we, or those around, ask whether God will step in and do something, it's good to remember that He already has. The events around AD30-33 have made the way for us to live differently and be different, even in the midst of a messed-up world. God's plan of salvation hasn't changed; it remains an invitation that we choose to either accept or reject.

Every generation has grappled with the truths of God and His eternal Word against a backdrop of conflict and fast-paced change which threatened to overwhelm them. It's nothing new. These questions have all been asked before, but they're still the wrong questions.

Surely the pertinent question is, 'What is God asking of us in the circumstances within which He has placed us?'

In such moments of focused reflection and stark self-awareness, we may make the uncomfortable discovery that our own instinctive reactions to the world around us don't actually align with God-inspired, kingdom reactions.

Are we reflecting Jesus or taking on the cynicism and pessimism of the world? Do we carry the assurance of those who have left their old lives at the foot of the cross, have sought and received God's forgiveness and are living their lives by being filled daily with His Spirit, listening for His voice and obeying, just as Jesus Himself did? Or have we made the unnerving discovery that there is a wide gulf between our doctrine and our reality, which is coming to light in these difficult days? If that is the case, perhaps we are followers in name only; giving cognitive assent to God's lordship in our lives, but missing the love, joy and peace which He promised. Alternatively, are we inadvertently slipping into a strange spiritual schizophrenia, where our reality fails to match the image we're trying to protect?

I'd like to encourage you to take the time with me to pause and re-examine ourselves and our faith; a spiritual health check, if you will. I believe that it's an expression of the kindness of God to bring these things to the surface so that, submitted to Him, we can seek forgiveness and pursue change. We have the perfect opportunity to lean in for a deeper and more mature connection with Him.

God is committed to making each of His children more like Jesus. He is working in us and through us so that as we are changed, we affect the world around us to see that change too.

Change is challenging; it takes time and is often uncomfortable; but we aren't supposed to be the people who roll over and give up, or the people who hide away, retreat into our Christian ghettos and pretend everything is OK, when we know it really isn't. God must surely have a bigger plan. He can't just intend that we simply hang on by our fingernails until Jesus comes back. We are made for so much more; and besides, that would not be consistent with what we know of Him, or how He has been at work through all the generations before us.

The writer of Hebrews agrees: 'we do not belong to those who shrink back and are destroyed, but to those who have faith and are saved' (Hebrews 10:39).

Inspiring words, but what might that look like?

God's call

I don't know what God is asking of you today, but I do know that He is the same faithful God who sustained the saints of old, stretching back to Bible times.

Our God is a God of hope; and every one of His people is, by definition, a hope-carrier, a joy-sharer and a life-bringer – things our world desperately needs. In the light of that, no matter what else may be true, God is certainly calling all of us to wake up, stand up and step up; to not simply acknowledge our faith in words, or by showing up at a Sunday service somewhere, but by walking the walk of radical Christianity which lives out biblical truth in every community, and in every facet of society, regardless of our geographical location, seven days a week, fuelled by a vibrant and authentic relationship with Him. We need to swim against the cultural tide and make effective impact where we've been placed.

It is definitely not a time to wear false humility or leave things to others who we feel are more qualified than ourselves to advance God's kingdom. We are each called to *be* the difference; to point to, and model, the Holy Spirit-empowered Jesus-life that sees us daily wrestling with our faith, listening, walking in step and ensuring that it's a three-dimensional reality; not just a set of cognitive ideas, philosophical aspirations or dry religious beliefs. Simply being a child of God makes us significant; dramatic exploits are not mandatory.

We're going to journey with the Old Testament writer Isaiah and his metaphor of a polished arrow, about which he wrote in chapter 49 of his book of prophecies. Isaiah communicated a layered message to the exiled people of Israel:

> Before I was born the LORD called me;
> from my mother's womb he has spoken my name.
> He made my mouth like a sharpened sword,
> in the shadow of his hand he hid me;
> he made me into a polished arrow

and concealed me in his quiver.
(Isaiah 49:1-2)

While Isaiah looked forward to the coming of the promised Messiah, his words also apply to the people of God throughout history. God's desire is that we become like Jesus; we too are metaphorical arrows.

I love how Isaiah repeated the theme of Psalm 139, in which David affirmed that we are each fully known by God, even before He put us together inside our mother's womb. Before our birth, He had plans and purposes for us in terms of both our words and our actions, but more importantly, He has always longed for connection with us. God is committed to shaping us to be more like His Son, Jesus.

Every parent knows that children are not trained by accident. To push a child out into the world to find their own way is irresponsibly foolish at best and devastatingly cruel at worst. It would be like releasing a boat from the safety of harbour onto the stormy seas with a cheery 'Good luck' to the crew, and expecting them to arrive unscathed on the other side of the world, having navigated thousands of miles of treacherous ocean without a compass, map, radio, supplies or any knowledge of how the boat works. Launching our children (physical or spiritual), or being launched ourselves, requires preparation.

In this book, our metaphor is not a boat, but Isaiah's handmade arrow. Why might we want to be arrows? The simple answer is that as children of God, we are being shaped to become more like Jesus. That's a process; it doesn't happen overnight, and the picture of an arrow under construction illustrates this well.

The life of an arrow from tree to polished weapon is a time of careful shaping. If that arrow is ever going to resemble something more lethal than a stick, there is a process to be undergone under the hands of a skilled craftsman to produce a weapon which will fly straight and true.

Arrows

Arrows remind us of the folk tales of yesteryear: Robin Hood and the like. These days, archery is a modern Olympic sport. The arrows are sleek and fast; made of a mix of carbon fibre, aluminium and tungsten. Everything about their design aims to reduce drag and increase accuracy. These arrows can be fired at phenomenal speeds of 160mph,[1] shot from technologically tweaked recurve bows made of carbon fibre composites. The arrowsmith's art has become a science.

This modern bow is a far cry from those of yesteryear too, though still based on the much-feared longbows of the English. Those bows, which helped give Edward III victory at Crécy in 1346 and gave Henry V's army their superior firepower at Agincourt in 1415, were once the scourge of Europe. Crafted from yew wood, they were carved with the heartwood on the inner side of the bow, while the sapwood – which was slightly more flexible – was on the outer side, where it had to bend a little more when the bowstring was pulled back.

Medieval arrows were crafted from various types of wood including pine, hazel and ash. The heads were originally made of flint, then fashioned into sharp blades, or barbs, and later made from iron, bronze or steel. Skilled fletchers added the feathers in precise arrangements to facilitate flight, using glue and thin cord.

History lessons, films and re-enactments are the only probable places that you are likely to encounter these arrows nowadays. Nevertheless, a quick trip to the internet will show that the skill required to craft them is alive and well. This is the process we will be exploring here.

To be useful and effective arrows ourselves, we will need to submit to the Creator's hands, and allow Him to shape us according to His pleasure and will.

---

[1] www.worldarchery.sport/sport/equipment/recurve (accessed 4th April 2023).

For most of us, the thought that our allotted lifespan – piteously short in the scale of human history – might be wasted, or might count for nothing, is abhorrent. We want to take hold of life, put our best into it, get the most out of it and be the people our hearts, and the Holy Spirit, tell us that we were born to be. Hence the importance of discovering both our identity and our purpose in life.

Becoming an arrow in God's quiver, ready, willing and obedient to His call, will mean that we can enjoy intimacy with Him and fulfil His purposes for us. There can be nothing else as worthwhile.

In the following chapters, we'll unpack the process of arrow-making together. Each chapter is followed by questions to help you engage with the stages of development, and to strengthen your faith.

Bear in mind that even by the end of the book, you won't be any more the finished article than I am, but I trust you will gain some insight into how God is working in your life. Perhaps you will also gain some fresh understanding of the ways along which He has already led you. Remember too that God can't love you any more than He already does, and He will never love you any less.

I have been walking with Jesus for more than half a century. I have known and enjoyed His grace, been grateful for His rebuke, surprised by some of the journey He has led me on, delighted by many of those I've met on the paths of sorrow and joy, while thankful that He has walked all of them with me. I come from a family of Jesus-followers, and I married a man who was in church leadership, with whom I now travel around the world encouraging and mentoring leaders in both the church and business spheres. I walked away from a potential career in the media to embrace this, and have never regretted that decision. Motherhood was a real time of character-shaping for me, and although my four children have grown and flown, I cherish the years when we were focused on raising them. In that time, I learned a great deal about forgiveness, patience, grace, mercy and unconditional love; things which have stood me in good stead as I sought to understand a little more of how God sees us and draws us onward with Him, and am now able to share that with others.

Our families get to see the unedited version of us, and mine would assure you, as do I, that God has not finished with me yet. I take heart from knowing that we are all a work in progress and that God is infinitely more patient and committed to making me like Jesus than I can ever hope to be; what a relief that is.

There are days when I feel an overwhelming despair that God's voice seems to be drowned out by the clamour of secular humanism in our post-Christian world, which appears to be determined to cut off the very branch on which it has stood so strongly for generations. I often feel small, insignificant and, quite frankly, fairly useless in the grand scheme, but God is still working in me, and I am safe in His hands. I too am an arrow in the making.

God's position

Regardless of the uncertainty in the world around us, we can be absolutely sure that God is neither surprised nor fearful. He is not wrong-footed by global events, nor threatened by the forces of evil that have been unleashed on the earth. His throne is firmly established; it cannot be shaken by any other power, neither natural nor supernatural. His promises are steadfast and enduring; He is faithful, kind and good. His desire is that no one should miss out on the opportunity to be part of His global family, that no one would spend eternity apart from Him.

If these are the last days, then so be it. That's irrelevant; I repeat: they are the only ones we have.

The question only remains: how will we use them?

Every generation has had its challenges and obstacles, times of conflict, economic collapse and social upheaval. History tells us too that there has always been opposition to the gospel, but followers of Jesus have continued to stand for Him. Jesus Himself promised that trouble would come our way,[2] but that in the midst of it He would walk closely with us, and that we would not be vanquished.

It's true that the battle is very fierce some days, and we've all known weariness, disappointment and probably times of personal defeat along the way. Spiritual battles have been fought with a mixture of victory and ignominious trouncing, but the spiritual war is not yet over. We continue to trust that God is working out His purposes through the men and women who He has created, known, chosen, called and equipped for the time in which He has placed us. We are His arrows, being fired into myriad situations with His redemptive message of hope.

Jesus' final promise before His ascension was that He would be with all of us, every day, through all of the days;[3] so we know that He has not abandoned us to gloom and doom. He has not given up on the plan of salvation, or the mandate to see His kingdom come and, one day, He will have all the nations and tribes of the world represented around His throne.

We are encouraged and inspired by the transformative stories of the Holy Spirit coming in power on people around the world; we take heart when we hear that dreams and visions of Jesus have initiated many a conversion, as precious souls have moved from death to life, from darkness to light. We weep with joy and celebrate when the prodigals come home. We rejoice to hear of 24/7 prayer initiatives,[4] of rescued addicts, families healed, crippling debts repaid and broken people restored as God works to reveal His boundless love and unmerited grace. We are thankful for every bridge-builder who has stepped out in faith to trust God and act as an arrow bringing good news to their neighbours and friends. Don't you long to be part of that heavenly project?

---

[2] John 16:33.

[3] Matthew 28:20.

[4] www.24-7prayer.com (accessed 26th February 2024).

God's desire

The minor prophet Habakkuk lived about seventy years after Isaiah's prophecies. He brought a message to the people in the southern kingdom of Judah, approximately 600 years before Jesus was born. In his book, he questioned God about the terrible flourishing of injustice he saw, and received a revelation that the Babylonian nation would be used by God to end it. Habakkuk expressed surprise that such a blatantly ungodly power could be used in this way, but he was reassured that God would work things out so that, ultimately, true justice would be meted out across the board. The prophet resolved to watch, wait and trust regardless of the things he'd seen, and he remembered how God had moved in the past. Recollecting Israel's history stirred his faith so that he was able to rejoice and trust in the present. We could do the same.

His book is a short one of just three chapters, but this verse punches above its weight with a sense of the 'now', right here in the twenty-first century:

> You uncovered your bow,
> you called for many arrows.
> (Habakkuk 3:9)

This verse makes me catch my breath. Can you hear the urgency of it? Can you sense a stirring of God's Spirit in your heart when you read it? In Habakkuk's context, he was seeing the arrows as Babylonians being fired by God as judgement. However, today God is calling for effective weapons to fire from His divine bow. He is calling us; you and me. We are those arrows bringing, not judgement, but God's life, promises and the sure hope of salvation. Can you hear His voice above the cacophony of other sounds clamouring for your attention?

Of course, God can step into history at any point; it is, after all, His-story. The Creator of the universe with all its spinning planets, supernovae and complex galaxies merely has to speak a word. Although He has armies of angels who could carry out His bidding far more effectively than ourselves, in His wisdom and grace He has chosen to use His children – the family of God – us – to see His kingdom come on earth.

As our culture unravels and kingdom values are carelessly discarded and trodden into the mud, He still calls us by name, to fix our eyes on Him, to stand up and be counted. We are not created to blend in, or to merely exist for however many years we have been granted. God has so much more for us, and for those who have yet to know Him.

There is a sharp, prophetic tone to Habakkuk's verse for modern readers. Right now, God is calling for us, for polished arrows – for Jesus-followers, who dare to believe His Word, who are ready and willing to be fired into the world – to have impact, find their target and make a difference.

Arrows are made to be fired. There is no point in having a quiver full of even the best-made arrows if they are never selected and used. Will you allow Him to shape you to be one of them?

My prayer is that whether you use this book as an individual, or in a group study setting, you would discover and appreciate more of who God is making you to be – not so that you can increase your cognitive knowledge, but so that you can allow yourself to surrender to the hands of the Master Archer, and be ready to truly fly wherever He desires.

> He shot his arrows and scattered the enemy,
> with great bolts of lightning he routed them.
> (Psalm 18:14)

1. Coppicing

A walk around any European forest of ash or hazel, willow or birch will soon show you that very few branches grow completely straight. Since this is the raw material for an arrow, that might be considered a major setback. Fortunately, hundreds of years ago, forest managers discovered the benefits and art of coppicing.

Coppicing is a method of pruning which involves periodically cutting a tree down to almost ground level; this stimulates fresh growth from the stump. New branches tend to grow straight upwards, towards the light, and have the useful flexibility of young saplings. Coppicing can be done every five to ten years and, fortunately for arrowsmiths, ash is a tree that responds very well to this treatment.

Done on a rotational basis, careful woodland management ensured a regular supply of suitable material for a medieval arms supplier. While not a mechanised industry, it did allow for arrowsmiths, blacksmiths and fletchers to work together to produce high-quality arrows, and was obviously many times more efficient than wandering randomly, if hopefully, round a woodland searching for suitable shoots and branches from mature trees.

Preparing an arrow in the old-fashioned way requires a lengthy sequence of preparation and perfecting, involving considerable violence to the potential arrow; but it produces a valuable, effective product in the end. Just as gold undergoes repeated heat treatments when it is refined in order to remove the impurities it carries, so an arrow must experience a sequence of processes at the hands of a skilled craftsman if it is to move from being a simple stick to a piece of lethal weaponry.

You may feel more like a rough stick than a sleek arrow, poised to penetrate the culture around you today; I know I often do. Reminding ourselves of God's truths is a way to lift our eyes off ourselves and our circumstances, stir our souls and reposition ourselves to move forward in faith, with our eyes fixed on Him.

God's search

Just as the forest manager searches for suitable wood to sell on to the arrowsmith, so God has searched for you. Whether you came to faith as a child, a youngster or in later years, He is familiar with every detail of our life's journey, and has seen our every step. In fact, God knows us through and through, and has done from conception.

You may find this comforting, or maybe it makes you uncomfortable. That probably depends on your view of God. If you've only known Him as a distant and severe headmaster-type figure, then I can assure you that you haven't truly met Him yet. God is a good, loving, present, engaged Father who cherishes, nurtures and champions us; we have no secrets from Him. He knows us thoroughly and fully – flaws, foibles, fractures and all – and yet, amazingly, He loves us and cares for us as well.

If He feels distant to you, then be assured that He truly cares for you, and longs to pursue a relationship with you. He's been watching, not to catch us out, but to draw us to Himself by putting markers along our path to point us towards Him. Keep seeking Him; He promises that He'll be found.[5]

---

[5] Jeremiah 29:13; Matthew 7:7-8.

God's choice

Not only does the forest manager see which coppiced trees are responding to his care, but he then picks out and chooses which ones are ready to be made into something both beautiful and useful.

God chooses us too. In fact, He chose us before time began on earth. Not an eeney-meeny-miney-mo, let's-see-who's-lucky-today kind of choosing, but a specific, deliberate, thought-out choosing. He also oversaw the entire miraculous pregnancy process which brought us into the world: from zygote to embryo to fully formed baby. The miracle of life has been in His hands the whole time.

I have four grown and flown children who are a delight to me. Each one was planned and anticipated with excitement; each was placed in my arms and greeted with a genuine joy and a fierce love, unlike anything I'd ever known. While my husband and I chose to have them, we didn't get to choose anything about their physical appearance, their academic aptitude or their personalities. We welcomed them and engaged in the wonder of seeing them grow, develop and flourish. Prior to their arrival, I was somewhat anxious on their behalf. What if we weren't the parents they would have chosen? What if they wished we were someone else? Fortunately, and thanks to the happy connective design of gestation and pregnancy, it wasn't a problem.

Sadly, some parents wish they had been given different children. Maybe they longed for a girl and a boy came along instead. There are disappointed parents who have expectations of a child which their offspring's inclination, intellect or DNA can never fulfil. Parents get what they are given: each child a unique combination of parental genes manifesting themselves in a distinct, never-to-be-repeated individual; and most of us are thoroughly enraptured by that. I have several friends whose unplanned children have brought just as much, if not more joy to their families, thanks to the surprise of their conception.

If you are an adopted child, whatever the story you carry, you have the privilege of being deliberately chosen by your adoptive parents. I can't imagine what that's like, or how such parents choose one child over another; but that element of choice is strong. You know what it is to be picked out.

There are currently upwards of 8 billion people on this planet, and thousands of years of human narrative precede us. Yet, God, in His wisdom sees, knows and loves you. You are not an accident. There are some mind-boggling statistics around this. Someone recently told me that the chances of any one of us being here with our unique DNA combination carries the same likelihood as 2 million people playing a game with a trillion-sided dice, and all throwing the same number at once. You really are a miracle!

You have been placed in history at this exact time and place to reflect God's glory, to enjoy Him and to demonstrate His nature and character in your particular context or sphere of influence. Those who are included in His family can all relax in the security that comes with the assurance that we have also been chosen by Him, not just as part of a crowd, but by name.[6]

The Bible says that God has called us 'out of darkness' (1 Peter 2:9) and into His plans and purposes for us, which are always good.[7] He uses the circumstances of our lives, including our relationships, to shape us and mould us, just as clay is worked into hundreds of different articles by the hands of a potter or, in the case of our arrowsmith metaphor, into a swift arrow.

That means that even if you spent your formative years within the care system, or in a series of foster homes without the safe space of a consistent, loving family, God still saw you, heard you, knows you, and His heart yearns to include you in His family, just as it has always done.

---

[6] Isaiah 43:1
[7] Jeremiah 29:11.

Perhaps you think that's far-fetched; after all, you reason, you don't seem like very promising material; but God thinks very differently. He has declared and shown His immeasurable love for us by sending Jesus into the world to bridge the gulf between us and to win us back to Himself.

The arrow is chosen, not because it already looks good. The Bible tells us that it was 'while we were still sinners, Christ died for us' (Romans 5:8). We don't need to try to clean ourselves up first, in a misguided attempt to impress God or to qualify for His forgiveness and grace. He accepts us as we are; but He loves us so much He will not leave us as we are.

Like the arrow, we are chosen, picked out and purchased at great cost. No woodsman would give his wood away; he would require a payment. There could be nothing more expensive than the life-blood of the Son of God which cleanses, or purifies, us from everything within us that falls short of His perfect holiness.

Everything – that means absolutely everything: the worst things you can think of – and the even more terrible things that your mind doesn't want to begin to contemplate – can all find forgiveness in the once-and-for-all perfect sacrifice of Jesus. No one is beyond His reach; nothing is too shameful, too brutal, too evil to be covered by that extraordinary spiritual detergent.

That is sometimes difficult to grasp; after all, surely some people don't deserve to be chosen, or to have a way back to God. But grace – mercifully – is not dependent on merit. Grace is not issued in proportion to the merit of our deeds. This is God's unique prerogative; it is not for us to decide.

Remember the dying thief next to Jesus at Calvary? We don't know his crime, but we know that crucifixion was the most excruciating death the Romans had been able to devise: slow, brutal and humiliating. We can only assume that he was a law-breaker of some sort; he certainly believed that his punishment was appropriate for his crime(s).[8] He may not have had all his

---

[8] Luke 23:40-41.

theological ducks in a row, but Jesus met him in those moments, knew his heart and assured him of a place with Him in heaven that very day.

A new way

Up until Jesus' time in history, men and women were obliged to make animal sacrifices to God as an offering for their sins. Blood was a requirement in order for forgiveness to be granted.

The Old Testament, Hebrew pattern of animal sacrifice required a substitutionary sacrifice, which symbolised the transferral of the people's misdeeds onto an animal which was slaughtered in their place; the spilt blood of the animal acting as an atonement.[9]

God has always been quite clear that death is the inevitable consequence of sin.[10] Our contemporary minds find this truth hard to get our heads around, but it's not such a surprise to see that a holy and perfect God cannot look on sin, when we understand the gravity of it. To revolt against our Maker, the King of the universe who has consistently provided for us, protected us and given us everything we could possibly need in perfection, is an appalling crime. How His heart must be broken.

Ever since Adam and Eve chose something other than keeping their open and pure relationship with Him, the repercussions of sin have tumbled down the generations for us as individuals, communities and nations. It's an immeasurable grief to God to see how sin harms us, and how we wound and hurt one another when we choose to live according to standards that are not His.

It's erroneous to think of God as silent, angry or, even worse, vengeful and vindictive. Anyone who is a parent suffers as and when and if their precious offspring make choices that bring

---

[9] Leviticus 4–5; 17:11.
[10] Romans 6:23.

them and their loved ones pain, sorrow and destruction. God feels the same hurt on a far greater scale.

Sin must be dealt with completely if we are to have any real, meaningful relationship with God. He's chosen us to have that relationship with Him, but the path between us gets blocked by sin. It's an impenetrable barrier. The nature of the sacrifice required to overturn this tells us the seriousness of our crime.

The Bible brings us the unpalatable truth that sin has infused us from conception; it is metaphorically imprinted in our DNA and has become part of the inheritance of all humankind, thanks to the disobedience of Adam in the beginning.[11] Sin is not just an annoying habit, or an inconvenient character trait. It strikes deep from, and into, our core being; it affects our lives in every area, and ultimately brings death, or separation.

Pastor and theologian Bruce Milne wrote:

> Sin affects the *whole* of a human being; the will … the mind and understanding … the affections and emotions … as well as one's outward speech and behaviour … no area or aspect of our nature is left intact by sin.[12]

This means that outside of Jesus Christ, we are unable to stand in God's presence, since we are indelibly stained with the sin which He cannot tolerate. We struggle to live according to God's will when He is not at the centre of our lives. When that place is taken by our own desires and wants, they dictate our decisions and choices, and fail to reflect God's kingdom. Our sinfulness leads to guilt and condemnation when we know we have broken God's law of perfection, and have no way of repairing it ourselves.

All this serves as an increasingly dense blockage in our ability to hear and discern the voice of God. Like white noise that drowns out everything else, our sin inevitably means that we become desensitised to His voice.

---

[11] 1 Corinthians 15:21-22.
[12] Bruce Milne, *Know the Truth* (Leicester: IVP, 1982), p106.

A new life

This all sounds fairly hopeless and miserable, but the good news is that the debt we owe has been paid for us by Jesus' death on the cross. Where our lives were forfeit, Jesus stepped in and gave His own instead. The gospel is not just a few books of the Bible or even a message; the gospel is Jesus Himself. God with skin on; a manifestation of the Father in human flesh. As the only sin-free person to have ever walked the earth, Jesus was the only one qualified to take our place, since He had no debt of His own.

At the cost of His own dearly loved Son, God bought us and brought us, back to Himself. Jesus' blood was spilt on our behalf. His once-and-for-all sacrifice made atonement for our wrongdoing.

This put an end to the ritual animal sacrifices of the past. When the temple in Jerusalem was destroyed in AD70, all those things which served as pointers and symbols to what was to come with the Messiah came to a natural end. They were no longer needed; Jesus had done it all.

> Unlike the other high priests, he does not need to offer sacrifices day after day, first for his own sins, and then for the sins of the people. He sacrificed for their sins once for all when he offered himself.
> (Hebrews 7:27)

Jesus' blood: so costly, yet so powerful.

What a wonderful thing that the Creator God should be interested in us at all. How marvellous that He should know us so fully, call us by name and choose to include us in His family. Our salvation is a fantastic miracle of grace, and we partake of it on God's terms, not our own. As a stick on its own carries no life away from the tree, it is not in a position to make its own terms with the one who tore it from that tree. Making bargains with God is a futile endeavour.

Just as every part of our nature was subject to sin before we knew God, now every part of our nature needs to become subject to Him after conversion. Complete lordship is His requirement; not to restrict us or hem us in, but to bring us more freedom than we've ever known.

Cutting sounds painful, but it's the beginning of our journey to arrowhood.

Target Questions

➤ 'God is a good, loving, present, engaged Father who cherishes, nurtures and champions us.' How have you known God in any of these ways?

➤ What is the significance of being chosen by God?

➤ How does knowing that Jesus has permanently dealt with the indelible stain of sin make a difference to your daily life?

➤ How can you ensure that every part of your nature is truly subject to God?

1a. Paul

Paul's change of heart, mind and life was so dramatic that his actual Damascus Road experience has become a euphemism for any startling turnaround or revelation that brings a conspicuous alteration to the *modus operandi* of an individual.

We first come across Paul when he still went by the name Saul. A Roman citizen from the port city of Tarsus, we find him looking on in approval as the first Christian martyr was killed by a violent crowd of furious religious leaders. Acts 6–7 records how Stephen was brought before the Jewish elders in a Sanhedrin court, where false witnesses were persuaded to lie about his activities in an attempt to get rid of him. The ploy worked and, despite one of the greatest oratories recorded anywhere in the Bible, the religious elite were infuriated by his claim that they had missed the longed-for Messiah they all claimed to be watching and waiting for. Incensed, they dragged Stephen outside the city walls and stoned him to death.

Saul had been born into a life of privilege. He was one of the religious elite himself and, having been educated in Jerusalem under the respected Jewish rabbi Gamaliel, Saul's CV was impressive:

> circumcised on the eighth day, of the people of Israel, of the tribe of Benjamin, a Hebrew of Hebrews; in regard to the law, a Pharisee; as for zeal, persecuting the church; as for righteousness based on the law, faultless.
> (Philippians 3:5-6)

He had been brought up from birth to conscientiously keep the Jewish law; important in that culture for finding favour with God, and the way to keep pure in His eyes. To him, the proposition that Jesus was the promised Messiah would have been a dangerous, liberal idea, which threatened the very fabric of Jewish society.

Saul would have thought of himself as chosen by God to seek out followers of Jesus and destroy them. He would have seen this job as doing God's work for Him. It's fair to say that in first-century Palestine, at the time of Stephen's death, he would have also been seen as one of the most unlikely propagators of the gospel. But then, quite suddenly, God met with him and he discovered that he had been chosen for a very different line of work.

Acts 9 gives a detailed account of how Saul was commissioned by the high priest in Jerusalem to continue his resolute quest to root out disciples and followers of Jesus. While he was still fuelling his anger against this group of people, and making all sorts of grisly threats, Saul obtained letters of authority to search synagogues around Damascus for believers who he would arrest and take back to Jerusalem for sentencing. They were considered to be apostates, betraying the long history of the Hebrew people, rejecting their culture and traditions.

Dr Luke, who wrote the book of Acts, recorded the extraordinary encounter that took place on the road to Damascus, when a bright light stopped Saul in his tracks and literally threw him to the ground. This was followed by a voice from heaven heard by no one except Saul, as God first questioned and then instructed him. The dazzled man remained blind for three days until godly Ananias came to visit, in response to hearing God during his own personal prayer time. Luke's account includes the initial reluctance of Ananias, based on all that he had heard about the focused brutality of this notorious Pharisee. However, obedient to God's call, he went as directed, found Saul, called him 'Brother', laid hands on him, and God healed him.[13]

God revealed to Ananias the heavenly appointed new task He had for this persecutor of believers:

> This man is my chosen instrument to proclaim my name to the Gentiles and their kings and to the people of Israel. I will show him how much he must suffer for my name.
> (Acts 9:15-16)

God chooses who He chooses; including me and you. Saul/Paul looked an unlikely candidate on paper, but nothing is too difficult for God. No one is beyond His reach, be they on the pavement, in the prison or in a palace. We may be surprised, but we are always grateful, if a little bit baffled, that His choice includes us.

How God chose Paul was a remarkable story which he told to a crowd in Jerusalem in Acts 22, and again in Acts 26 during his trial before the governor Festus, King Agrippa and Bernice. It's fascinating to read about his experience in his own words.

Saul started being called Paul in Acts 13, after he and Barnabas were sent by the believers in Antioch on their first missionary journey together, starting in Cyprus.

Paul's change of name indicated the extent of his radical change of heart and his life's focus. From persecuting the fledgling Church to evangelising, discipling and planting church communities across the Mediterranean in various teams, Paul's teaching brought revelation to hundreds of converts who, in turn, affected hundreds and thousands of others searching for life, hope and purpose.

You may know of other conversions in which the element of God's choosing is as strong. Most of us undergo incremental change over a long period of time, and we have less-exciting stories, in which the before and after contrasts are not so

---

[13] Acts 9:10-18.

pronounced. There may well be people within our own faith community who have dramatic stories of how Jesus met them, and the consequent changes which took place in their lives. It's always a great conversation starter to ask others about their own experience, and an effective way of learning more about their journey and who they really are. It's important to remember, though, that all our stories are just as valid as anyone else's. The level of drama is irrelevant to the reality of the heart transformation, or the fact that God, for reasons we cannot explain beyond knowing that He loves us, also chose us.

Everyone in God's family has moved from death to life; no one was any more dead than anyone else before we responded to His Spirit at work in us. God graciously meets with us as He chooses; but all of us, like Paul, need to die to an old life and embrace the new one, nourished and nurtured by the life of God.

As soon as Paul had his sight restored, he was baptised and began to preach in the local synagogues, much to the concern of the disciples and believers in the area. Not surprisingly, they were fairly incredulous that such an obsessive oppressor, so committed to the violent eradication of believers, should be accepted as a brother in Christ. Their caution is understandable; their fears were only allayed when Barnabas befriended him. This godly man, known for his gift of encouragement, made time to reach out to the ex-persecutor and fledgling believer. It was Barnabas who took Paul to meet the apostles and introduced him to other followers of Jesus.

So, straight away, in a complete turnaround, Paul began to preach the good news of Jesus, debated with scholars, and used his education and learning to prove that Jesus was who He had said He was. Despite death threats and suffering, beatings and imprisonments, storms and sleepless nights, encounters with bandits and multiple dangers, Paul never reneged on his faith.[14] He knew that God had appointed him for the task of widening

---

[14] 2 Corinthians 6:4-5; 11:23b-28.

the net of the gospel message, and that fact gave him the resolve to carry on.

He ended his days in a prison in Rome from where he wrote some of his most impactful words of encouragement to various churches, which today form a substantial part of the New Testament. So, in that way, his transformed life is still helping to transform other lives almost 2,000 years later. His teaching, exegesis, explanation of doctrine and application of godly principles into real life are as powerful now as they ever were.

Paul was ripped out of his old life in a miraculous way. After that blinding encounter with God, he threw off his past, embraced forgiveness, submitted himself to a new Master and became a willing and obedient servant, welcoming his new life of faith with vigour and focus, refusing to be distracted by anything else. He knew that he had been chosen by God to go and serve across a swathe of the Mediterranean by bringing the message of hope, life and joy to unreached people. He knew too that others had been chosen by God, they just didn't realise it yet; he knew the encounter he had had could impact others, and open their eyes to who Jesus really was. In his own letters, he often introduced himself as one who was called and chosen by God; he knew that there had been no mistake.

Although it wasn't a promising beginning, Paul became a giant in the faith; an arrow fired effectively not just into first-century Palestine and Europe, but way beyond that, into the twenty-first century, finding its target and pleasing the One who prepared and 'fired' him.

2. Goodbye to the Old

The journey begins

Our coppiced stick, or branch, has now begun its journey to become an arrow. It has been selected and broken off from the tree where it has spent its previous life. This is the first step. The arrowsmith can do nothing until this is done.

Break off a leaf, a twig or a branch from its living parent tree and the inevitable happens. Without connection to the roots, life-giving sap and a vital water supply, it dies. Death is inevitable for us would-be arrows too. This sacrifice of leaves, twigs and blossom will lead to something of much greater worth. We are not talking about a physical death, but a dying to our old life; the selfish, me-orientated life we lived before we submitted to God and allowed Jesus to take the reins.

We become someone entirely new – changed from the inside out – when we come into God's family. This is not about turning over a new leaf or making a New Year's resolution; neither is it about a personality change. It's far more radical than that!

This is the new birth that Jesus spoke about to a frightened religious leader under cover of darkness. Nicodemus didn't understand it fully. He was so confused about the physical implication of being 'born again' that he struggled to make the spiritual connection (John 3:1-21), but it's an accurate term for something so extreme. We don't just say 'Goodbye' to our former way of life; we ask God to kill it off completely.

More metamorphosis than makeover.

This is symbolised in the act of believer's baptism, in which a person is literally immersed under the water and then emerges to a fresh chapter as a new person in Christ. The water is not special in any way at all. It's just water; it's wet. But baptism is an act of obedience to the command of Christ, which demonstrates publicly that a believer has come into a new life with God.[15]

Salvation, effectively, gives us a spiritual heart transplant.

In that moment of entering a new life by faith, and by acceptance in the finished, completed work of Jesus on the cross, we make a dramatic move from a place of death to a place of life.[16] You can't get more polar opposite than that! It's as different as moving from a place of darkness to a place of light. We were far away from God, but now we're close enough to metaphorically sit on His lap in intimacy.

This is not a cognitive, theoretical understanding, but a living relationship. We are not signing up to a list of doctrinal requirements; nor do we need a degree in Greek, Aramaic or Latin. Theology can helpfully illuminate our spiritual journey, but it is not mandatory for an authentic life-changing revelation of God, or for what Jesus has accomplished for us and in us. It is not about an experience for its own sake either, nor an emotional aberration; it's a life-changing, solid fact.

Remember, this is not a self-help pilgrimage; we have not simply 'turned over a new leaf' or begun to engage in a mind-over-matter haze of psychological unreality. At the same time, we do not kiss our brains goodbye; far from it. We enjoy a robust faith which provides ample opportunity for debate and thoughtful processing.

---

[15] Some traditions baptise by 'sprinkling', but here we are talking about the biblical format and symbolism of baptism by full immersion.
[16] Ephesians 2:5.

When we submit our lives to Christ, we have moved from one kingdom to another, lock, stock and barrel. Paul explained it this way: 'For he [God] has rescued us from the dominion of darkness and brought us into the kingdom of the Son he loves' (Colossians 1:13). That's clear and conclusive.

Some of us can recognise how, or where, our spiritual journey began. It may have been a specific day, or defined by a particular moment. Others recognise a slow, cumulative change over a prolonged period of time. Either way, we know that a day will eventually come when the journey will end; there is a destination. While we have no idea when that day will arrive, for those in God's family the end point is assured.

Spiritually, regardless of the questions and searching that brought us there, our journey begins at the foot of the cross with salvation. From there we are set to explore our life of faith, having turned our back on our old life and embraced the gift of the new life God has given us.

Spiritually, we are a new person.

So, too, the 'arrow' has been irrevocably broken from the tree. It is destined for purpose.

The next stage for our emerging arrow involves removing any extraneous twiggy branches and leaves from the coppiced wood, which it may have been growing while it was attached to the tree. Beautiful as they may be in situ, they are of absolutely no use on an arrow. By definition, the arrow needs to have a straight shaft without any extra bits on it that might interfere with its weight, balance and trajectory.

If allowed to remain, the arrow's design would be intrinsically flawed. It couldn't possibly make a direct flight from the bow without deviating off course – pretty useless in times of peace or war.

What does this look like?

Losing the baggage

In John Bunyan's old allegory, *The Pilgrim's Progress*, the sincere traveller, Christian, sees his heavy burden of sin roll away down the hill, never to be recovered, when he comes to faith in Christ. Try though he might, Christian could never unfasten it himself and it became a great weight on his back. Getting rid of that crushing load was a moment of pure joy and relief. It's a powerful picture, illustrating how God takes our sin and has put it as far from Him as one horizon is from the other. In other words, it's been dealt with completely.

Our sin is totally gone forever. God Himself says, 'I will forgive their wickedness and will remember their sins no more' (Jeremiah 31:34; Hebrews 8:12).

This doesn't mean that He forgets about sin in the way that you or I forget where we put the car keys; it's not about being absent-minded. God simply chooses not to bring any of our sins to His remembrance. Neither will he drag up our old failures, mistakes and moments of outright disobedience. He will never rub our noses in what's done, covered and forgiven. This is absolutely, staggeringly amazing; and all the more so when you think of the sort of grudges we tend to have against others or, more pertinently, how often we remind ourselves of the misdeeds of our past. Sometimes, our memories are triggered by other events, encounters or associations and we find ourselves plunged back into maelstrom emotions of regret or distress. Most of us are our own worst critic. We torture ourselves by rehashing things that God says are forgiven, dead and buried. We need to learn how to 'remember [them] no more' as well.

God's intention is that our focus be elsewhere; on the prize at the end of our race of life.[17] That prize is being with Him for all eternity in the place of perfection where tears, pain, suffering and death are mere shadows of the past. We can only do life

---

[17] 1 Corinthians 9:24; Hebrews 12:1.

that way if, like all good athletes, we leave everything else back in the metaphorical locker room, focus on the lane we're allotted, run with every fibre of our mind and body involved in the race, and fix our eyes on the finishing tape ahead.

When we leave our old life fully behind us, not only can we rejoice in the freedom of God's forgiveness, but we may find the necessity of forgiving ourselves as well.

This is crucial if we're going to remove the things that weigh us down in our arrow-forming process; excess baggage from the past will only get in the way. Where that baggage exists, it increases its drag factor when we nurse regrets about the past. We must be done with those, and be rid of their burdensome effect on us. This requires a further change of heart, a change of mind and a change of focus.

Although it's absolutely true that, like the pilgrim in Bunyan's story, all our sins and wrongdoings have been rolled away, we come into God's kingdom little prepared for our new life in God. We usually retain our old patterns of behaviour and thought until, like the extraneous branches, our old loyalties to sin are torn away from us.

Defaults

Just like our phones or computers, we come with default mechanisms that are our instinctive reactions – our first thoughts – and, if not checked, they dictate the speech and actions that follow.

Until we have made new default settings in our lives, we will generally continue to use the old ones which are so well established. Our hearts have a new loyalty, and now our minds need to follow or we will end up in a tangle of guilt, despair and self-flagellation as we urge ourselves to do better – out of our own effort – and miss the grace of God. Only Jesus allows us to permanently change our default settings as we carve out new neural pathways.

The Bible tells us that it's the grace of God which 'teaches us to say "No" to ungodliness' or unrighteousness (Titus 2:11-12). But if we're saying 'No' to that way of life, we need to be saying, 'Yes' to something else.

Paul talked about this in his letter to the Christians in Ephesus.

> You were taught, with regard to your former way of life, to put off your old self, which is being corrupted by its deceitful desires; to be made new in the attitude of your minds; and to put on the new self, created to be like God in true righteousness and holiness.
> (Ephesians 4:22-24)

The same passage is translated in *The Message* like this:

> Since, then, we do not have the excuse of ignorance, everything – and I do mean everything – connected with that old way of life has to go. It's rotten through and through. Get rid of it! And then take on an entirely new way of life – a God-fashioned life, a life renewed from the inside and working itself into your conduct as God accurately reproduces his character in you.

Paul's picture of taking one thing off and putting on another is very helpful. Our old life is like a big, heavy winter coat that we take off and get rid of when we come to Christ. He gives us new metaphorical clothes to wear, which symbolise forgiveness, wholeness, healing and holiness.

It would be pretty silly to try to put these new clothes on over the top of the old ones. They would be bulky, restrictive and uncomfortable; they simply wouldn't fit. That old coat needs to be completely removed, and then the new clothing put on. We're not left with nothing, just as we're not left living in a spiritual vacuum. There needs to be an exchange: old for new.

Paul spelt it out for the Ephesian church: those who used to lie must stop doing that, but now they must start telling the truth; those who used to steal must also stop and do – not nothing – but 'something useful' with their hands (Ephesians 4:25-28).

The key to this is the little phrase he puts in between the putting off/putting on instruction; it's about changing the attitude of our minds.

The Message again, puts it helpfully like this:

> Don't become so well-adjusted to your culture that you fit into it without even thinking. Instead, fix your attention on God. You'll be changed from the inside out. (Romans 12:2)

The NIVUK translation says:

> Do not conform to the pattern of this world, but be transformed by the renewing of your mind.

Renewing our minds

Science has shown us how incredibly complex and powerful our brains are. When the Bible talks about the mind, it is talking about more than simply the control centre of the body, much more than nerves and synapses sending and receiving messages to and from the rest of the physical body. Someone who has no brain function is only kept alive by a life-support machine; their mind is no longer active.

What goes on in our minds determines the choices we make about absolutely everything. We choose which thoughts to ponder; which emotions will hold sway, and which will be reined in; what comes out of, and goes into, our mouths; how we use our time; with whom we spend that time; on which images we allow our eyes to dwell; which sounds, music and conversation we allow our ears to hear, and every other action involved in day-to-day living.

This is where our default mechanisms are seated, and it's where we must confront them in order to change them as we grow in Christ.

How do we renew our minds?

This is not something that can happen by sitting in a church service once or twice a week. No sermon or preacher can do this for us. It requires each of us to take responsibility and conscious action. It's a practical outworking of aligning our thinking with God's thinking.

Most of the time we aren't aware of individual thoughts: they're a splurge of impressions and ramblings as we navigate our day at different levels of consciousness. We can be highly alert, or switch off. Those rambling thoughts can turn into harmless daydreams that take us back in time or to desert islands and sun-drenched beaches, or they can become more unhelpful fantasies: the dangerous 'what ifs', as we toy with scenarios which might have been.

Paul gave some good advice to the church in Corinth that can benefit us as we change our spiritual culture, and ensure that we are not ruled unhelpfully by what happens in our heads (2 Corinthians 10:5). He suggested that we view thoughts as potential intruders into not just our heads but our whole lives. In verses 10 to 18 of Ephesians 6, we read his explanation that we are in a spiritual battle, and therefore obliged to fight if we are to be victorious. He wrote that while we don't have conventional weapons of war, we are equipped with spiritual weapons which have enough power to bring down all sorts of apparently well-defended spiritual castles. God's Word is more than able to withstand the debates, questions and countercultural values that fly in the face of His values and the importance of connecting with Him.

A crucial part of this warfare concerns fighting for our minds. In other words, we start to filter our thoughts. We challenge them as they enter our heads with the words of any guardsman worth his salt: 'Who goes there? Friend or foe?'

We can't stop the spectrum of thoughts that come into our heads, but we do have a choice in what we do with them, and we certainly won't want to be welcoming all of them in to stay and make themselves comfortable.

We can train ourselves to check our thoughts in this way – a kind of 'self-censoring' in order to discipline our minds and create new defaults. Just as people train themselves physically for a fitter, healthier body – often spending hours at the gym – we need to train ourselves spiritually, and that requires both time and dedication if we are going to master these things. In the same way that physical muscles respond to training and, over time, find exercise easier as stamina increases, so spiritually we will begin to find it easier to make good choices as we have our minds renewed.

Much of the time our thoughts are very helpful nudges to a course of action: 'I'm cold'; 'I'm tired'; 'I'm hungry'; 'I'm so proud of my kids'; etc. These alert us to situations to which we can give an appropriate response: 'I'll put on a jumper'; 'I'm going to bed'; 'I'll have some toast'; 'I'll be sure to communicate that to my child'.

If we're on our guard when the unhelpful thoughts crop up, we will be ready to challenge them, capture them before they wreak havoc with our minds, and respond with characteristics of the kingdom. Thus, 'She's getting on my nerves,' can become, 'Father, I find her irritating, but give me Your grace right now, and help me to see You at work in her.' Or some equivalent.

Capturing thoughts helps us respond to them in a decisive way, whatever they're about.

A thought prescription

If thoughts need to be taken prisoner and thrown out, then do it; but be sure to replace them with something else. Regardless of what your parents or your teachers may ever have said, your head was never designed to be an empty space! Emptying your mind completely is a method used in Eastern meditation, relaxation classes and the like, to supposedly de-stress. But, unless we have a guard at the door of our mind and some healthy replacement thoughts, all sorts of rubbish can come surging in to fill it, much of which can nudge us off course. Some things just don't deserve house room or headspace.

If you can't think of anything to exchange those unhelpful thoughts for, then try Paul's prescription that he dispensed in a letter to the church at Philippi:

> Whatever is true, whatever is noble, whatever is right, whatever is pure, whatever is lovely, whatever is admirable – if anything is excellent or praiseworthy – think about such things.
> (Philippians 4:8)

I like to think of these as an old-fashioned five-bar gate, which used to be standard for farmers' fields before they were replaced with bulky metal ones. They have five horizontal wooden bars, representing things that are true, noble, right, pure, lovely. A diagonal bar reinforces those five, to give strength to the construction; that stands for admirable things. The swinging part of the gate is attached either side to solid wooden gateposts, driven into the earth sufficiently deeply to ensure that the gate stands upright securely, and does the job of enclosing livestock on one side or the other. They symbolise the excellent things on one side, and the praiseworthy things on the other; substantial and enduring.

As a child with a busy head, I used to ask my parents what to dream about each night. They would regularly prescribe me a dose of this 'mind medicine'. Rather than have my mind wander into anxious thoughts, this proved to be a great antidote and preventative treatment for bad dreams, consistently giving me positive things to dwell on as I drifted off to sleep. I highly recommend it – not just for bedtime, or only for children. You can prescribe yourself a few doses each day, and eventually it will become second nature to you.

This is what real meditation is all about: chewing over God's truth. It's all about keeping Jesus at the centre of everything. Just as guy ropes and stakes keep a tent secured so it can't blow away, or a ballerina concentrates on a fixed spot before she begins to pirouette, a mind that is tied to God cannot be blown away, allowed to drift into unhelpful territories or end up in a dizzy, ungainly heap on the floor. An athlete in a race will fix their eyes not on the hurdles, their feet or the other competitors, but on the finishing tape. In the race of life, we need to keep our eyes locked on to Jesus so that we don't run off course, or into the wrong lane.

If God is our fixed point among all the hurly-burly of life, we won't be knocked off the straight path we're on.

Having our hearts and minds changed is a process, and it means that we need to know God's heart and mind. How do we do that? Well, the Bible is the revealed Word of God, and that's where we can learn how to live this new life that we have come into.

Reading the Bible

Getting to know the Bible can seem a monumental task if you've never read it before. Starting at Genesis and slogging chronologically through all sixty-six books to Revelation is probably not the best way to go about it.

I suggest: find a modern translation and begin with one of the Gospels – Matthew, Mark, Luke or John – which cover the life and ministry of Jesus up to His death, resurrection and ascension into heaven, from four different perspectives. They are followed by an account of the early Church in Acts, and then a number of Paul's letters to the churches with whom he had a relationship. These are a great place to discover how to get our minds truly transformed, as Paul explained things to real Christians struggling with real-life issues, just as you and I do in our own cultural context.

God's principles for living transcend time and cultures; they are always applicable, always relevant.

Our minds are first of all changed when our hearts have changed. Basically, we have dethroned ourselves and enthroned God as Lord and King, and so we submit our whole beings to Him. He has become our treasure, that which has most value to us, and consequently our focus will be on Him.

The extraneous twigs are being torn off our prototype arrow. They are worthless, since it's no longer functioning as the branch of a tree. Once in God's family, what is important to us alters; our values and priorities change. We are liberated from the relentless, crushing Western cultural drive for a bigger house, a better car; even climbing the career ladder by hook or by crook has probably lost its appeal; the latest gadgets and designer wardrobes lose their lustre. Jesus' followers in other cultures are often horrified by the materialistic drive that fuels so much of what is valued in Europe and the USA, in particular. Challenges elsewhere are different, but just as real. Where following Jesus is forbidden, our spiritual brothers and sisters face daily threats of which we have little understanding and no experience.

A change of perspective

Our perspective is radically altered as we're taken up with our relationship with God through Jesus and His plans for a messed-up world. We recognise that daily filling and communion with the Holy Spirit is a powerful reality, and necessary if we are to take our place within that plan.

We've understood that He has plans and purposes being worked out through His people across the world, and we are delighted to discover our place within them. We've grasped the value of reading our Bible, praying, searching out truth and investing in our relationship with God. We find a concern for our fellow believers that we never had before, as we start to see them as God sees them,[18] and now experience a fresh compassion for those who don't yet have a saving relationship with God. We are genuinely concerned for their eternal destinies, their fractured relationships and their damaged lives. Our hearts and minds prioritise the things of real spiritual importance and weight.

None of this means that we have had a personality bypass. It certainly doesn't mean that we have become dull and boring. If we have, then we have somehow missed Jesus completely. Our priorities, our values, our outlook have all been revolutionised. It's not about me, me, me any more. I can no longer be the centre of my world. Christ has taken that place, and now it's become a far bigger world than we realised. It also comes with a watertight promise: 'I have come that they may have life, and have it to the full' (John 10:10).

This is not a life of quiet piety as depicted in stained-glass windows or on religious Christmas cards where characters wear dinner-plate-sized halos. We neither walk nor float several inches above the ground with a weird glow of pseudo-holiness around us. There is, however, a jam-packed, abundant and exuberant 'life in all its fullness' (NCV) prepared for us by God, to be thoroughly enjoyed by us as we walk in step with Him. Why would we want to miss that, or to settle for less?

Everyone, without exception, is looking for a way through life that brings more than insipid existence; one that is based in truth rather than lies – be it the false promises of so many political and social programmes, the multiple cults on offer – or the seductive woke culture where 'personal truth' denies objective realities. I don't believe there is a single person on earth who doesn't want to know love, joy and peace in their life; no one who isn't yearning for affirmation, self-acceptance and purpose. The only place anyone will ultimately find those things is in Jesus, who categorically claimed, 'I am the way and the

---

[18] 2 Corinthians 5:16.

truth and the life. No one comes to the Father except through me' (John 14:6).

Having come to Him, we are now being 'transformed into his image' (2 Corinthians 3:18) and becoming more like Him by having our minds retrained to think in a Jesus-like way. The Word of God is our handbook as we grapple with this and begin to understand the truth. Our arrow is under construction, at last.

Knowing about, and really knowing

Jesus, John said, is the Truth, so in knowing Him better we become better acquainted with truth. But God wants more for us than that. He wants us to really know it, or rather, know Him. This is a far deeper, more intimate knowing than cognitive knowledge or accumulated information. This is the word used in more archaic translations of the Bible where, for instance, we can read that Elkanah 'knew' his wife Hannah, and she then became pregnant with Samuel (1 Samuel 1:19, KJV). This kind of knowing means, to have intimacy with and subsequently bear fruit, ie life.

Amazingly, we are now in an intimate relationship with God that has brought us real life. We are also invited to have a depth of intimacy with the truth of God's word in such a way that it looks like something in our lives – it bears fruit. It must make a difference to be authentic. It should not simply wash over us in the way that so much information does, without being retained or affecting our lives in any discernible way.

If we are going to set new neural pathways, we need to dig into truth. Jesus said, 'If you hold to my teaching, you are really my disciples. Then you will know the truth, and the truth will set you free' (John 8:31-32).

As we continue in our day-to-day routines, it's amazing how that dead and buried person tries to exert their influence over our new life; but it's an experience every Christian shares. However, Jesus' assurance is that the truth sets us free from all that. That's great news. Imagine being free of all that baggage that you brought into the kingdom in terms of old patterns and old behaviour! More great news: you don't need to imagine it; it can be a reality. If we keep consciously, or unconsciously, carrying that baggage through life, then, like the 'twigs' on our arrow, they will pull us off course and weigh us down. Truth makes a difference because it liberates us to follow wholeheartedly after God.

The writer of Hebrews encourages us to break out of old patterns like this:

> Let us throw off everything that hinders and the sin that so easily entangles. And let us run with perseverance the race marked out for us, fixing our eyes on Jesus, the pioneer and perfecter of faith.
> (Hebrews 12:1-2)

Isn't sin like that? It can wrap itself around us like a piece of seaweed that gets caught between our feet and causes us to fall flat on our face time and time again. It's no use simply unwrapping a bit of it. We need to disentangle ourselves completely and toss it firmly aside so it doesn't have the chance to trip us again.

This is what being transformed by renewing our minds looks like. It won't be done in an instant, but it's a worthwhile discipline to keep us on track and in the abundant life Jesus promised us. The twiggy branches are discarded as we embrace new defaults, casting off those things that hold us back and could disrupt our spiritual journey. The stick is becoming an arrow.

Target Questions

➢ What is the difference between turning over a new leaf and coming into God's family?

➢ What does it mean to 'be made new in the attitude of your [mind]' (Ephesians 4:22-24)?

➢ Which methods have you discovered to establish new spiritual defaults and keep your eyes fixed on Jesus? Does Philippians 4:8 help?

➢ What fruit is growing in your life as a result of increased intimacy with Jesus?

2a. Peter

Peter is like the Everyman among Jesus' twelve disciples. He's a breath of fresh air in some ways; he wasn't an academic, or an obvious candidate for discipleship, but he's thoroughly relatable because of his mistakes. We see ourselves in him because he's not so very dissimilar to many of us.

Simon (as he was then called) had a fishing business with his brother, Andrew, who was the one who introduced him to Jesus after a tip-off from John the Baptist. Eager and excited to have discovered that the promised Messiah was actually alive in his own era and vicinity, Andrew didn't want his brother to miss out, and straight away went to find him and bring him to meet Jesus too.[19] The first thing Jesus did was change his name from Simon (meaning 'to hear', or 'listen') to Peter (meaning – not to peter out, or fade – but 'rock'; a substance solid and firm).[20]

Jesus saw something in Peter that no other rabbi had done. Rabbis often picked out individuals to join them as pupils; until Jesus came along Peter and the others whom Jesus called had been overlooked. Under his rough exterior and volatile personality, a good heart was beating, along with a genuine hunger for the things of God. Peter seems to have been a natural leader, maybe prone to bossiness, and quite probably the oldest. When Jesus was asked a question about the temple tax,

---

[19] John 1:40-42.
[20] www.thebump.com/b/simon-baby-name (accessed 19th January 2024).

he pointed Peter to a miraculous provision via a fish, which covered the payment for the two of them.[21] According to Old Testament law, this tax was payable only by people over the age of twenty.[22] The rest of the disciples may well have been much younger than the way we usually see them portrayed.

It was Peter's boat that Jesus chose as an impromptu pulpit when a crowd around the lake of Galilee was pressing in on Him. Once Jesus had finished preaching, He told Peter to put out the fishing nets again into deep water 'for a catch' (Luke 5:4). This was foolishness for a seasoned fisherman who knew that a) this was the wrong time of day to go fishing, and b) he was in front of a lot of noisy people who would have disturbed the fish. Peter was on the verge of telling Jesus at least some of this as he began to protest that they'd been out all night long and caught nothing. But even as he said it, you can almost see how Peter checked himself, and perhaps remembered the look Jesus gave him when Andrew had introduced them. There was something very different about this rabbi from Nazareth that drew Peter to Him. So, somewhat against his professional judgement, he agreed to give it a try. The subsequent haul of fish threatened to break the nets and capsize the entire boat.

Jesus wanted Peter to know He was interested in his business and everyday life; but more importantly, He was interested in him.

Overwhelmed by such a massive catch, Peter fell at Jesus' feet, all too conscious of his own weaknesses and flawed humanity in the presence of something so 'other' that it absolutely had to be sacred and holy. His natural fear prompted him to ask Jesus to leave them. Life with Jesus around was not going to be comfortable. Yet, Jesus invited him to leave his fishing business and follow Him instead. Peter never looked back.

It was Peter who wanted to walk on water with Jesus, as we read in Matthew 14. No one else in the boat on Galilee that dark

---

[21] Matthew 17:24–27.

[22] Exodus 30:14; 38:26.

night attempted the feat. The other disciples thought the figure walking on water towards them was a ghost, which rendered them terrified. 'Good for you, Peter,' we say. 'You're the only one who took that courageous step.' But we miss the point. While Peter, like any good rabbinic student, wanted to be like his Master, he wasn't quite as far on in his journey with Jesus as he thought. Whether impetuous or initially full of faith, Peter was distracted by the elements of wind and rain; he began to panic, and sink. Did he doubt Jesus, or himself, or perhaps his capacity to be empowered by Jesus? Yes, he was the only one who did walk on the water (if only for a couple of steps, it was more than anyone else has done), but Jesus didn't commend him for that, even though he was clearly trying to copy his rabbi. Such students were in training for this very thing: to copy their masters and emulate them in every way. On this occasion, Jesus rebuked Peter for his lack of faith.

Keeping our eyes on Jesus is paramount, whoever we are.

Peter's impulsive nature often prompted him to state the obvious, or to speak without thinking, but, once again, it was Peter who first boldly stated that Jesus was unquestionably the promised Christ; the longed-for Messiah.[23] The other eleven were prepared to repeat what the locals were saying – that perhaps He was the embodiment one of the old prophets – but only Peter went out on a limb and spoke out what the Holy Spirit had revealed to him. He had a deep conviction of Jesus' true identity.

Yet, almost immediately after this monumentally important statement, for which Jesus pronounced a great blessing over Peter, Matthew 16 cites a very different conversation between Peter and Jesus. Knowing what lay ahead of Him, Jesus began to talk to His followers about what would happen when they next went to Jerusalem. He broke the news to them that He would suffer at the hands of the religious elite, and be killed

---

[23] Matthew 16:16.

there. He also introduced the mind-stretching fact that three days later, He would rise from the dead.

Peter found this whole narrative offensive. His default reaction was an indignant one. Rather than pause and ask an appropriate question, he forgot himself completely as he took Jesus to one side and began to remonstrate with Him. Instead of listening to the One He had just recognised and publicly acknowledged as the promised Christ, Peter went all-out in insisting that Jesus' prediction could not be allowed to happen.

It was a misguided attempt on Peter's part to protect his Master. A fierce loyalty was rooted in seeing what was in front of him, rather than what God had in mind. His refusal to contemplate the future, which Jesus had long known was in line with His Father's will in order to open the door to salvation, brought Peter the most sobering of stinging rebukes. 'Get behind me, Satan! You are a stumbling-block to me; you do not have in mind the concerns of God, but merely human concerns' (Matthew 16:23).

It must have stopped him in his tracks. Peter had a lot to process in reflecting on these two contrasting conversations. Esteemed one moment, and a verbal slap in the face the next. I wonder how he weathered the curious stares and probable barbed remarks of the other eleven after the humiliation of Jesus' dressing down. His pride may have been wounded; he might have given in to his old defaults, packed up and gone home, but Peter never walked away.

Not long after this, Peter, James and John witnessed the amazing transfiguration of Jesus into His heavenly glory on top of a mountain. Everything about Jesus became a dazzling, bright, white light, and suddenly, Moses and Elijah were somehow present, talking to Him there. The appropriate response from the three disciples would probably have been to crash face down on the ground in awe and trembling, and indeed, that's what they did after the voice of God Himself spoke from a thick cloud. Prior to that, however, Peter opened his mouth at a time when it would have been better to say nothing, and just listen.

> Peter said to Jesus, 'Lord, it is good for us to be here. If you wish, I will put up three shelters – one for you, one for Moses and one for Elijah.'
> (Matthew 17:4)

What on earth was he thinking? Apparently overwhelmed by the extraordinary moment, his mouth ran away with him into utter nonsense. Did he really think this was some kind of divine camping trip? Or perhaps he was harking back to the kind of shelters the Israelites used during their forty years in the desert, or even the construction of the original tabernacle. Peter wasn't being flippant – that's not consistent with what we see of him in other situations – I believe he genuinely wanted to help, to be involved and participate in this strange gathering, and maybe to make it last as long as possible. Even while his words were tumbling somewhat incoherently from his mouth, the presence of God covered them all in the form of a cloud as He spoke divine affirmation over His much-loved Son.

Poor old Peter; he was probably quite relieved that Jesus told them not to tell anyone else about what they had just seen. He was spared the embarrassment of retelling his inappropriate part of the strange experience, although Gospel-writer Matthew must have found out about it somehow.

In the days leading up to the crucifixion, it was Peter and John who were sent to make preparations so that Jesus and the disciples could celebrate the Passover feast together. They found a furnished upstairs room, just as Jesus had indicated, and proceeded to make the appropriate preparations.[24] It was here that Jesus washed His disciples' feet in a visual act of service, and effectively squashed their squabbles about who was the greatest.[25]

---

[24] Luke 22:8-13.
[25] John 13:3-11; Luke 22:24-27.

Once again Peter's old self broke out. He disagreed with Jesus, telling Him that He would never get to wash his feet, like some household servant. He had completely missed the point; this washing was more than a question of hygiene. This was Jesus demonstrating secure servanthood because He was so comfortably assured of who He was, why He was there, where He'd come from and where He was going. He set a pioneering example of the kind of leadership the apostles were to embrace in the days ahead.

'Unless I wash you, you have no part with me,' said Jesus (John 13:8), and immediately Peter changed his position completely. In a total about face, he declared that since that was the case, Jesus had better include his hands and head as well, and basically wash all of him. It's actually quite endearing, yet Peter still missed the point.

Again, Peter came under Jesus' spotlight when his rabbi reverted to using his former name, Simon, as He shared how He had been praying for His impetuous disciple.

> Simon, Simon, Satan has asked to sift all of you as wheat.
> But I have prayed for you, Simon, that your faith may
> not fail. And when you have turned back, strengthen
> your brothers.
> (Luke 22:31-32)

How amazing to know that Jesus had prayed for him by name, even in such a serious context. Using his old name was a way of highlighting how well Jesus knew Peter and his predilection for allowing his old life to leak out. Jesus wouldn't be taken by surprise by the events that would unfold that night. Because we know what happened, we cringe at Peter's overly enthusiastic reply as he claimed he was unafraid of what lay ahead; how he was prepared to join Jesus in prison if need be, or even to die with Him.

Another sobering reply from Jesus in front of everyone: 'I tell you, Peter, before the cock crows today, you will deny three times that you know me' (Luke 22:34). Did Peter notice how

Jesus reverted to the name He had given him at their first meeting, or was he too busy wishing the ground would open up and swallow him, I wonder? Was his resolve strengthened by his misplaced pride to prove himself to the disciples, to show that he had truly put that old life firmly behind him, and even to prove that to Jesus Himself?

What is certain is that Peter had one of the two swords that were brought to Gethsemane with them, and when Judas arrived with a crowd of people including soldiers, he was prepared to use it. Peter may have fallen asleep while Jesus prayed, but in a tight spot, his default was to fight his way out of trouble. Swinging wildly, he sliced off the ear of the high priest's servant, Malchus;[26] but you can be sure he wasn't aiming for that ear. The chances are that Peter would have taken the head off this man if the servant hadn't had such good reflexes.

Jesus called a halt to the aggressive retaliation, and graciously healed that ear. I'd love to know the rest of Malchus' story. One week later, what might his reflections have been on the events of that Passover week, and what would he have answered had anyone bothered to ask him who he thought Jesus really was?

Although the disciples scattered at that point, John had connections with Caiaphas' household and was able to access the courtyard of the high priest's house and get Peter in as well. While Jesus went through abuse at the hands of the Sanhedrin in that illegal night trial, Peter 'warmed himself' (Mark 14:54) by a fire outside, his ears open for news.

Here he was recognised twice by one of the servant girls as having been in the company of Jesus. Once again, Peter's defaults let him down as, intimidated by women who had a very marginalised, peripheral role in that society, he claimed to not know what they were talking about, and that he didn't even know Jesus. When he was challenged again because his Galilean accent gave away where he was from, Peter felt the pressure increase. Instead of following through on his expressed

---

[26] John 18:10.

intentions of earlier in the evening, he upped the ante by invoking curses and swearing that he had no knowledge of the man on trial.

Wherever Jesus was, He had Peter in His sights at this moment, and in eight little words of descriptive writing, Peter's world crashed around his ears: 'The Lord turned and looked straight at Peter' (Luke 22:61).

If ever a look said a thousand words, this one did. But what did it express: anger, regret, disappointment, rebuke, or a selfless love so deep that even Peter's betrayal couldn't thwart it?

Whatever it communicated, in that instant Peter remembered Jesus' words, and he was overwhelmed. Running from the courtyard, the man who was theoretically prepared to follow Jesus to death broke down in inconsolable tears of contrition and deep sorrow.

Peter could have been the arrow that just couldn't break with his past; and yet Jesus restored him, forgave him, commissioned him and reassured him, as we see in John 21. He underwent an extraordinary transformation by the power of the Holy Spirit at Pentecost; from fear-filled to genuinely fearless. He became an anointed leader of the emerging Church, a preacher, master-builder/apostle and teacher, primarily to the Jewish people. He saw God change lives, and he performed miracles; he also experienced a miraculous escape from prison himself, documented in Acts 12. His two letters were written to believers – some undergoing persecution – scattered across an area known as Asia Minor, urging them to keep in mind who Jesus really was, and to stay faithful to His truth.

Peter became a mighty and effective arrow once he really put his past behind him and allowed God to change him from the inside out.

3. Stripping the Bark

Making an arrow is a rough process as far as the arrow is concerned. God once told Jeremiah to watch a clay pot being squashed and moulded under the pressure of the potter's hand.[27] The discomfort of the process was necessary to produce something of worth.

Under pressure

We've been led to believe that pressure is a bad thing, to be avoided at all costs. Statistics tell us that more people than ever before are suffering from stress; this may manifest itself as ulcers, migraines and breakdowns brought on by the pace and pressures of life. For many, such symptoms are consequences of the struggles during the pandemic lockdowns.[28] Supermarkets and pharmacies offer a staggering array of stress-busting goodies: bath essences, aromatherapy candles, essential oils, muscle relaxants, energising teas, herbal remedies… the list seems endless. Bookshops and libraries devote entire sections to self-help volumes that promise to divulge the secrets that will free us from the constraints of pressure. We are invited to de-stress everything from our wardrobes to our diaries to our diet.

---

[27] Jeremiah 18:1-4.
[28] iris.who.int/bitstream/handle/10665/356119/9789240049338-eng.pdf?sequence=1 (accessed 1st March 2024).

But pressure is not always a bad thing; it can be helpful in the right context. A dirty lump of coal can only become a sparkling diamond if subjected to the right conditions; some of the most valuable treasures on earth are the result of extreme pressure in very dark places. Likewise, the pressure cooker is a useful piece of culinary equipment that cooks food in an artificial environment of good stress.

Again, stress produced by an encounter with danger is vital for the adrenal glands to produce the adrenaline hormone required in the body's fight or flight reaction; it can be a literal lifesaver. Working to deadlines for a project, or exams, can be stressful, but it can also be a great motivation to focus with a view to achieving a result of a higher standard than if the environment were more relaxed.

Our arrow is nowhere near ready to be polished yet, and it is going to experience its own kind of stress. It's been broken off the old tree and the extraneous pieces removed. Now it must have the outer layer of bark stripped off too.

Bark as a protection

While the arrow is still a functioning branch on a tree, the bark serves as a protective wrapping. It's a tough enough coating to take bumps from the outside, as the tree is buffeted by aggressive weathering and curious browsing cattle but, crucially, it stops the inside from drying out and manufactures nourishment in an environment of evaporation.

Some bark is tough, thick and gnarled; other bark can be peeled off in long strips – much to the delight of children in the park. Either way, if the stick is ever going to fulfil its potential as an arrow, then this is the next stage in its journey.

We have begun the lifelong process of being transformed to become like Jesus by renewing our minds. Now we face a new challenge.

Earlier, we noted that the stick could not 'make its own terms with the one who tore it from that tree'. Similarly, we cannot negotiate with God, barter or make conditions with Him now. He paid a high price for us, and while *we* may not believe He got much of a bargain, He disagrees. Now we've put Him in His rightful place as King in our life, He is King of all of it. Not just a bit of it; not just on Sundays; not everything except the bank account/television remote/schedule... all of it; everything.

God's relationship with us is one in which His desire is always to break through self-erected barriers; to bring healing, life and wholeness.

Motivated by His great love and concern for us to flourish and become all He has made us to be, God will gently peel away the layers of our self-defences to get to the 'real' us, if we surrender to Him. Once those barriers are down, He can bring His gentle healing to damaged places. His love nurtures us; it never shames us, embarrasses us or humiliates us. The goal is to get Him *in* to every area and us *out* of every area, if He is to truly be King in our lives. This means there are no 'no-go' areas as far as He is concerned.

'No-go' areas are not just geographical; they exist in relationships too. There are marriages in which the topics of parents, finance or sexual intimacy are never discussed; areas of hurt and disappointment which can't be resolved because the subject matter is too emotive to explore. Consequently, apparently uncrossable chasms open up over the years, stealing joy and robbing the relationship of the intimacy God intended. Friendships can remain shallow when we erect inappropriate boundaries. We may carry past hurts which have caused us to be defensive in our connection with others; these usually end up isolating us, making us vulnerable to dark thoughts and damaging introspection. It's impossible to sustain deep, meaningful friendships with a large number of people, but it's important to have some kindred spirits with whom we can be open and honest.

This can feel unnerving, especially if we've spent many years being in charge of our own life; it's not surprising that we might become defensive if we're challenged. Our default may still be to keep our hand on the rudder. We may not be controlling as such, but it's surprising the lengths we can go to in order to hang on to control in various areas of our lives: finances, eating habits, social preferences, time management, etc.

Breaking through the barrier of self-sufficiency

Handing over governance of our life to God is a milestone of massive significance in our life's history. But when push comes to shove, we may find that the reality of having Jesus' reign extend into every part of our life is rather hard to swallow; that's why God will insist on peeling back those protective layers of self-sufficiency so that our decision becomes an authentic, three-dimensional, all-encompassing, living truth.

In an age that applauds self-sufficiency – in every facet of life – this is massively countercultural. Those who make it alone in life through sheer self-will, energy and determination are lauded as heroes worthy of public recognition. Sadly, many of these role models cannot sustain their success; all too often they fall prey to broken relationships or financial misdemeanours, or are found to have been little more than bullies, projecting an image rather than a reality.

Self-sufficiency is nowhere to be found in the Bible. We can't walk with God or live our Christian life from our own skills or ability. There is nothing in us that can sustain a level of righteousness by our own effort, so self-sufficiency is a nonsense.

Righteousness is a gift from God, and He won't take that back; but to live in the good of it we must allow Him access to all areas of our lives.

When I first met my husband, I was fairly guarded in what I was prepared to talk about regarding myself. I had been used to living on my own; I enjoyed my own company, and I would keep a lot of things to myself. I didn't let people get too close because, quite frankly, I'd had some experiences of disappointment which led to me strapping on some emotional armour for protection; I didn't want to get hurt again. I thought it was pretty effective, but I was wrong; it was doing me no good at all.

I remember sitting in the car with him after an early date, and him saying, 'I'm not going to let you get away with not talking about things with me.' Initially, I was indignant. What a cheek, I thought. Who does he think he is, anyway? What surprised me, though, was the unexpected feeling of welcome relief that came over me. Perhaps I didn't have to carry all this 'stuff' on my own any more. The need to be defensive or on my guard the whole time vanished as a weight I didn't even know was there, lifted from me.

Bernard wasn't being cruel or dictatorial; in fact, it didn't take long for me to realise how fortunate I was to have found someone who cared enough about me not to let me continue in that rather malfunctioning, self-destructive default. Rather than feeling offended, after that first recoil I slowly began to open up. It was safe; I wasn't going to be rejected, so I could finally be myself. Far from being restricting, it was actually very liberating. I found a new lease of life as my crude self-sufficiency began to be stripped away.

That's a very real representation of how God comes alongside us and does the same thing.

Saints who sometimes sin

Becoming a Christian doesn't turn us into flawless people overnight – perfection is a long way off – but the wonderful truth is that God has planned for this. He knows that even though we yearn to live lives that bring Him glory and pleasure, there will be times that we mess up. That's one reason why I love the Bible so much; it doesn't try to gloss over the mistakes and outright disobedience of even some of the greatest heroes of the faith.

See what I mean by taking a look at these examples, which span the Bible from Genesis through to the New Testament:

Adam, the first blame-shifter, couldn't stand up to the peer pressure of his wife.

Abraham, the patriarch and Father of the Faith, lied on two separate occasions to save his own skin. He also compromised by sleeping with his wife's maidservant, the result of which was a tribe which was in almost constant conflict with God's people in the years to come.

Rebekah favoured one son (Jacob) over the other and helped him to deceive his father, Isaac, thus cheating his elder brother, Esau, out of his birthright.

Jacob deceived both his father and his brother without protest, qualm or apology. He later deceived his uncle Laban as well.

Reuben, Jacob's firstborn, slept with his father's concubine.

Aaron gave in to peer pressure and led the Israelites into despicable idol worship.

Moses murdered an Egyptian right at the start of his journey towards leadership, and tried to hide the evidence. Years later, he got so angry with the Israelites that he misrepresented God to them and so forfeited his place in the Promised Land.

Miriam allowed jealousy and resentment to lead her into discontent and complaining against God. The consequence was a bout of leprosy before Moses prayed for her restoration and healing.

Samson got involved with notoriously bad women, despite God's particular call on his life.

Naomi nearly forfeited her destiny after giving in to intense and crippling bitterness.

King Saul had some serious anger issues, which included trying to pin young David to the wall with a spear. He consulted with a medium, despite knowing it was contrary to God's law, and, tragically, he ended his life by his own hand.

David committed adultery with Bathsheba and arranged the death of his close friend to try to cover his tracks. He also failed to train his children in God's ways.

Solomon, despite being the wisest man in history, had hundreds of sexual partners through his seven hundred wives and three hundred concubines (1 Kings 11:3), many of whom came from nations with whom God's people were forbidden to intermarry, and he was led astray from his walk with God in consequence.

Peter, who, as we've seen, in spite of his vociferous support for his rabbi Master, denied he even knew Jesus; not once, but three times. Later on, Peter was called out on his inconsistency when, having ministered effectively to the Gentiles, he withdrew from them when he allowed his fear of a small group of Jewish believers known as 'the circumcision group', to get the better of him' (Galatians 2:11-14).

Thomas doubted Jesus could have been resurrected, despite the testimonies of reliable witnesses.

That's quite a hall of fame. I'm so grateful that the Bible gives a warts-and-all account of these individuals, who would have the modern tabloids falling over each other to get an 'exclusive'. It reminds me that we are all on a journey of faith, not a quick dash to perfection. The Bible doesn't glamorise them or dwell unnecessarily on their bad choices in a voyeuristic way, but it does make it clear that they sometimes had to bear the consequences of their sin. What they didn't have to do, and neither do we, was to continue to live under the burden and guilty weight of that sin.

Sorry, or really sorry?

At the point of conversion, our sin was taken from us; we're washed clean from the inside out, but God has also made provision for us to keep clean. It's called repentance, and it keeps us soft towards God – bark-free, as it were.

This is more than just saying, 'Sorry.'

My children learned to say 'sorry' when they were still very little. The difficulty for us parents was differentiating between them being 'sorry' they had been found out and being 'sorry' that they had behaved in a particular way. For example, if one of them told a lie (regrettably, they were not angels after all), was the 'sorry' a calculated move to try to avoid the disciplinary consequences, or was there a genuine heart sorrow about their misdemeanour, accompanied by a change of heart – a resolve not to do it again?

That's the difference between an apology and repentance.

Repentance involves a change of mind, a change of heart. It admits that we were not merely misguided, or unfortunate to act as we did; it was not a mistake or an error of judgement. We consciously chose a non-Jesus path, and now there is a clear action taken of turning around in a different – a kingdom – direction.

We are no longer 'slaves to sin' (Romans 6:20) in the way that we were before Christ had control of our lives, and we now have provision for the times when we do sin. The diagram shows how this works:

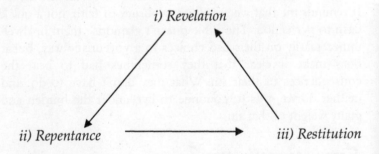

i) Revelation

ii) Repentance   *iii) Restitution*

God puts His finger on something in our lives and we receive a revelation, or insight, about where we have missed His way. Our natural reaction is to want to sort it out, to put it right and make amends. But if we seek to do so by our own efforts, we can bypass the whole process of repentance, so are still not right with God. In other words, we never admit to the uncomfortable truth that we were wrong.

If we simply resolve to try to do better next time, it will prove to be as effective as pulling ourselves out of a bog by our own bootlaces. It may appear to work in the short term, but we'll soon be back at the same place. Why? Well, because in bypassing repentance we also bypass grace.

> For the grace of God has appeared that offers salvation to all people. It teaches us to say 'No' to ungodliness and worldly passions, and to live self-controlled, upright and godly lives.
> (Titus 2:11-12)

Paul explained to his good friend and fellow worker, Titus, that it's God's grace that helps us to refuse to allow ungodly, sinful things into our lives. If we don't access grace then we're moving in legalism, which merely engages our brain while bypassing our hearts, and so leads to death.

Repentance allows us to receive His grace, which then resources us to make restitution in an appropriate and effective way.

Since God's love for us, and His acceptance of us, is not based on our performance, it means that He is delighted, even eager, to forgive us when we repent. Even when we have to come back to Him about the same thing, He doesn't wave it in our faces. God is not just the God of the second chance, but of the third, fourth, fifth and beyond. That doesn't mean that He has stopped taking sin seriously; but, 'If we confess our sins, he is faithful and just and will forgive us our sins and purify us from all unrighteousness' (1 John 1:9).

Sin brings judgement from God, as Adam and Eve found out in the Garden of Eden. God did not sympathise with their deception by Satan; He held them responsible, but He also provided them with a means of redemption.

Realistically, we all fall short of God's exacting standards on a daily basis, so repentance will probably become a healthy way of life for us. Fortunately, God's grace is big enough to handle it. It doesn't have a sell-by date and it will never run out.

> For it is by grace you have been saved, through faith –
> and this is not from yourselves, it is the gift of God – not
> by works, so that no one can boast.
> (Ephesians 2:8-9)

Master of my own destiny

It's interesting that so many New Age philosophies revolve around 'self'. It's a subtle but destructive form of human pride. It claims that we are effectively our own gods; that there is no power beyond or outside ourselves; we become our own truth, deciding what is right or wrong for us. Everything is subjective; there are no absolutes, no objective realities.

The teaching of our current culture does not allow for the biblical truth of an Almighty God, who holds the universe in His hands, who desires relationship with us and who has made the way for that to happen through Jesus, to be taken seriously. It's much more mystical and vague than that; a self-service religion where, like a buffet, you can select the parts that appeal to you and disregard the rest, but still walk away with a 'valid' meal.

The real blockage to God's grace is the thinking that allows our pride to take centre stage. 'I am master of my own destiny,' it declares. 'Look within: I possess everything inside me to be whatever I want to be.' In reality, it is the embodiment of supreme arrogance; it is self-worship. That makes it a form of idolatry which God says is 'detestable'.[29]

The Bible flies in the face of that philosophy. We contribute nothing to our salvation except our own sin; nothing to be proud of at all. It also says that 'God opposes the proud, but gives grace to the humble' (1 Peter 5:5, RSV).

---

[29] 1 Peter 4:3.

Not only does God take a poor view of this kind of arrogance, but He actively opposes it.

Indulging in pride in any form means that God will stand against us. By definition, we will be cut off from accessing His grace and find ourselves in a pitiful condition. Without the grace that helps us to say 'No' to unrighteousness, we will end up saying 'Yes' to it, and find ourselves on a route that leads away from God rather than towards Him. The only way back is along that humbling, yet wonderful, road of repentance which God mercifully provides for us.

It would be foolishness to think that we can have a foot in both camps. All vestiges of pride, self-reliance and self-sufficiency need to be stripped away.

If I have truly submitted my life to Christ, then He must now hold that number one position; He takes centre stage, not me. If I try to usurp that place and take back the throne of rule for my life, I am not only heading for trouble; I will actually be slipping into some devilish activity.

Devilish pride

Satan himself, originally an angelic being the Bible calls Lucifer, was thrown out of heaven for trying to usurp the throne of God.[30] Fuelled by pride, and dissatisfaction with who God had made him to be, he led a rebellion in heaven, the consequence of which was that he was ejected, along with his fellow schemers. Together they have been causing havoc on the earth for generations. Such an attempt at divine revolution was rooted in jealousy for the glory that rightly belongs to God alone. Neither a comic nor imaginary being, 'Satan is a malignant reality, always hostile to God and to God's people'.[31] He is

---

[30] Luke 10:18; Isaiah 14:12-15; alluded to in Ezekiel 28:12-19; 2 Thessalonians 2:4.

[31] N Hillyer, *The Illustrated Bible Dictionary, Volume 3* (Westmont/Carol Stream, IL: IVP/Tyndale House, 1980) p1396.

actively at work in the world today opposing the gospel in any and every way possible, and besmirching the created image of God in humanity – the pinnacle of creation – wherever he can.

Ever since that heavenly disruption, it has been the goal and purpose of the devil to dethrone the King of kings. He cannot do it literally, since God's throne is established – it cannot be shaken – but he'll happily do it in my life, or yours, or the life of anyone who is following Jesus, however he can. His strategy has not changed over the millennia; he still has an agenda to 'steal and kill and destroy' (John 10:10), and he will seek to achieve that in a no-holds-barred onslaught on the people of God.

As God strips the metaphorical bark from us human arrows-in-the-making, He reveals what's really in our hearts. Having access to all areas means there is no dark corner where His light cannot shine. We are exposed in every part. Known fully inside and out.

There is something both thrilling and unnerving about such absolute knowledge. No more masks; no more pretence.

Wearing the right yoke

It is time to sacrifice our self-sufficiency on the altar of humility, and walk the path ahead of us as God intended; not alone, relying on our own abilities, but with Him, dependent on His unfailing strength.

In the New Testament Jesus offers a compelling invitation:

> Come to me, all you are weary and burdened, and I will give you rest. Take my yoke upon you and learn from me, for I am gentle and humble in heart, and you will find rest for your souls. For my yoke is easy and my burden is light.
> (Matthew 11:28-30)

None of us has ever been as self-sufficient as we perhaps like to think. We've all been physically and emotionally tired, weary in our spirits. The invitation of Jesus is to put on His yoke and walk with Him. This is not a yoke of doctrine but of friendship, relationship, son/daughtership.

Jesus knew what He was talking about. He must have made many of these wooden yokes in His father's carpenter's shop back in Nazareth.

Before the industrial revolution, when farmers relied on horses and oxen rather than machinery to get jobs done, tilling a field required the strength of two animals to pull the plough. To ensure that they pulled in step, they were lashed together by a wooden yoke shaped to fit across their shoulders and strapped in place so that the weight of both the yoke and the plough were distributed evenly. The result was an efficient unit, working together to make a straight furrow ready for planting.

Jesus says we need to be wearing His yoke and walking with Him. He promises that it is both easy and light; doesn't that sound attractive? If we wear His yoke rather than our own, then, unlike the cattle, we are in a very uneven but far more effective partnership, in which Jesus takes all the weight on Himself. The implication is that the yoke Jesus is offering us is made to measure, and finished to a high level of quality so that there are no harsh edges to cut into us, and no rough straps to cause chafing; a bespoke yoke. Whatever yoke we fashioned for ourselves and wore through life before we submitted to God, it needs to be taken off and replaced with this one if we're to live in the rest that Jesus offers.

This isn't the same as lazing about on the couch doing nothing. Having God at the centre of life isn't like winning the lottery so all your problems are over; it's not a soft option. Life will not suddenly become one long picnic in the park; there will still be difficult times, distressing situations, personality clashes, irritants and circumstances that challenge us and stretch us further than we thought possible.

One of the most famous passages in the entire Bible was written by King David, of David and Goliath fame. In Psalm 23:4 he wrote: 'Even though I walk through the darkest valley,

I will fear no evil, for you are with me.' Even in the shadows where death lurks, we can know this, and that's the life-altering difference. Jesus will be walking right next to us through it all, however dark.

If you are weary through carrying the problems of others on your shoulders, then give them to Jesus and let Him carry your worries and anxiety on His broad, strong shoulders. He cares about you, so He cares about those things that trouble you. Let Him strip back your bark and meet with you where you are vulnerable.

If you are overwhelmed with fears of the future fed by the headlines and hysteria of the media, then be encouraged by reminders in several psalms that none of those protagonists will live forever. They may appear to have defied God but, secure in heaven, He laughs. God knows that time will move them on and their earthly strutting will be assigned to the dusty corners of history, while He endures forever.

If you find yourself consumed by financial concerns, then turn to Jesus' words in Matthew 6, and take heart:

> Therefore I tell you, do not worry about your life, what you will eat or drink; or about your body, what you will wear. Is not life more important than food, and the body more than clothes? Look at the birds of the air; they do not sow or reap or store away in barns, and yet your heavenly Father feeds them. Are you not much more valuable than they? Can any one of you by worrying add a single hour to your life? ... do not worry ... your heavenly Father knows that you need them.
> (Matthew 6:25-27, 31-32)

Anyone who is walking yoked to Jesus in this way cannot return to self-sufficiency unless they choose to pick up the old yoke. Since that one was not designed to fit, then it will be awkward, uncomfortable and painful. Why would anyone want to return to it?

Walking in step

One of the most comforting verses to me in the whole of the New Testament is recorded by Luke, after Jesus' death and resurrection. Jesus appeared to two of His friends as they made the long journey from Jerusalem to Emmaus. Deeply distressed by the events of the previous hours, and confused by the women's report of an empty tomb and angels, they walked along the road together, still at a loss to understand what had happened, which made no sense to them. Suddenly, 'Jesus himself came up and walked along with them' (Luke 24:15). The two friends were kept from recognising Him until after they'd reached home and sat down to supper with Jesus.

What I love about this verse is that first, Jesus came to them Himself. He didn't send an emissary, or a letter, but came in person. Not only that, but He 'came up', or 'drew near'; He came close and walked along beside them, listening and talking as they went along the road. He didn't stand behind them and rebuke them for their lack of understanding. Neither did He stand in front of them and urge them to 'do better', or to 'hurry up'. Nor did He stand at a distance and shout instructions so they could try to work it out on their own. No; God is primarily relational, and so Jesus came right into their space to help His friends wrestle through their difficulties and hurts. Then, He walked with them; side by side, step by step, addressing their worries, sharing their pain and finding their hearts.

He does the same with us.

Be encouraged; even though you may wince and smart a little from having that protective bark removed, you are becoming more like a polished arrow with every step.

Target Questions

➤ How do you see pressure in your life: positive or negative? Think of examples of constructive and destructive stress in your own life.

➤ Which of the biblical examples resonated most with you? How does it help you to know that none of the characters listed was a perfect saint?

➤ Why is repentance so key to a healthy spiritual life?

➤ Which yoke are you currently wearing? Is it the one Jesus wants you to wear? How can you change yokes?

3a. Naomi

Naomi's story is found in the little book of Ruth. It's just four chapters long, and we focus primarily on Ruth herself when we read it because, at heart, it's a beautiful love story between her and Boaz. The themes of harvest and community are strong too, which is why it's often read during Feast of Weeks, Pentecost, or Shavuot, as it's also called in Jewish tradition.

Naomi lived during the time of the judges, before Israel's monarchy was established. This was a period during which there were repetitive cycles of idol worship, followed by God's discipline and a consequential return to Him, before the nation tragically but predictably hardened their hearts and slid once more into the worship of foreign gods. Famine was one of the tools God used to alert His people to their destructive choices, cause them to look up from their lives, re-evaluate their circumstances, become aware of Him again, and to call them back to a path of righteousness.[32]

The book opens by citing an apparently natural disaster as the trigger for Elimelek and his wife, Naomi, to take their two sons and leave their home town of Bethlehem – which, ironically, means 'House of Bread' – and head for Moab, as the famine in Israel became unbearable. Historically, the Moabites descended from an incestuous relationship between Abraham's nephew, Lot, and one of his daughters; the Moabites and

---

[32] Leviticus 26:18-20; Deuteronomy 28:22-24.

Israelites had been in conflict for generations. Not only that, but it was the Moabites who had hired Balaam to curse the entire Hebrew nation as they journeyed from Egypt to the Promised Land under Moses' leadership; and it was the Moabite women who seduced the Israelite men into a pagan lifestyle by inviting them to their immoral and detestable religious practices.[33] All in all, Moab may not have been the best destination for a God-fearing Hebrew family; perhaps this is an indication of the desperate situation in which they found themselves.

Nevertheless, Elimelek and Naomi flouted God's specific instructions when they allowed their two sons, Mahlon and Kilion, to take wives from the Moabite people. The timeframe isn't clear and no explanation given, but before long both Naomi's husband and her boys died, leaving her as a grieving migrant widow with two daughters-in-law to feed and care for. Their status as women and widows made them doubly vulnerable as a bleak future stretched out ahead of them.

Back home in Israel, the famine had ended, so Naomi strapped on some emotional armour and resolved to go home where, while still susceptible to mistreatment, at least she would not be regarded with the horrible stigma of being a stranger and a foreigner. Perhaps this is why she blessed her two daughters-in-law and urged them to head back to their own families where they might seek refuge and consolation, and maybe one day find another husband too. Although initially reluctant to leave Naomi, Orpah did just that, but Ruth couldn't bear to abandon her. Despite Naomi's anger and grief over losing both her husband and her sons, Ruth had seen something in the life of her mother-in-law that motivated her to stick with her through whatever was to come.

Ruth wanted to both live and die with Naomi under the banner of God's blessing. By this declaration, she rejected the gods of her homeland, and embraced the faith she had been introduced to through her husband's family.

---

[33] Numbers 22–25.

Naomi's heart must have been comforted by not having to face the humiliating journey back to Bethlehem on her own. However, her circumstances had turned around so dramatically that she no longer wanted to be known as the woman everyone in her home town had known before. Naomi means 'pleasant' or 'gentle'; it was the name she wanted to renounce in the light of the things that had happened in her life over the recent years. Her situation had changed, but her physical appearance must also have been considerably altered, since people genuinely no longer recognised her. Was it really Naomi they were seeing back in town? Her response to them was:

> Don't call me Naomi ... Call me Mara, because the Almighty has made my life very bitter. I went away full, but the LORD has brought me back empty. Why call me Naomi? The LORD has afflicted me; the Almighty has brought misfortune upon me.
> (Ruth 1:20-21)

Can you hear the resentment, the seething rage and vitriol in her voice? Naomi blamed God for her situation and the cruel loss of her family. She was full of self-pity and self-loathing, distant from God and wondering what the point of her life now was. Still grieving, her words betrayed the fullness of her heart as her disappointment spilled over in the street. Naomi was dead to her; now she was Mara. She put up a barrier between herself and God, deeming Him culpable and laying the responsibility of her bereavements at His door. It's as though she determinedly turned her back on Him and refused to seek Him in her anguish and pain.

Naomi had no idea what her life might look like in this next season; without the men in her family, she could see no reason for purposeful living. Like many of us who go through trauma or experience a terrible blow, she retreated into herself and fell into the slough of self-pity, from where she nursed her grievances against God.

To keep themselves alive and provide a temporary income, Naomi realised that she would have to sell the land her husband had owned. Meanwhile, Ruth clearly realised it was her turn to care for her disgruntled mother-in-law; it was her initiative that started a new thread of the story.

It was Ruth who suggested that she should go and glean some leftover grain in a farmer's field so that they could have something to eat, even though she was now the one who would bear the consequences of being an outsider. Bereaved women would find it hard to support themselves in this society, and often ended up on a slippery slope to prostitution as they struggled to earn some sort of living.

While she was quickly identified as a foreigner by the farmer's workers in the field where she ended up, in a wonderful God-incidence (as opposed to coincidence), it turned out that the owner of the harvest field was from the same clan as Elimelek, so had a natural compassion for his relative's family. Boaz showed great concern and generosity towards Ruth, giving explicit instructions to his workers that she not be harassed or molested (an indication of the usual treatment extended to women in her position). He had heard on the Bethlehem grapevine how the two widows had arrived in Bethlehem, and how Ruth had left her homeland to stay with Naomi. Moved by her sacrifice, he invoked God's special blessing over her.

On her return in the evening, Ruth explained the fortuitous events of the day, including how Boaz had provided lunch for her and given her extra barley to bring home. When Naomi heard that it was Boaz's field in which Ruth had been gleaning, it's as though she received a spiritual jolt. She remembered that he was a family relative, and therefore qualified as a 'guardian-redeemer' (Ruth 2:20). This meant he could take up certain responsibilities laid out in the Old Testament law, including marrying the widow in order to have children on behalf of the dead man, and to buy back land that a family member may have had to sell if they fell into poverty. The same applied if a person had been compelled to sell themselves as a servant or hired worker to another.[34] In this way, Boaz himself stands as a forerunner of Jesus, the ultimate guardian-redeemer.

It seems that this was the moment when Naomi was roused from her self-pity and saw a flickering light of hope; a reminder that God had not abandoned her, as she had previously thought. Her self-applied bark peeled back just a little.

It was not luck that brought Ruth to Boaz's field, but the guiding hand of God. No wonder that Naomi was keen that Ruth should stay working in those wheat and barley fields, where she was confident of Boaz's protection, and hopeful for something more.

Naomi wisely gave her daughter-in-law instructions on initiating the process of redemption by having her present herself to Boaz, washed and perfumed, and lying at his feet (Ruth 3:3-4). This submissive and symbolic act was welcomed by the older man. In fact, the story takes on a greater depth and softer hue when it becomes clear that Boaz was not just willing to undertake this as a necessary duty of care for Naomi, but because Ruth had become very precious to him.

Another closer relative had first refusal on Elimelek's land, but when that man realised that the transaction would include taking on his widow as well, he backed off, concerned that his own estate would be endangered by the inheritance laws. So the way was cleared for Boaz to step up and buy the property, as well as to shoulder responsibility for Naomi, and to take Ruth as his wife, which would keep Elimelek's family name alive. This legal transaction was ratified by the elders, who blessed the deal prophetically:

> We are witnesses. May the LORD make the woman who is coming into your home like Rachel and Leah, who together built up the family of Israel. May you have standing in Ephrathah and be famous in Bethlehem. Through the offspring the LORD gives you by this young

---

[34] Leviticus 25:24-28, 47-49.

woman, may your family be like that of Perez, whom
Tamar bore to Judah.
(Ruth 4:11-12)

This reference to Jacob's wives and offspring demonstrated the weightiness of their words, tied as they were to the honoured history of the people of Israel.

Not only does Naomi and Ruth's story have this almost fairytale-like ending, but the closing verses reveal something more wonderful still. God had graciously stripped away all that defensive bark which Naomi had erected around her bruised and hurting heart.

Naomi's friends rejoiced with her when her first grandson was born. They praised God that she would be looked after in her old age, and for the blessing of having a treasured daughter-in-law who was so devoted to her that they considered her better than a complete complement of 'seven sons' (vv14-15).

Naomi's life had purpose again. She looked after her grandson Obed, doting on him to such a degree that people joked that he was actually her own son. Not only that, but the family tree shows how Obed later had a son named Jesse, who in time became the father of David, the best and most celebrated monarch Israel ever had. That makes Naomi King David's great-great-grandmother, and Ruth his great-grandmother. What a tremendous honour to be part of that family line which generations later would include the promised Messiah Himself. That a Moabite woman – someone from outside God's chosen people group – should be included in that genealogy is further testament to the immeasurable grace of God, who saw Ruth's devotion and rewarded her in this extraordinary way.

How wonderful, too, that rather than leave Naomi wrestling with her unresolved anger and bitterness of spirit, God stepped in to gently strip away her defensive 'bark', extinguish her resentment and revive, replenish and restore her heart, mind and spirit to a place of contentment in His hands.

Naomi would have forfeited so much if she had hardened her heart and continued to justify her rancour, holding on to her grudges about the way God had led her. It was His mercy that stripped the hardness from this particular arrow, painfully exposed what was festering inside her and brought her into a place of healing and wholeness from where she could be a blessing again.

4. Abrasive Grace

Our journey with God is ongoing, of course. We each have a unique story to tell, which will have multiple twists and turns, highs and lows. It's easy to see the parallels with our arrow, which is still in the process of being transformed from a simple stick to a weapon ready to be used in effective warfare. Having been broken and torn, it's now been stripped. Its natural defences have been broken, exposing that tender inner core. It still isn't ready for firing, though.

Now comes the first of the smoothing processes.

In the times when we feel overwhelmed by the rigorous nature of some of God's dealings with us – and we've all probably felt that at some time or another – it's good to remind ourselves that God is seeking to make us into something spectacular for His pleasure and purpose. He is committed to completing the process He has begun in us.[35]

You've heard of amazing grace; now we're going to look at abrasive grace as God takes us arrows on to the next stage, which will begin to smooth out the parts that hold us back. It sounds harsh, but it's His love that compels Him to do so with infinite tenderness, patience and grace. Our God is a God of excellence and He does all things well.[36]

---

[35] Philippians 1:6.
[36] Mark 7:37.

God's best

In spite of the global pandemic and the ease of internet services, I am not yet an online grocery shopper. While I am seldom eager to visit the supermarket, inevitably when supplies are low, I go to trawl the aisles again. There, I am presented with a vast array of products. Any single item can probably be purchased in several forms, at a variety of prices reflecting the quality of the product. I can choose my purchases according to my budget, from a no-frills range, through the supermarket's own brand, right up to the pricier product designed to communicate the superior nature of the item compared with all the rest; it's the one with all the superlatives on the label: finest, best, connoisseur, etc.

Although I've yet to find a supermarket selling polished arrows, I'm willing to bet that God would have them labelled at the classier end of the range. When He set Himself to turning our rough and not-yet-ready stick-like selves into these living works of art, He was not going to be satisfied with a shoddy product. He's not a God of half-hearted, lacklustre activities.

This next stage of grating, or grinding, certainly sounds like a painful process, but it's necessary if that arrow is going to fly straight and smooth. An arrowsmith would place his arrow in a jig – a block with an arrow-shaped groove running lengthways down it – fix that in a vice and use a basic, flat plane for this job. God, as we will see, uses His inexhaustible, immeasurable grace.

In Bible times, milling was a daily job for women. They took portions of their harvested cereal crops and put them into a stone quern – a long dish-like piece of equipment, shaped to accommodate the repetitive back and forth movement of a grinding stone across the grain. Women would have to kneel down for this rigorous and rather tedious task. A relatively small amount could be ground at any one time, but grinding breaks the wheat, barley or maize down into a fine powder of flour, ready to be made into sustaining bread; crucial for daily sustenance.

Now the arrow has had its bark stripped off, it is soft enough to have the lumps and bumps ground out of it. Very few sticks are dead straight – not even the coppiced ones – even without those twiggy offshoots that have now been broken off. Once the bark is removed as well, any remaining bulges can be dealt with to take it a step closer to aerodynamic usefulness.

Fortunately, God's intervention is not going to be done with anything as brutal as a stone rolling pin or a modern-day angle grinder. He comes to us with His wonderful, gentle grace. This process is not designed to wear us down destructively, but to straighten us out as He continues to transform us into the image of Christ. The more we look to Him, the more we reflect Him and become like Him.

God's grace

What is this grace that God lavishes on us?

As children back in Sunday school, we learned this phrase about grace: 'God's Riches At Christ's Expense'. It's become rather a cliché now, but in the 1970s it was a popular explanation among pastors, ministers and youth workers. I knew it was the right answer to a multitude of questions but, honestly, I still didn't understand what it really meant for a number of years.

Bruce Milne defines grace this way:

> the free display of favour, particularly by a superior to an inferior. Referred to God, it is that free decision of God, apart from all constraint and in no way compelled by our merit, to have mercy upon His sinful creatures, saving his people from all the effects of their sin through Jesus Christ.[37]

One of the best definitions of God's grace that I've ever heard is the simple, child-friendly one which states, 'Mercy is not

---

[37] Milne, *Know the Truth*, pp181-182.

getting what I do deserve; grace is getting what I don't deserve.' That's probably the one which has helped me understand grace the most clearly, and realise that grace goes a step further.

All these definitions help to shed light on the wonder of God's grace. Sometimes grace is easier to grasp by examining what it isn't. The opposite of grace is law, and the Bible has a lot to say about this.

Man's law

The pious people of Jesus' time thought that they could gain, or earn, their salvation through strict observation of the law. The original Old Testament Law was given to Moses by God on Mount Sinai, embodied in the Ten Commandments which served as a Freedom Charter for the people, after their crushing years of slavery in Egypt. They were expanded and added to over the course of time until, instead of freedom, every part of life was wrapped up in a set of suffocating rules which had to be followed rigorously. Not doing so laid yourself open to accusations of ungodliness. Now the people not only had the Torah – the first five books of the Bible – or Moses' law, but extra teaching and laws covering religious, ceremonial and civil law matters.

The Pharisees were particularly conscientious about keeping their interpretation of the law, which took so much of their time that it became more about 'doing' than 'being'. They often took principles to an extreme degree. They truly believed that keeping every last detail of the law would win them merit with God. It was like looking through a telescope the wrong way round: their focus was no longer on pleasing God, but on their own efforts at being holy – an impossible standard for anyone.

It was over this point that they so frequently came into conflict with Jesus. He condemned them for their pious exterior and self-righteous deeds, which bypassed their hearts and left them without compassion for the poor, the downtrodden, the sick and the marginalised; all groups to which Jesus Himself was drawn.

Some of Jesus' harshest words were directed at the religious rulers of the day:

> Woe to you, teachers of the law and Pharisees, you hypocrites! You give a tenth of your spices – mint, dill and cumin. But you have neglected the more important matters of the law – justice, mercy and faithfulness ...
> Woe to you ...You clean the outside of the cup and dish, but inside they are full of greed and self-indulgence ...
> Woe to you ... You are like whitewashed tombs, which look beautiful on the outside but on the inside are full of the bones of the dead and everything unclean. In the same way, on the outside you appear to people as righteous but on the inside you are full of hypocrisy and wickedness.
> (Matthew 23:23-28)

Meeting Jesus

Jesus won no prizes for diplomacy, and didn't make many friends among the Pharisees. Even the curious Nicodemus chose to talk to Jesus about His teachings under cover of darkness to avoid censure and the distracting challenges to Jesus' authority which his colleagues often employed.[38]

This group of religious leaders was mostly so involved in their legalistic lifestyles – including making sure everyone else lived the same tortuous way – that they completely missed the grace of God, and simultaneously failed to recognise who Jesus really was. Sadly, the same might still be said of many so-called religious people today.

Many who are searching for truth in our generation reject the Christian faith because they believe it is a faith based on a

---

[38] John 3:1-21.

list of dos and don'ts. The idea of living a repressive, restricted life according to such stringent rules is not, unsurprisingly, a life that is attractive to them; consequently, they often walk away without truly understanding who God is or what a relationship with Him is really all about. There are even those who resolve to live as full a life as they can on their own terms now, free (as they perceive it) from all the restrictions that God might want to put on them. They reason that, maybe when they're old, they'll consider it again; a kind of later-life insurance policy.

It's so sad to witness such an erroneous perception of God as a severe and harsh disciplinarian who frowns on anything that might constitute fun. Satan, the enemy, plays on this, propagating the image in as many places and contexts as he can. The truth, however, is quite different.

A good place to understand what God is really like, is to look at Jesus. He explained it to His own disciples like this:

> 'If you really know me, you will know my Father as well. From now on, you do know him and have seen him.'
>
> Philip said, 'Lord, show us the Father and that will be enough for us.'
>
> Jesus answered: 'Don't you know me, Philip, even after I have been among you such a long time? Anyone who has seen me has seen the Father. How can you say, "Show us the Father"? Don't you believe that I am in the Father and the Father is in me?'
> (John 14:7-10)

Just as a child often resembles a parent, Jesus resembled His Father, but it was far more than a physical resemblance. Jesus remained part of the Godhead but took on human flesh. God is Spirit, but the nature and character of the Father and the Son are the same.

We see Jesus spending time with the prostitutes and outcasts of society, and therefore see that God loves those on the fringes who we might perhaps find hard to love.

We read about Jesus forgiving sins, and we understand that God is a God of boundless mercy and immeasurable love.

We find accounts of physical healings and people being delivered from evil spirits that tormented them, so we get a glimpse of God's overarching compassion and His tender heart.

We discover Jesus at a wedding,[39] providing a new supply of fantastic wine, so we can be sure that God loves parties, laughter, fun and families; He clearly cares about the details of life. We frequently find Jesus engaged in eating meals and enjoying life with family and friends around food and fellowship.

We see Jesus talking to a despised tax collector[40] and understand that He meets each of us just where we are.

Jesus' good friend John got it right when he declared, 'See what great love the Father has lavished on us, that we should be called children of God!' (1 John 3:1).

Love and grace are all mixed up together in generous quantities, and God smothers us with them. Far from being restrictive, the Jesus life is one of real life, liberty and joy which is not dependent on our circumstances. In submitting to Him we enjoy the benefits of a past that has been forgiven and dealt with – all shame and guilt completely washed out of our story – and a future full of purpose, all set in the context of of God's unshakeable promises and empowered by His Holy Spirit.

When God 'set his love upon [us]'[41] – a distinct decision of the will – it was simply because He *chose* to do that. It had nothing to do with our personal merit, our skills, our performance, our heritage, our academic achievements or our bank balance. It was *nothing* to do with us and *everything* to do with Him.

---

[39] John 2:1-12.
[40] Luke 19:1-10.
[41] Psalm 91:14, KJV.

God's family

Jesus said He wouldn't call those who loved Him 'servants', but 'friends' (John 15:15).

Moreover, Paul used the picture of adoption when he explained to the churches at Ephesus and Galatia that God has gone even further than this (Ephesians 1:5; Galatians 3:26-37). We are not associates or employees; not even colleagues, but members of the family: sons and daughters of the King of kings. When the Bible calls us sons, it's not a deliberate attempt to exclude women, but rather to include them as inheritors and heirs; flying in the face of Jewish tradition. Such a promotion of status is based on God's grace alone. We cannot earn it, and this is where so much of our misunderstanding of grace comes from.

All of us were born into the world thanks to the union of a mother and a father. Some have never known their fathers; some were abandoned by their fathers and brought up by a mother who managed to a greater or lesser degree on her own. Some had fathers who were present physically but were emotionally absent, who didn't engage with the family. Others had fathers who abused them physically, mentally or sexually. Many people had fathers who did an OK job, and some had fathers who were genuinely good. No one has ever had a perfect father; such a man does not exist outside the pages of storybooks.

How each of us views our own father can colour how we see God as heavenly Father. Truth to tell, the vast majority of us spent a great deal of our childhoods looking for the approval of our fathers. Some got it, some didn't; some still look for it even though they are well into adulthood themselves; and some still yearn for it long after their biological father has died. Our desire to please may have been demonstrated on the sports field, in our schoolwork, in our ability to master a skill or to make money and gain success in business. However we expressed that desire, it's more than likely that it had to do with our performance; it was all based on what we did or didn't do.

Gaining affirmation and approval in this way is probably evident in every generation. Parents who offer substantial rewards for outstanding achievements may inadvertently perpetuate it by trading prize money for good exam grades. In trying to encourage diligent study, they may perhaps be emphasising that performance brings affirmation. This fiscal motivation may be a good incentive to work hard, and it's certainly how the business world operates, but if it's the only expression of parental love, it's severely flawed.

Being not doing

God's love is very different. He loves us because He loves us. He just does, and that's it; end of story. Although, truly, it's only the beginning of the story.

His love is not dependent on our performance; it is undeserved and can't be earned – that's why it's called 'grace'. It never runs out and is totally reliable and consistent.

Our heavenly Father is the truly perfect Father we've longed for all our lives, whether we knew it or not. His grace is a gift, a generous present that brings joy to God the giver, as well as to the receiver.

Every parent knows the joy that comes from watching their offspring open a present on their birthday or at Christmas. Even the anticipation of seeing them rip off the paper to discover the treasure inside is an exquisite pleasure. We watch their facial expression as it dawns on them that they're now holding in their hands the exact present they've been hoping for over the past months. At last, it's a reality. Amid hugs, kisses and yells of thanks, we celebrate with them. That's how God feels when we truly get hold of His grace and respond with joyful thanksgiving.

More grace

Every giver likes to receive thanks for their gift; an acknowledgement of the time and effort involved in picking out a suitable gift. How disappointing it can be when a word of thanks is withheld, or if the present is thoughtlessly discarded, put in a box for the charity shop or simply left unused to gather dust.

So it is with grace. What's the point of receiving this marvellous gift if we're not going to use it? Worse still, what if our initial thrill evaporates like the dew, and we return to a dreary life of legalism? What a pointless, miserable way of life.

Here's another definition: 'Legalism is the pursuit of God by humankind, based on anything other than grace.'[42] When we try to impress God, in our own strength and by our own efforts, again we fall into legalism, and are doomed to disappointment and misery.

Paul rebuked the young Christians in the church in Galatia for exactly this behaviour. They had been taught, and understood, a basic foundation of grace for their new lives in Christ, but squandered this wonderful gift by neglecting it.

> You foolish Galatians! Who has bewitched you? Before your very eyes Jesus Christ was clearly portrayed as crucified. I would like to learn just one thing from you: did you receive the Spirit by the works of the law, or by believing what you heard? Are you so foolish? After beginning by means of the Spirit, are you now trying to finish by means of the flesh?
> (Galatians 3:1–3)

Paul was baffled and distressed by the way legalism was still the default setting in the behaviour patterns of the Galatian church. He longed for them to discover the liberating grace of God and

---

[42] Bernard Sanders. Used with permission.

to live in the good of that every day. It was to be a lifestyle, not just a doctrine.

Let's unpack some of those rich facets of grace.

Unmerited

This is possibly my favourite attribute of God's grace, because it underlines again how very little it has to do with me! Whether I am having a good day, a bad day, a hormonal day or a routine day, I can know God's favour on my life. When I focus on this, I have great cause to be thankful, worshipful, and can choose to walk through the heaviest of demanding days with a lightness of spirit, rooted in the security of knowing that my relationship with God is never under threat from my slips and stumbles. I cannot disqualify myself from grace, no matter what happens during the course of the day, regardless of how I may feel.

No wonder John Newton, the former slave trader who came to faith in Christ, called it 'Amazing Grace' in his famous hymn! A fresh revelation and solid understanding of this grace will stir you to sing that old hymn with fresh gusto; you can plumb the powerful truths of every rich stanza.

Grace is truly amazing:

> The fact that God in His sovereign mercy has condescended to give Himself in His very being in the Spirit to our feeble, broken and sinful lives is supreme cause for worship and thanksgiving. All that God has done, is doing and will do through our union with Christ in terms of our election, calling, regeneration, repentance, faith, justification, adoption, assurance, sanctification, and perseverance is reason to adore, bless and worship Him.[43]

Absolutely.

---

[43] Milne, *Know the Truth*, p206.

Unending

Grace has no sell-by date and no 'best before' date. Grace is as enduring as the Giver Himself. It never runs out and, however much we use, there is always more available.

Unlike so many so-called 'special offers', it's not just valid 'for a limited period only'. Somewhere at the bottom, so many of these flyers and emails have the ominous words in tiny print: 'Terms and conditions apply'. If your eyes are good enough to read it all, you'll soon discover that the offer is seldom quite what it appeared to be at first. God's grace definitely doesn't come with that tiresome tag at the bottom.

The only terms and conditions that apply are that we come in repentance and faith, and give Him lordship of our lives. There are no exclusions, nor a list in microscopic type at the bottom barring dictators, mass murderers and the like. God will accept repentant drug pushers, arms dealers, rapists and fraudsters. 'Outrageous!' we may say. Is God really saying that there is no one beyond His reach when it comes to belonging in His family and enjoying His grace? Absolutely; and if we're honest, that is hard to wrap our heads around. It can offend us, because it doesn't align with our own limited views of fairness and justice.

Unlimited

There is no quota system involved with grace. You are not allotted a specific portion for your lifetime, and then, once you've used it up, that's it; finished. Not at all. We can confidently enjoy God's grace twenty-four hours a day, 365 days a year, including Bank Holidays and Christmas Day. It's not only available between the hours of 9am and 5pm; never closed at weekends. Neither is it only available during the times we've messed up and seek to put things right with God again by way of the well-worn path of repentance.

Grace can be enjoyed fresh every day. The prophet Jeremiah wrote:

> Because of the LORD's great love we are not consumed,
> for his compassions never fail.
> They are new every morning;
> great is your faithfulness.
> (Lamentations 3:22-23)

There's a fresh supply each and every day. Grace doesn't get tired, or go limp, like the lettuce in your fridge. It's available around the clock regardless of time zones, and is best enjoyed when it spills over into every part of our life, all of the time.

Unfailing

Have you ever tried to drive out of a car park, having paid the appropriate fee in the machine, only to find that your ticket is rejected at the exit, leaving the barrier resolutely closed against you? It's not that you were trying to leave without paying; you put in the correct money and have a ticket to prove it, but at the last stage of exit you are denied safe passage out by an electronic 'glitch'. The system has failed.

God's grace is *not* like this! His love, mercy and grace are always flowing; His arms are always open to us.

Even at first glance, that is fantastic; to know that nothing and no one is beyond the reach of God's grace is astonishing. However, if truly no one is beyond accessing God's grace should they choose to do so, that must apply to some seriously unpromising candidates, which might not sit so well with us.

I wonder who you think of as the worst person who's ever lived. We know that God doesn't have a 'sliding scale' of merit. We'd probably all put Mother Teresa pretty far up the scale, thanks to her selfless service to the poor in the slums of Kolkata over many years; and perhaps you know missionaries who've made great sacrifices to work in far-flung places, who persevere in the face of monumental challenges. At the opposite end of the scale, trailing far, far behind in goodness we would probably place the likes of Hitler, Stalin, Pol Pot, Idi Amin, Mao and Saddam Hussein.

It seems incredibly unfair that God might be interested in the villains on our list. Compared with them, we can reassure ourselves that we're not so bad; therefore, we reason, perhaps it's not quite so surprising that God would choose to love us after all.

Grace simply blows that argument away. It's available for whoever may come and drink deeply from God's well of mercy, forgiveness and restoration. That's grace.

New patterns

When we fail to enjoy grace, we are failing to break our old pattern of living and end up in legalism. In his excellent book *Enjoying God's Grace*, Terry Virgo illustrates the point by imagining that legalism and the law were our first husband to whom we were irrevocably joined. He calls him Mr Law. The bond of that stifling marriage was broken by Jesus' death: 'you … died to the law through the body of Christ, that you might belong to another' (Romans 7:4). No longer bound to that husband, we are now bound to a new one called Grace.

Terry goes on to explain:

> The difference between the two husbands is phenomenal. Mr Law was an overbearing and demanding individual. He wearied and burdened us with rules yet refused to help us. Jesus on the other hand is 'gentle and humble in heart' and He gives us rest for our souls, an easy yoke and a light burden … Christians, however, often fall into a terrible trap. Although we have been freed from our old husband, we find it hard to break with our former attitudes to ourselves and our negative self-worth.

Having enjoyed the glorious liberty of our new marriage, we can still become vulnerable to the pressures of feeling unworthy and even condemned. The devil then becomes very active and tries to tell us that we are not working hard enough to please our new husband.

Tragically, we believe him. Before long, we are desperately trying to please our new husband by observing the sort of rules that our old husband required of us. By doing this we hope to shake off all the feelings of condemnation

What has gone wrong? Simple. The wife has returned to her old husband. The loving relationship she once had with Jesus has turned into a legalistic striving to fulfil the demands of evangelical law. It's spiritual adultery and it will never work.[44]

As we begin to see grace for what it truly is, we can start to see how crushing legalism has been, and how repugnant it is to God. We need to ensure we don't return to that burden.

Grace brings life.	Legalism brings death.
Grace brings liberty.	Legalism brings enslavement.
Grace brings joy.	Legalism brings misery.
Grace brings confidence.	Legalism undermines my self-worth – who Christ has made me.
Grace means that when I fall I don't have to stay down in a place where self-loathing, fear, recrimination and despair will run riot with me. All I have to do is stand up again.	Legalism tells me I've messed up forever; that I am a useless failure who can never recover.

---

[44] Terry Virgo, *Enjoying God's Grace* (Eastbourne: Kingsway, 1999), pp27-30.

See the difference:

> When we live by law, we obey because we have to.
> When we live by grace, we obey because we want to.

It might look the same on the surface, but in reality there is a world of difference. The motivation, as well as the roots of all we do, has altered beyond all recognition; the spirit in which we live is of another kind altogether.

People who consistently walk in grace are a joy to know. Everyone wants to be near them and catch the infectious spirit of their lives. Somehow, you can see Jesus in their faces.

Those who walk in legalism are not good company and are likely to find themselves lonely, and often bitter, individuals.

So fantastic is God's grace that, over the years, the message of grace has sometimes been watered down because it was considered so outrageous. Clergy were bothered that the liberty preached about grace would become a licence for people to simply do whatever they wanted without feeling guilty any more. That felt threatening, especially in contexts where damaging, coercive control was wielded. Is it possible to have too much grace? Some people refer to this as hyper-grace.

The New Testament churches came across this question as well, but Paul addressed this too.

> Just as sin reigned in death, so also grace might reign through righteousness to bring eternal life through Jesus Christ our Lord.
>
> What shall we say, then? Shall we go on sinning, so that grace may increase? By no means! We are those who have died to sin; how can we live in it any longer? ...
>
> Count yourselves dead to sin but alive to God in Christ Jesus.
> (Romans 5:21–6:2, 11)

We will begin to feel the liberating results that come as God smooths us out with His grace. Far from being a wearisome experience, this abrasive part of the character-shaping process turns out to be uplifting beyond our imagination.

God's grace straightens us out. The more He gently, lovingly grinds us with that grace, the more we are unrecognisable from the awkward stick which formerly promised to only be useful as firewood. Now we're shaped for action, and enjoying life so much more as we embrace who God made us to be, and what He created us for.

Target Questions

➢ What's the difference between trying to do better and living in grace?

➢ What does the life and ministry of Jesus tell us about the character and nature of God?

➢ How has your own father influenced your view of your heavenly Father?

➢ In what ways do the four descriptive elements of grace impact you?

4a. Elijah

When you think of Old Testament prophets, Elijah may well take centre stage. He had an extraordinary ministry, most spectacularly during the reign of King Ahab and his notorious wife, Jezebel. These were among the stories that kept me on the edge of my chair in Sunday school. Sprinkled with conflict and drama, they were tales of God's power dramatically demonstrated, and the fear of God falling on His people (and on us too) as the miracles that Elijah performed under the inspiration of the Holy Spirit were retold.

We know Elijah was especially significant, because in the account of Jesus' transfiguration on top of a mountain in Matthew 17, he appeared alongside Moses; these two giants of the faith spoke with Jesus, as witnessed by Peter, James and John.

Born 900 years before the birth of Jesus, Elijah is first mentioned in 1 Kings 17, when he audaciously announced a national drought to the formidable king of Israel, which was a divine judgement on the land. The prophet delivered the message and then promptly disappeared from public view. God instructed him to go and hide away by the Kerith Ravine, where he could drink from the brook and be brought food by ravens operating under God's command. It doesn't sound very hygienic or appetising to me, but there's no doubt it was supernatural. None of this was dependent on Elijah doing anything at all. Both morning and evening, God graciously provided for him as the birds brought him bread and meat from who knows where. Considering how aggressive ravens can be, it conjures up quite a picture.

Day by day, Elijah must have watched the flow of that brook diminish to a trickle, and then nothing. There's no hint that he doubted God or concluded that the supply of grace had also dried up. Far from it, for then he was directed to the home of a widow and her son in Zarephath, where God once again miraculously ensured that they all had enough to eat. Elijah also raised the boy to life after a strange fatal illness left his mother bereft. He cried out to God in prayer on behalf of the grieving mother, and his prayers were answered; the boy was restored to life in another demonstration of God's grace and kindness.

My favourite Bible story has to be the famous competition Elijah hosted on top of Mount Carmel with the prophets of Baal. After the drought had dragged on for three desperate years, God told Elijah to go and see King Ahab again. Ahab was very well aware of Elijah's credentials as a prophet, since the drought had begun, and continued, just as Elijah had decreed. Unsurprisingly, Ahab was less than pleased to see him, calling him, 'you troubler of Israel' (1 Kings 18:17).

Elijah showed great boldness in addressing the king: 'I have not made trouble for Israel ... But you and your father's family have' (v18). He then invited Ahab, and all the people of Israel, especially and specifically the 450 prophets of Baal and the 400 prophets of Asherah, who were resourced and provided for by the pagan queen, Jezebel, to the summit of Mount Carmel. There, he rebuked the people for vacillating between their worship of Yahweh and false idols and gods. He announced an exciting competition that would decide once and for all which divinity was real.

Instructions were given to bring materials to build two altars, along with two bulls for sacrifice. The rules were that each team would prepare their altar but not light it; their god must supply the necessary fire as they called on him.

The prophets of Baal laboured all morning to catch the attention of their god, but nothing happened. The Bible, in wonderful understatement, says, 'Midday passed, and they continued their frantic prophesying until the time for the evening sacrifice. But there was no response, no one answered, no one paid attention' (v29). We can almost feel their frustration. Elijah had begun to tease them, suggesting that perhaps their deity was in deep thought somewhere, busy, travelling or maybe just asleep. His mockery incensed them further as they indulged in barbaric self-harm in a frenzied effort to prove their devotion to Baal. Still nothing happened.

It was evening by the time Elijah had had enough of their antics and called everyone to pay attention to his altar. Building his altar with twelve stones, which represented the twelve tribes of Israel, he dug a trench around it, piled some wood on it and placed the animal sacrifice on top. Four jars were filled with water three times each, and the contents poured over the whole lot, soaking the entire structure. For that soggy mess to catch fire it would certainly require a miracle.

In a simple spoken prayer, Elijah appealed to the Almighty as the generational God of Abraham, Isaac and Jacob – a reminder to the crowd of Israelites of their honoured history and shared story. He made sure the spotlight was firmly on the living God, not on himself, so that the crowd would be exposed to His dynamic power and know for sure that this was the God they needed to return to again.

Immediately, heavenly fire fell, consuming everything on the altar including the water. The impact was instantaneous. People fell flat on their faces in repentance, confessing the majesty and authority of the God they had rejected for so long. It was a mighty victory for Elijah, and for the other believers in the nation who were hidden away. None of this was a result of Elijah's effort or an indication of his own effort. God demonstrated His power in order to win back the people He loved so dearly; grace all over again.

This display of divine pyrotechnics was followed by the slaughter of the 850 occult prophets, ridding the land of their abhorrent desecration of a nation on whom God had had His hand for generations. In a physical sign of this foundational change, the mother of all rainstorms arrived, breaking the drought at last. God's grace literally poured out from the dark skies in life-giving water again. More grace!

You'd think Elijah would have danced his way home, rejoicing after this personal high point and such a mind-blowing encounter with God. However, we read in 1 Kings 19 that all it took was a short note from Queen Jezebel, furious to hear that her prophetic minions were dead and threatening to kill him within twenty-four hours, to send Elijah literally running for his life.

After a day of travelling into the barren desert, he found a scrubby tree, sat underneath it heart-sore, broken and depressed; there, he prayed to die. Exhausted and overwhelmed by the earlier spiritual warfare of the mountaintop, Elijah fell asleep.

God might have rebuked him, disciplined him or withdrawn; but He did none of those things. Instead, he sent an angel with the miraculous and pragmatic provision of food and drink, after which Elijah slept again. Another nourishing meal was provided when he woke up, which gave the prophet enough strength to continue his journey to Mount Horeb. There, he had another encounter with God that gave him new focus for the next part of his prophetic commission.

God manifested His power on this mountain in gale-force winds which shook the landmass and shattered rocks, followed by a massive earthquake and a rip-roaring fire. Elijah must have felt very small and very frightened, but then God spoke to him in the softest of whispers.

There is a refreshing practicality in the way that God gave Elijah exactly what he needed when he needed it. In one moment, breath-taking fire from heaven; in another, a simple meal of nourishing bread and refreshing water. That's grace.

God pouring out His mercy and kindness on a loved child, whether they're experiencing a spiritual high, or under the intense pressure of evil demonic forces; running like a trained athlete, or simply exhausted physically, mentally, emotionally and suffering from spiritual burnout.

Grace categorically cannot be earned; it's a generous gift from our loving God. In this instance, rather than demand more than Elijah could give, the gentle, compelling voice of God granted grace upon grace in both a spectacular and a practical way, both instances reminding the prophet that the One he served was greater than any other deity.

Elijah wasn't done after Mount Carmel. He mentored his apprentice prophet, Elisha, and remained a godly thorn in the side of wicked King Ahab, prophesying his death in battle as well as the grisly demise of his evil wife.[45]

This arrow was effectively fired into the nation of Israel to call them back to worship the true God. Had he not experienced God's grace, particularly in the desert, Elijah's ministry might have come to a juddering halt as he fell into long-term depression. Without God's guiding hand, he could have been prey to Jezebel's trap and been physically destroyed. As it was, that grace gave him the resources he needed to continue in the calling God gave him.

It's easy to be dazzled by Elijah's life and ministry; for most of us, the things he did and saw are far beyond our experience. However, a letter written by Jesus' half-brother, James, to the scattered Jewish believers from each of the twelve tribes not only encouraged them to persevere through trials and sufferings, but also to engage in the important discipline of prayer. He held up Elijah as an example for them as he reminded them:

> The prayer of a righteous person is powerful and effective.

---

45 1 Kings 21:19-23.

> Elijah was a human being, even as we are. He prayed
> earnestly that it would not rain, and it did not rain on the
> land for three and a half years. Again he prayed, and the
> heavens gave rain, and the earth produced its crops.
> (James 5:16-18)

Elijah was just as prone as we are to discouragement; remember, he was so depressed at one point that he wanted his life to be over, even though he'd just witnessed a fiery miracle of gargantuan proportions on top of Mount Carmel. Remember too that grace is given, not earned. Elijah knew it, and so can we.

His gripping story ends with a jaw-dropping finale, in which he was taken up to heaven in a whirlwind, accompanied by flaming horses and a 'chariot of fire' (2 Kings 2:11-12). Elijah hit his target time after time because he kept walking and talking with God, daring to believe His words were true, and drilling deep into the source of unmerited, unending, unlimited, unfailing grace.

5. The Splinters of Expectation

God's amazing grace has been grinding down the lumps and bumps that spoilt the shape of our arrow shaft. It's also been loosening some natural splinters which break from the main body of wood and will need to be removed as well. We all know that even the smallest fragment of a splinter under our skin causes a disproportional amount of pain. Splinters need to be removed promptly to ensure that there is no opportunity for infection to take hold within the wound.

In our allegory, splinters serve to illustrate the way we inadvertently cause pain, both to ourselves and others, by the pressure of expectations. They may be perceived expectations or genuine ones; either way, they can cause devastating damage. Most of us frequently place unrealistic and ridiculously high expectations on ourselves as well, which can be crippling.

Wearing a mask: playing a role

Living up to expectations, whether our own or those of others, causes us to live in unreality. We can end up playing a part, or living a role, exchanging one mask for another.

It's not only actors who know how to play a role.

From an early age we learn how to do this. Indeed, important and healthy child development comes through imaginary play. Cast your mind back far enough and you'll probably remember your play school, or kindergarten, with its standard provision of a 'home' corner and, almost certainly, a dressing-up box. Supplemented by a few cardboard boxes or a couple of old sheets, these served as rockets, trains, desert islands, tents, planes, tractors and dungeons; all providing hours of innocent adventure.

The Greek civilisation was among the first to include drama and theatre into its culture, long before the birth of Christ. Masked actors played out the stories of legendary heroes, and heroines, in vast amphitheatres, depicting their struggles against the Greek gods. The masks symbolised the nature of the character – a hero or villain – in much the same way as they do in Japanese theatre, accompanied by a chorus who filled in the narrative and emotional responses inherent in the well-known tales.

The Greek word for a play actor is *hypokritēs*, from which our own word 'hypocrite' is derived; the essence of which is simulation, or insincerity.

No one wants to be a hypocrite in this sense but, shockingly, we can still spend a great deal of our adult lives play acting. Teenagers tend to unconsciously use this behaviour as a healthy means of exploring who they really are as they face the basic questions of life: 'Who am I?' and 'Why am I here?' More and more in the modern era, these questions become embroiled in sexuality, which was never meant to be the centre of who we are. We know this, because there is no marriage in heaven and therefore it's irrelevant in terms of who we are at heart.[46] However, there are foundational questions of identity and purpose; God wants us to be clear on both, but we do need to ask the right questions if we're to avoid disappearing down irrelevant rabbit holes.

Most of us are required to fulfil an extraordinary number of demands every day. We juggle the roles of cook, housekeeper, laundry service, taxi driver, first-aider, counsellor, interior designer, gardener, personal shopper, babysitter, tutor,

---

[46] Matthew 22:30.

confidante and lover, with varying degrees of success, usually while pursuing our own job or career outside the home. Even then, other weighty demands clamour for our attention as we seek to be provider, adviser, protector, engineer, mechanic, raconteur, DIY-er, sports coach and financial planner, all within the same twenty-four hours. No wonder so many of us are exhausted!

The point is that all of us feel the compelling need to be a great many different things to, or for, a great many different people. Frankly, it's well-nigh impossible to do that consistently well. The supermen and women we read about in glossy magazines exist only between those pages. Reality is rather different, and if we buy into the expectation of not merely 'having it all', but 'doing/being it all' as well, then we're bound for disappointment. Expectations are a force to be reckoned with.

Expectations: good or bad?

Before we abandon them altogether, it's worth remembering that not all expectations are bad. As a child I was expected to be polite; I was proactive in teaching my own children good manners. Those expectations were helpful in preparing them for positive interaction with the world.

Some expectations are significantly less helpful. These are the ones that can penetrate deep into our beings, causing the same intense pain as those lethal little splinters.

Years ago, I met a lady in the same maternity unit as myself, who confidently told me that her newborn son would be going to a very particular school where both his father and his grandfather had been; the tradition would stand. I couldn't help feeling sorry for this small bundle of life as I wondered whether he would ever be consulted on the topic. It was announced as a non-negotiable fact, but what if he proved not to be suited to the rigours of such an establishment?

Perhaps something similar went on in your own family. Maybe you went along with it; or possibly the desire to protest broke out in full-blown rebellion and an abandonment of all the family's values. Another splinter lodged under the skin.

Swimming against the tide

Adolescents experience a huge amount of peer pressure regarding what is expected of them in their social and academic lives, far more so than their parents and grandparents ever had to bear before the relentless influence of social media. While peer pressure has always been in play, the culture has made a seismic shift, and the tragic consequences are playing out in terms of mental health across a generation.

It's tough to be a follower of Jesus in the kind of environment where godly standards are mocked and flouted so relentlessly, but it's not dissimilar in that sense to the environment in which the early Church took root and spread across Europe, and beyond. It remains a reminder of the necessity to be walking with God in the power of the Holy Spirit each and every day. Our young warriors need to be able to do a whole lot more than merely survive if they are to walk confidently and victoriously through this season of their lives. We don't want to see them damaged by the negative influences that abound, so it's hard not to be reactionary by battening down the hatches and being so overly protective that they can't cope outside the Christian ghetto.

Our young people have a mandate to shake things up, challenge, declare truth in a winsome fashion and open the way for God to make a difference among their friends. They are arrows too. We don't want them destroyed, but we do want them to be powerfully living out God's standards with gritty determination, focused integrity, unshakable conviction and profound, life-giving joy. That's why it's important they see examples of authentic faith in people in their lives.

There's a whole generation of arrows who haven't come into God's family yet, and who are waiting to hear the good news and meet Jesus for themselves.

It's not just young people; adults aren't exempt from peer pressure either.

Contemporary culture advises and shouts at us through news feeds, social media, magazines, talk-show hosts and secular colleagues, to look out for number one. If your marriage is getting a bit sticky, has 'run its course' or 'isn't working for you', then the popular advice is to get out of it. Never mind your partner, children or promises, they say: you need to concentrate on yourself. Your own fulfilment is paramount. Don't be held back and miss out on the fun in life. That would be a waste; after all, you only live once.

Then there's the expectation of what is required of you in the work environment in order to get on: a white lie here; an exaggeration there; denigrating a colleague who's become a rival; being economical with the truth somewhere else; engaging in office politics to manoeuvre your way up the career ladder. It's just part of the world of work. Or is it?

Within the Church community, the expectations are different, but just as real. Based on the fact that we assume that if we are all following Jesus we should be, think and act a certain way, we can be horribly disappointed in one another. Since none of us has yet reached heavenly perfection, we can set each other up for a fall if we imagine that everyone is a super-saint. We each have our strengths and weaknesses, our faults and foibles which God by His grace is still shaping. Each of us is a work in progress. Sadly, we often fail to extend the same grace to others that God has extended to us. If we weigh one another down unhelpfully with unrealistic expectations, we'll miss the unique giftings we do have.

Growing fruit in our character

The truth is that as we allow God to change our hearts and minds, we do become more like Jesus. The more mature we are in Him, the more consistent and healthy will be the fruit of Jesus-like character in our life. Paul highlighted, 'the fruit of the Spirit ... love, joy, peace, patience, kindness, goodness, faithfulness, gentleness, self-control' (Galatians 5:22-23, RSV). All these things were evident in Jesus' life.

Fruit grows; it doesn't just appear overnight. A tree needs time, care and nutrients if it's going to consistently produce quality fruit. On uncomfortable reflection, I know that most of these aren't as well developed in my life as I'd like them to be.

Take patience, for instance. I find an astonishing lack of this particular fruit when I'm driving, or stuck in a queue anywhere, while time ticks on. I'm a linear thinker and am all too easily exasperated if I'm thrown off course. Such irritants don't excuse bad behaviour on my part; I'm still learning and growing. However, I'm sorry to say that anyone in the car next to me, or beside me in the line, who expect me to simply smile benignly and bless the other drivers and the till operator in sincere and inspired tones, might be disappointed.

Likewise, there are times when I don't exhibit the self-control that grows from a Spirit-filled life. I may be tired; I may have had a rough day of accumulated stress, or find myself faced with a situation I thought had been resolved earlier in the day/week, and... before you know it, my mouth has given vent to a reaction in which no thoughts were '[taken] captive' (2 Corinthians 10:5) at all. Almost immediately, I am disappointed with myself.

It's no good trying to justify, rationalise or excuse my behaviour. I have to humble myself and follow the triangular diagram of Chapter 3 in repentance, and ask God to forgive me and help me grow these things in my life. Unlike the *gifts* of the Spirit' that Paul talks about (1 Corinthians 12:1, my emphasis), which (as the name implies) are given, or imparted, fruit takes time to develop and is dependent on the health of the tree. Good strong roots are a must for healthy growth and, consequently, healthy fruit. In other words, in order to display these characteristics in my life I need to be walking closely with Jesus 24/7; I need to be rooted into His Word and teachable too.

At the same time, I take heart from the late Tim Keller's words, reminding myself – in the unlikely event that I could forget – of how good the good news really is:

> The gospel is this … We are more sinful and flawed in ourselves than we ever dared believe, yet at the very same time we are more loved and accepted in Jesus Christ than we ever dared hope.[47]

Outbursts of impatience or anger, while reasonably rare, could nevertheless confuse another Jesus-follower who might have an expectation of me that is not grounded in reality. They may have heard me speak from a platform or via a media page, and if they had expected me to be a stained-glass window sort of saint, then they may be shocked to discover the truth. Unless that is addressed, it could cause them real problems in their own spiritual walk. I would have inadvertently become a trip hazard on their path of faith. They may wonder whether my own faith is real, or whether I am just another hypocrite and fraud. Disillusionment or cynicism could easily creep in.

Jeff Lucas agrees:

> Cynicism … flourishes when our expectations are unrealistic, which is a common problem amongst idealists like us. We all have unspoken expectations about the way things should be, and rightly so. But we can forget that those we walk with are flawed human beings, just like us. If you've been in a church for more

---

[47] www.christianitytoday.com/news/2023/may/tim-keller-dead-redeemer-new-york-pastor-cancer.html (accessed 12th September 2023).

than six months, and nothing about it or nobody in it has ever irritated you, then you're probably clinically dead. We do need to adjust our hopes into line with realistic understanding of the frailty of human nature.[48]

This makes me smile ruefully, because it's so patently true. None of us is infallible, and all of us get irritated with other people, especially if they have different ways of thinking and doing from ourselves. Once we get to know people as friends rather than labels or roles, life becomes a lot more navigable and honest. But it's also true that we need to counter cynicism with grace. Cynicism is a harmful canker that needs to be kept out of the Church. It ill befits the bride of Christ.

Cynicism doesn't need a second invitation. It is an epidemic disease that is being found more and more among those who used to be called the hopeful. What shall we do with it? Find the more perfect church?[49]

There is no such place. Move to another church and we'll find it is still peopled by a mixture of redeemed sinners, each as imperfect as ourselves, but each as loved as ourselves and to whom the same mercy has been extended by the same loving heavenly Father. Jesus said that those who show mercy are the ones who will also receive it.[50] That gives me a solid motivation for extending mercy to others, since I am very keen for God's mercy to be extended to me.

Grace and mercy are great antidotes to cynicism, and to unhelpful expectations.

---

[48] Jeff Lucas, *Gideon: Power from Weakness* (Milton Keynes: Authentic Media, 2004), p49.
[49] Ibid.
[50] Matthew 5:7.

Ouch!

Here's another example of the painful splinters that expectations can cause.

A minister and his wife once moved their family to a new city, where the husband was going to take up the pastorate of a traditional evangelical church. To his wife's horror, she discovered on arrival that a number of positions in the church had been left vacant specifically for her. She was expected to embrace each of them with enthusiasm. Had she done so, she would have found herself taking a weekly women's meeting, running the children's work and crèche, overseeing all the catering and refreshment requirements of the church, as well as organising the weekly flower rota. She was thrown into panic, temporarily overwhelmed by what was expected of her. Capable as she was, she didn't feel that's where her strengths lay, and she had neither expectation nor intention of being involved in any of these intimidating things. Extricating herself from them was not easy.

The expectation had fallen on her so heavily because the previous pastor's wife – clearly a lady of boundless energy and resources – had juggled all of these responsibilities without batting an eyelid, so it was assumed that the new pastor's wife would do the same. In reality, she was committed only to setting up home in a strange new place, giving time to her young family, hoping their regional accents didn't alienate them, tentatively trying to make some friends and find her way around in a new place, while supporting her husband in his role.

It's easy to see how that assumption of expectations caused a problem among the church family. Her expectations were miles apart from those of the church members, and consequently the way was opened for all sorts of potential hurt and misunderstanding. Those expectations were a spiritual splinter that needed to be removed swiftly. To ignore them would have been folly, opening the door to resentment, anger, bitterness and cynicism from either, or both, parties concerned.

Grace and mercy were required in large quantities, on both sides.

Expectations tend to hem us in, suppress and even suffocate us. It's all too easy to become a prisoner to the expectations of others rather than finding a place of peace, rest and purposeful living within the promises and presence of God.

God's expectations

What is it that drives us, and whose expectations are we entertaining and allowing to dictate our choices?

Questions that dig a little deeper might be: 'What does *God* expect of me?' 'What is *He* looking for?' and, 'What does *He* want from me?' Do the answers to these questions indicate that we are reacting to the felt expectations of others, or living in the freedom of obedience to the expectations of our loving heavenly Father?

These are questions that *need* to be answered; they lie at the heart of the matter.

Jesus had clear guidance on tuning into what God expects and is wanting from us, recorded in chapter 4 of the Gospel of John. A politically incorrect conversation between Jesus and a Samaritan woman of dubious morals took place by a well in the heat of the day. She had made her trip to the water source at a time when she knew that no other women would be there, in the hope that she could avoid their censorious gossip and ill-disguised disgust. Jesus' presence would have been a surprise at any time of the day; men were not seen at this place of women's work. The fact that He started talking to her at all was a significant break with traditional Jewish–Samaritan culture. If He'd stuck to the rules, He should not even have acknowledged her presence.

At no time in this encounter did Jesus condemn the woman or make a judgement about her; He simply stated the facts about her domestic arrangements, which were startlingly accurate –

five husbands and, currently, a live-in lover – and so gained her attention.

As they continued to talk about faith and worship. Jesus told her, 'A time is coming and has now come when the true worshippers will worship the Father in the Spirit and in truth, for they are the kind of worshippers the Father seeks' (John 4:23).

The Samaritan woman could not have been under any illusions. Jesus was quite clear, and that has not changed; God is looking for worshippers.

He is not looking for actors, people who go through the motions or those with a nominal Christianity. God has a passion for people to be passionate about Him. He is actively searching for men and women across the globe who will bring Him real worship from their hearts, which accords Him honour and praise. He is not interested in songs, hymns or Sunday services per se, but in lifestyles that reflect His lordship, in genuinely changed, authentic followers who have laid aside their own agendas and preferences for the things that please Him.

John Piper declared this profound truth: 'God is most glorified in us when we are most satisfied in him.'[51] We will find true satisfaction nowhere else.

Old formulas, trite words and super-spirituality are externals that easily bypass the heart. They are things we *do* rather than a reflection necessarily of *who we are* or who we are *becoming* as God shapes us. Without the Holy Spirit they are dead and useless. God is always more interested in who we are than what we do, or do not do.

What is clear is that we need to worship both 'in the Spirit and in truth'.

---

[51] www.desiringgod.org/messages/god-is-most-glorified-in-us-when-we-are-most-satisfied-in-him (accessed 12th September 2023).

Worship God enjoys

All truth (Word) and no Spirit is in danger of becoming indigestible stodge; all Spirit and no truth (Word) can be perilously close to insubstantial froth.

Even that's not the whole picture, because real biblical truth is marinated in the Holy Spirit; without Him we are only being presented with partial truth. Equally, when the Spirit is at work, He will draw out biblical truths. This is one way in which things can be weighed and assessed.

If traditions become the mainstay and expectation in a church service, they too can become spiritual splinters that burrow under our spiritual skin, bringing pain and robbing us of the abundant life that Jesus has promised us. They can stick fast, deep in our hearts, and cause all sorts of hurt as what was once vibrant life becomes predictable habit – a shell from which the life has ebbed away.

Is it any wonder that so many young people abandon church in their late teens and early twenties? They can smell a fraud a mile away. The real tragedy is not the fact that they dislike some of what happens in our churches, but that in discarding those things they discard the living Jesus, in whom they could find everything their hearts long for. The enemy is laughing in smug satisfaction.

It's amazing how quickly things that once carried life can become dead, dry routine.

During the 1970s and 1980s, many churches made a shift in their worship practice by replacing the organ with keyboards and guitars. Ancient hymnals with antiquated language were replaced with something more modern and accessible. They were frequently met with resistance and the cry of, 'But we've always done it this way!' Personal preferences and expectations threatened to take precedence over seeking God on how He might like to be worshipped. Throughout history our structures have threatened to eclipse our Saviour. Yet He has always been more interested in hearts than hymnals.

People look at us in disbelief now when we recount such stories. 'No way!' they laugh and splutter. 'Who would get so worked up about that?' These days, having a live worship band is almost as commonplace as having an organ used to be. How quickly a new tradition has become just as entrenched as the old one.

Neither an organ nor keyboards are wrong in and of themselves, of course; each is just as irrelevant as the dress code, but it's easy to see how traditions have a habit of putting down roots very fast. When our style of operation becomes 'The Way We Do Things' over the 'Who' that we do them for, then we've probably stopped asking what God wants, and may find ourselves out of step with Him.

It's horribly easy to coast along without engaging our hearts or our minds and to end up with worship that's neither in the Spirit nor in truth. Whatever you might think about it, God is not going to be impressed. He's going to be disappointed and grieved.

It's not even that God needs our worship. After all, He is surrounded by the hosts of heaven; angels and archangels who are supremely equipped to render appropriate worship beyond our wildest imaginings. The Old Testament prophet Ezekiel's glimpse of what goes on in heaven, recorded in the first chapter of his book, is enough to assure us of that. Compared with angelic praise, our feeble offerings are almost embarrassing. They are as vastly different as Michaelangelo's inspired works of art are when compared with the wax crayon scribbles a toddler coming out of play school waves so enthusiastically at their parent or carer. How amazing that God receives genuine heart worship from us with the same warmth as a carer receives that crumpled drawing.

But Jesus was talking about more than simply the way a church conducts its weekly gatherings. Worship is far more all-embracing than that.

Paul explained it in his letter to the believers in Rome like this:

> Therefore, I urge you, brothers and sisters, in view of
> God's mercy, to offer your bodies as a living sacrifice,
> holy and pleasing to God – this is your true and proper
> worship.
> (Romans 12:1)

In other words, our whole life is worship. We don't switch it on and off for the benefit of those around us in a church environment; it oozes out of us day by day. We are so full of Christ that He spills out on everyone around us through the course of every day. If He doesn't, then we're not full.

The Message puts the same verse so simply:

> So here's what I want you to do, God helping you: Take
> your everyday, ordinary life – your sleeping, eating,
> going-to-work, and walking-around life – and place it
> before God as an offering. Embracing what God does
> for you is the best thing you can do for him.

God isn't fooled. We can conform to expected behaviour patterns, but God sees way beyond those. As the Samaritan woman found when she spoke with Jesus at the well that day, He is interested in what's happening in our hearts, where real truth lives. Try as we might, we will not be able to disguise that from Him.

The heart reveals what's really inside us, what we're truly like. Anyone can go through the motions, but God is looking for something more.

Known by God

God still looks for men and women whose hearts hunger and thirst to truly know Him. He can spot a phoney a mile off, but He longs to have us respond to Him fully and sincerely, from the depths of our hearts. He knows all about us – every detail, every secret: the good, the bad and the ugly – and He loves us anyway.

We, on the other hand, don't have that depth of knowledge yet. In the well-loved chapter 13 of Paul's first letter to the Corinthian church, he put it like this: 'Now I know in part; then I shall know fully, even as I am fully known' (v12).

One day, in heaven, when our finite minds have been cast off in favour of new ones that can handle the infinite, we will see things and understand things with a clarity we can't even imagine in the confines of our humanity.

Being fully known is a scary thing, because there is a part of us that remains fearful of rejection, based on what will be discovered in the deepest, darkest parts of our hearts. This is what we unpacked as we explored how the bark must be stripped from the arrow shaft, revealing its inner parts. It brings a vulnerability as we stand exposed before the God who knows us through and through.

Looking God in the eye will probably never be possible, since we'll probably be flat on our faces in awe and worship in His presence. However, there is also a thrill in being so fully and thoroughly known that all remnants of fear are banished by love and acceptance. That's true even in human relationships; how much more so in the face of such pure, strong, enduring love.

The Bible tells us that, 'perfect love drives out fear' (1 John 4:18). Being known so absolutely and accepted without reservation gives us a freedom that means that the expectations of others are now irrelevant, whatever their source.

The Old Testament prophet Joel understood this when he appealed to the people of Israel to return to wholehearted worship of God. He urged them to:

> Rend your heart
> and not your garments.
> Return to the LORD your God,
> for he is gracious and compassionate,
> slow to anger and abounding in love.
> (Joel 2:13)

Joel knew that simply going through a ritual would make no impact on the spiritual lives of the nation of Israel. God would not be taken in by the mere appearance of remorse and repentance. There needed to be a reality in their repentance and godly sorrow that came from their hearts, if any serious change were to happen.

The same is true for us. A polished arrow can bear no splinter; so let's get rid of all those unhelpful expectations, real or imagined. We must stop pretending to be someone we're not, and were never meant to be.

God wants the real, authentic us, as He made us to be; that's who the world needs to see, because then we can reflect Him authentically too.

Target Questions

➢ Living up to expectations, whether our own or those of others, causes us to live in unreality. How has this been true in your life?

➢ What is the difference between the fruit of the Spirit and the gifts of the Spirit?

➢ Can you identify habits or traditions in your sphere of experience which no longer carry the life of God? What might you do to begin to change this?

➢ How can we resist living under the expectations of others and find peace, rest and purposeful living within the promises and presence of God? What does God expect of you?

5a. Samuel

Samuel came to prominence as the last judge to serve the people of Israel. He was the answer to the fervent prayers of his mother, who bore the shameful stigma of barrenness in a culture where fecundity was celebrated.

Hannah was brought to tears by the personal pain of her condition and, overwhelmed with sorrow, poured out her heart to God during one of the family's annual trips to the tabernacle. Her anguish took her to fervent prayer and to the decision to dedicate her son, should God be so gracious to grant her petition, to the service of God for all the days of his life. God answered her prayer and opened her womb. She named her newborn 'Samuel' (1 Samuel 1:20) because it meant 'heard by God'.

Keeping her promise, Hannah sent Samuel to be trained under Eli's supervision at the same place of worship where she'd prayed so fervently that God would grant her a child. God honoured her pledge, and Hannah's beautiful song of praise and thanksgiving in 1 Samuel 2 is a forerunner of the song Mary sang in Luke 1.

Even as a boy, Samuel learned to recognise and respond to the voice of God. This trained him in his prophetic calling as a man who would bring God's Word to a people who were more or less inclined to listen, depending on the circumstance. In many ways, it was Samuel who led the nation back to appropriate worship, back to the ways and will of God for how to live. Everybody recognised this. His words weren't wasted, and the whole country took note of what he had to say.

It must have been quite a dispiriting task for Samuel to watch that repetitive cycle of national behaviour in which the nation turned away and towards God.

In later years, Samuel's sons were appointed as judges too, but they fell prey to corruption by taking bribes and allowing injustice to flourish. Unsurprisingly, the people were disgruntled about that, so went to Samuel together to ask for a king instead of judges. All the nations around had them, so why not Israel? Their request meant they were rejecting God's rule; Samuel wasn't wrong when he saw trouble ahead.[52]

Despite warning the people of how a king would subjugate them in taking the best of everything – land, livestock and people – they kept clamouring for such a man, and God gave them what they wanted. Sometimes that's the worst thing that can happen.

Samuel was instrumental in anointing the young man Saul for kingship; a man the Bible calls: 'as handsome a young man as could be found anywhere in Israel, and he was a head taller than anyone else' (1 Samuel 9:2). This impressive-looking man would be the very first king in a new chapter of the nation's history, but, sadly, he failed to maintain God's standards.

Saul's forty-two-year reign unravelled as he slipped further and further away from God's paths. He stepped out of line when, in a burst of impatience, he decided to usurp the priestly role which Samuel carried and offered a burnt offering without being qualified to do so. It cost him the kingdom. His blustering excuses did nothing to avert Samuel's rebuke that he had acted foolishly.

> You have not kept the command the LORD your God gave you; if you had, he would have established your kingdom over Israel for all time. But now your kingdom will not endure; the LORD has sought out a man after his

---

[52] 1 Samuel 8.

own heart and appointed him ruler of his people, because you have not kept the LORD's command. (1 Samuel 13:13-14)

The contrast between Saul and David was marked. Whereas Saul had been so striking to look at – taller and more handsome than his contemporaries – David was handsome and healthy[53] but, relative to his brothers, the smallest in his family.

Once Saul forfeited the throne with which God had entrusted him, he seems to have become increasingly sulky and irrational, open to the influence of evil spirits and nursing a grievance against the shepherd boy who saved the nation from the threats of the Philistine giant, Goliath.

Tragically, the Bible says that God 'regretted' allowing Saul to be king (1 Samuel 15:35), and Samuel grieved over it. In the light of Saul's spiralling mood swings and resentment against God's decision, Samuel didn't want to leave his house in case Saul had him killed. We read in 1 Samuel 16 that God had to speak to him strongly.

The prophet was given instructions to go to a family in Bethlehem, taking the special horn of anointing oil with him to be administered to whomever God indicated. Obedient as ever, Samuel went to the little town where, generations later, other shepherds would worship the angel-heralded Saviour, Himself a descendant of this rural family.

Perhaps Samuel felt uncharacteristically unsure of himself after all that had happened with Saul, but when he invited Jesse and his sons to a special sacrifice, he was immediately impressed by the physical appearance of the young men.

To Samuel's ageing eyes, the eldest was the obvious choice for a new king, but fortunately his hearing was more finely tuned to heaven than his sense of sight was. God's reminder to him rings as true for us as it ever has done in the intervening years:

---

[53] 1 Samuel 17:42.

Do not consider his appearance or his height, for I have rejected him. The LORD does not look at the things people look at. People look at the outward appearance, but the LORD looks at the heart.

(1 Samuel 16:7)

Seven sons were scrutinised by Samuel: Eliab, Abinadab, Shammah (all three were present, serving in Saul's army when David felled Goliath), Nethaniel, Raddai, Ozam and one other passed by, but Samuel felt no prompting to anoint any of them. Somewhat baffled, he asked whether Jesse had any other boys. David seems to have been a bit of an embarrassment, hidden away shepherding the flock. Perhaps, knowing that seven is the biblical number of completeness, the family was felt to be just that, before son number eight came along unexpectedly. It's inferred but not stated that David was the extra, or superfluous one, dangling at the end of the family: the youngest son; insignificant, always trailing behind his brothers.

'Not so,' said God, as He saw the integrity of David's heart and prompted Samuel to anoint him as a future king. If Samuel had allowed himself to be ruled by his expectations, the wrong man would have been picked for the job. Those splinters could have set Israel on a different trajectory, but this arrow flew true as Samuel submitted to God's smoothing process and found the correct target to see God's purposes fulfilled.

6. Knotty Issues

Our arrow is now looking less like a stick and more like the deadly weapon it will ultimately be. The Master Craftsman has tenderly, deliberately, carefully and lovingly taken the rough wood and shaped it into something of both worth and purpose. One would hardly mistake this piece of wood for brushwood or kindling any more. The shape is defined, and the surface is almost smooth.

But not quite.

Within the patina of the wood, there are invariably knots. Less common in coppiced wood, these are the scars from where a branch has fallen off, but the tree has cleverly encompassed it as it's continued to grow around that exposed join. They are the hard, resistant parts of the wood. While they give it great character, they need to be sanded down so that they don't jut out inappropriately. An arrow must be smooth to be swift. It's a fiddly job, because the very nature of the knots means that they are naturally opposed to this kind of treatment.

As far as our metaphor is concerned, the knots represent two different things.

1. Created uniqueness

First, the fact that irregularities of knots remain in the wood is a reminder to me that God never gives us a personality transplant. While all of us are being changed and shaped to become more like Jesus, He does not erase all traces of our individuality. We are not machines or automatons; we are uniquely created beings. The family of God comes in all shapes, sizes and colours, and that's the way it's supposed to be. We are not identical, and that's deliberate. There is no cookie cutter to be used on Jesus' followers, as though they come off a spiritual conveyor belt, indistinguishable from one another.

All the differences we have in personality, gifting and the application of unchanging kingdom principles in our lives, at work and at home, exist to enhance our corporate impact on the world.

Paul talks about this in 1 Corinthians 12, specifically in regard to the different spiritual gifts that exist in any church. He compares the church with a body.

> And so the body is not made up of one part but of many.
> Now if the foot should say, 'Because I am not a hand, I do not belong to the body,' it would not for that reason stop being part of the body. And if the ear should say, 'Because I am not an eye, I do not belong to the body,' it would not for that reason stop being part of the body. If the whole body were an eye, where would the sense of hearing be? If the whole body were an ear, where would the sense of smell be? But in fact God has placed the parts in the body, every one of them, just as he wanted them to be.
> (1 Corinthians 12:14–18)

In the kingdom of God, we can truly say that it takes all sorts.

I'm so relieved that although God changes us radically from the inside out, He leaves the knots of our personalities to show through. It is no mistake that He's made some of us very loud, some of us shy, some of us funny and some of us dreamers. Some of us are natural pioneers and adventurers, while others are more like supportive pillars who relish the stability that can come with settling in one place long term. Think how terribly dull it would be if we were all the same.

A helpful illustration for this is based on how the spectrum of light works. Light itself appears to be white, yet we see in colour. This is because light reflects off surfaces that absorb light differently. Thus the same light from above reveals a vast array of colours below: blues and reds, yellows and oranges, purples and greens; in fact, the whole spectrum is revealed. I'm not a big fan of thinking of people as flowers but, for the sake of the example, imagine that every coloured flower stands for an individual. Each one reflects the light of God differently, and so we appear as the unique individuals God made us to be. God's people truly cover the spectrum of the rainbow. This is as true of our personalities as it is of our giftings, just as Paul explained in 1 Corinthians.

I remember a lady who came to Jesus through an outreach. She was evidently delighted about her new life and the revelation of what Jesus had accomplished for her, but she seemed rather nervous about something. Gentle questioning led to her nervous enquiry, 'Does this mean I have to like Cliff Richard now?' We laughed together. This precious lady was clearly relieved to discover that this was not a condition of entry to the family of God! Some of us are fans of Cliff's music; others are not; but God would not be substituting her own musical preferences for those she perceived to be the standard tastes of Christians. If she liked Country and Western music before she surrendered her life to Christ, she would still like it afterwards. It's not everyone's cup of tea, but that's the point of our wonderful individuality.

In spite of this, it's clear that as God shapes our hearts, our personalities may be moulded too. We cannot dissociate the one from the other, since we are whole people. If you have a naturally boisterous personality, God may simply teach you how to be more sensitive to others to avoid the possibility of steamrollering everyone around you. If you are naturally shy, you are unlikely to have a career as an international platform speaker and preacher ahead of you – short of serious divine intervention. However, you may find that God speaks to you about reaching out to those around you with care and compassion, in a way that both stretches you and challenges your shyness. You may discover a new level of confidence without being bullied into being someone you're not.

Sanding down these knots is necessary, but removing them is not.

2. Stubborn pride and bad attitudes

Some knots respond well to the sanding process, but others are more resistant. The second thing they represent is pride; that's the hard, unyielding stubborn part of us which really needs attention.

This ugly trait can be so deeply embedded in us that we may not even be aware of its presence. There it sits, ensconced in the darkest part of our hearts, apparently harmless, but ready to spring into action at a moment's notice in opposition to the Master Craftsman who labours to see us changed.

Pride takes all manner of forms; it's the part of us that continues to work in opposition to what God wants for us. We've looked, in earlier chapters, at how easily we can put 'self' at the centre of our lives and so knock Christ off the throne. That's a form of pride too, but the knotty pride that God wants to sand down in our lives is the kind of pride that manifests itself primarily in our attitudes.

Anyone who's been a parent for more than a month or two knows that their children are not perfect angels. One of our primary tasks is to teach them to live in a way that is appropriate to the world they occupy. Training in behaviour is one thing; training in handling attitudes is a whole different area of challenge. Bad attitudes tend to show themselves more frequently – but far from exclusively – in older children. These manifestations are usually far more subtle than blatant bad behaviour, outright rebellion or barefaced disobedience; but our youngsters need to be taught how to handle big feelings and attitudes, as well as to learn good manners, honesty and a host of other values we cherish. An ugly attitude that is allowed to flourish can all too soon become an acceptable way of life that adversely affects behaviour, and can poison both the atmosphere and the lives of all family members as well as spill out further afield. Not only that, but if those attitudes are allowed to continue into adulthood, we won't be doing our loved ones any favours; it's best to tackle these things while they're still young, if we can.

Personally, I found parenting teenagers far more challenging than parenting toddlers or young children. It seemed more like a battle of wits, trying to discern what was actually going on. Some days I felt I needed an advanced degree in psychology. A bad attitude can creep up on the household like a fog, and it can be hard to discover where it came from. Getting rid of it and helping a young person find the tools to replace it with a good attitude is both time consuming and exhausting, but a rewarding investment of time and energy.

It's not surprising that many parents find this one challenge too many, and throw in the towel somewhere around this point in the vain hope that if they leave bad attitudes alone they will go away, or that the teenager will grow out of them on their own, giving everyone else a more peaceful life as a result. It's a flawed theory; if you're in that season, I encourage you to hang in there, keep praying and push through. It will be worth it.

Truth to tell, we adults can sometimes be just as guilty of having bad attitudes as teenagers are. Perhaps we've never conquered them, if our own parents failed to teach us how to cultivate and maintain good ones. None of us had perfect parents, just as none of us has perfect children, and it's absolutely certain that, in turn, we are not perfect parents ourselves; the truth is that we all have bad days.

I've lost track of the number of people I've met who are suffering from the destructive consequences of simmering bad attitudes that linger on, whether towards people or to situations. They've persisted through life with chaotic thought patterns that lead primarily to their own misery, and which have the unfortunate effect of pushing other people away. Can we be the friend who loves them enough to help them without judgement? Having such friends is rare, but precious; being such a friend is a privilege.

Another attitude, as prevalent in adults as in adolescents, is sulking. This is evident in those who don't get their own way and can't handle it, those who are poor listeners, or those who can't disagree constructively, as well as those who fall back on the 'It's not fair!' refrain, and stay there. It's horrible in a child, but somehow worse in an adult. Either way, it fails to reflect the character and nature of God.

The root of this is that hard kernel of pride that persists in resisting the rule of Christ. Sulking is an indulgent behaviour that keeps 'me' at the centre of everything. It refuses to contemplate the perspective of anyone else, even God.

It's pride that keeps us from saying, 'Sorry.' Pride tends to push us into a defensive stance, to resist finding a way through a situation for fear that we might be the one who needs to change. Change is uncomfortable and demanding. Pride also fails to honour or respect other individuals, because its main thrust is to ensure that I justify myself at all costs.

Fault-finding

It's this ugly pride that is the culprit when it comes to that judgemental demeanour that is so quick to see faults in others but so slow to see the fault within. Jesus put it this way: 'Why do you look at the speck of sawdust in your brother's eye and pay no attention to the plank in your own eye?' (Matthew 7:3).

It's a vivid and even humorous picture, but also an effective warning about hypocrisy. Most of us find it so much easier to see what's wrong with everyone else than we do to see the faults in ourselves.

Again, *The Message* puts it eloquently:

Don't pick on people, jump on their failures, criticize their faults – unless, of course, you want the same treatment. That critical spirit has a way of boomeranging. It's easy to see a smudge on your neighbor's face and be oblivious to the ugly sneer on your own. Do you have the nerve to say, 'Let me wash your face for you,' when your own face is distorted by contempt? It's this whole traveling road-show mentality all over again, playing a holier-than-thou part instead of just living your part. Wipe that ugly sneer off your own face, and you might just be fit to offer a washcloth to your neighbor.
(Matthew 7:1-5)

This is such an evocative picture story; it probably had Jesus' listeners rolling around with tears of laughter pouring down their faces. It makes me smile too, until I see myself included in the story and feel the just rebuke.

Comparison is practically a national pastime here in the UK. It's as if by pushing everyone else down, we think that we can somehow elevate ourselves a little more. Just another excuse for rotten, stinking pride to rear its ugly head. No wonder God wants to make sure He's sanded it down in our lives.

Paul told the church in Corinth that certain people get into the comparison game ill-advisedly. 'When they measure themselves by themselves and compare themselves with themselves, they are not wise' (2 Corinthians 10:12). This sort of talk goes on in church communities just as much as it does in the work canteen, or anywhere else. It may not always be verbalised, but we've all done it. 'I may not be perfect,' we say to ourselves, 'but at least I'm not like so-and-so.' So we allow our pride to plump us up a little, reassuring ourselves that we're not so bad after all.

Our pride is fed when we can find comparisons that put us in a better light. Before we know it, we're believing our own press, as it were, and feeling that we're spiritually superior.

The flipside of the same coin is evident when we compare ourselves unfavourably with others. It's not unusual to hear someone say wistfully, 'If only I was more like so-and-so. She's so much prettier/cleverer/more popular/more well-off/more spiritual than I am.' 'He's so much more capable/smart/eloquent/impressive than I am.' Such talk basically accuses God of having made a mistake when He created us, and the root of it is still our own pride.

Peacocks and turtles

We often talk about two kinds of pride.

The first is 'peacock pride', so-called because of the way it struts about, preens itself and generally admires its own self. This kind of pride is put on display; it doesn't try to hide itself or dress itself up as anything else. It's an in-your-face kind of arrogance. While it has a rather nauseating effect on everyone else, it is supremely confident in itself.

The other type of pride is 'turtle pride'. This kind of pride functions by causing an individual to retreat back into their 'shell' in much the same way that a turtle does. It's less obviously on display, but it still responds as if it is at the centre of everything; just less on show. It manifests itself as the inappropriate – or false – humility demonstrated by someone who is continually looking for affirmation from others. It is still generated from a place of pride since it is just as self-absorbed.

As a child, I remember the word 'pride' was simply explained as a problem because of that persistent 'i' in the middle of the word. 'I' is literally at the centre of a pride-filled attitude.

The Bible has quite a lot to say about pride and none of it is good! Here's the most sobering verse of them all, which I quoted earlier: 'God opposes the proud, but gives grace to the humble' (1 Peter 5:5, RSV).

It's not simply that God doesn't like pride; He actively opposes those who live from this place. I find that enormously sobering. If God is opposing me – if He is actively working against me – because of the pride that is operating in my heart and spilling out into my life, then I am in serious trouble. I will be thwarted at every turn. I cannot possibly win against God; I would be mad to try.

If God is for me, however, then even if I am outnumbered on every side I am still in a majority; but to have Him deliberately resisting me, blocking my endeavours and countering what I do is too dreadful to contemplate. Not only will that way lead to disaster, but it also tells me of the seriousness with which God sees and responds to pride.

Take heart, however, because the verse also tells us that God does give His grace to the humble. The humble person is happy to submit to their Creator. It means that we take our eyes off ourselves and put on our 'God-glasses' in acknowledging that we are submitted to Him. Then we can see Him, others and ourselves as He does. Humility, it has been said, is not thinking less of yourself; it's not thinking of yourself at all.

Resisting temptation

We've already looked at how much we need God's grace, want His grace and have experienced His amazing grace. It's not just about the past tense. I've already quoted this verse, but let's look at it again:

> For the grace of God has appeared that offers salvation
> to all people. It teaches us to say 'No' to ungodliness and
> worldly passions.
> (Titus 2:11-12)

Grace is the means of escape when we're tempted. In other words, we need to access the grace of God every single day if we're to walk righteously. We cannot resist every pull that draws us away from God purely by our own strength. Although our willpower may be strong, it's not an effective long-term solution to the problem of resisting temptation. Regrettably, none of us is that strong.

There are many options that present themselves to us each day which seem to be attractive paths, whether they are verbal, attitudinal or behavioural. If we simply go with the flow and respond on the basis of our feelings, then we will almost inevitably end up on a road we don't want to be on. Our life's trajectory, if plotted on a graph, would lurch up and down alarmingly; more thermometer than thermostat. If we choose to leave God's path, we immediately put ourselves in a vulnerable position.

It is only the grace of God that gives us the strength to refuse this kind of easy reflex response, which bypasses our thoughts altogether and helps us to resist the ominous entanglement of pride. Once again, we can see the practical importance of changing our default mechanisms. If we dig in to His unmerited, unending, unlimited, unfailing grace, we will be reminded of who He has made us to be and what He has done for us; then we will discover a rekindling of the desire to stay clean.

We don't say 'No' to things because we're afraid of God's rebuke. We say 'No' because, as we know the joy and security of being loved fully and completely, we don't find those things that He dislikes attractive any more. We cannot put ourselves beyond the reach of His love, and neither do we want to. Nevertheless, we don't want to treat such lavish love with carelessness. That would cheapen His love. We cannot repay His love; but with His strength and in His power, we aim to walk worthily of it even though we know we're far from worthy in and of ourselves.

Pride will impede our walk with Jesus, and trip us up time and time again if we don't root it out. It certainly helps if we understand the destructive effect it has, not only on ourselves, but also on those around us.

Interestingly, even admitting to pride is hard for us, which simply underlines how active it can be. The irony is that it's pride that won't allow us to admit that we struggle with pride.

Listen to Paul again:

> For by the grace given me I say to every one of you: do not think of yourself more highly than you ought, but rather think of yourself with sober judgment, in accordance with the faith God has distributed to each of you.
> (Romans 12:3)

Pride in any shape or form challenges the lordship of Christ in our lives.

Be on your guard

We know that there is an enemy at work who would love to see God's Kingship contested and, preferably, destroyed in our lives. He is happy to quietly nurture that ugly piece of our character for his own ends, and to our own hurt.

The Bible tells us that this enemy, Satan, 'prowls around like a roaring lion looking for someone to devour' (1 Peter 5:8).

That's graphic imagery, and a dramatic statement. The Bible doesn't beat around the bush in its explanation of the evil agenda at work against us. We saw in Chapter 3 how Satan's mandate is still to 'steal and kill and destroy' (John 10:10) in any way he can, because when we're following Jesus, obeying God and walking in the power of the Holy Spirit, we are a major threat to his kingdom of darkness.

Satan doesn't always need to do anything dramatic. Sometimes he will disguise himself, in a sly effort to inveigle his way into our lives; at other times he will be blatant in an all-out attack against us.

A believer who lives their life indistinguishably from their contemporaries poses no such threat to the enemy, since they are not actively working to see the kingdom of God established in their life: their marriage, kids, workplace, national government, school board, local football club, aerobics class, among their neighbours, or wherever they spend their time.

However, believers who recognise that Jesus is serious about changing hearts and lives; who pray in faith and expectation that God's 'will be done, on earth as it is in heaven' (Matthew 6:10); those who earnestly and diligently seek to share the love of God, His salvation and abundant life through Jesus with those around them, will inevitably stir up discontent in the spiritual world.

Satan's plan has not changed one iota over the millennia. Whether literally or not, he will just as happily steal your joy, kill your passion and destroy your hope as actually take your life. And he has a thousand ways to do it, including stirring up your pride. He'll trash your certainty, laugh at your faith as presumption and destroy every God-given dream you've ever had. He will chip away at your self-esteem and sense of worth until you doubt whether all those promises from God really applied to you at all.

One of the most effective tools in his armoury is that of the lie. This is a hugely effective piece of deception that brings confusion to people's minds day after day in every part of our communities. Jesus alerted His Jewish listeners to this strategy:

> [Satan] was a murderer from the beginning, not holding
> to the truth, for there is no truth in him. When he lies,
> he speaks his native language, for he is a liar and the
> father of lies.
> (John 8:44)

Just as he did at the beginning of history, in a garden with Eve, Satan will plant an idea here, sow a seed of doubt there; anything that will get you to believe that God is holding out on you. He loves to deceive you into thinking that God has lumbered you with a second-best life.

He will lie to you about the veracity of God's promises and the sufficiency of His grace. He'll stir up doubt and insecurity; attritioning your soul until you're tied up in such knots that you can hardly even see Jesus any more, let alone fix your eyes on Him. The devil will feed that knotty pride, or appeal to it however he can if it serves to dislodge Jesus from that primary position in your life. Like guerilla warfare, he relentlessly seeks the opportunity to stage an ambush, to take back the ground that once legitimately belonged to him.

We can rejoice that God has given us our unique personalities, but let's cheerfully submit to having our knotty pride sanded down. Then we can see ourselves as God truly sees us. We won't allow ourselves to be tripped up, defeated or discouraged by the enemy's tactics because we recognise them for what they are.

How we see ourselves needs to be aligned to the truth of how God sees us.

Paul told the believers at the church in Colossae that 'you died, and your life is now hidden with Christ in God' (Colossians 3:3). That being so, when God looks for us, we are not hidden from His sight, but we are covered, surrounded or engulfed in a sense by Jesus. So God looks at you and me and sees Jesus: righteous, holy and pure. How wonderful.

Pride has no place here. It cannot be allowed to spoil the arrow, or it will never find its target.

Target Questions

➢ What are the character traits that show themselves most strongly in a) your family? b) you? How has God softened and shaped those in you?

➢ Do you recognise either peacock or turtle pride in your own life? What does godly humility look like?

➢ In which areas of your life have you encountered the enemy attempting to 'steal and kill and destroy'?

➢ Satan is 'the father of lies' (John 8:44). What untruths has he told you that have caused you to stumble? How can you counter those attacks?

6a. Naaman

The story of Naaman in 2 Kings 5 is another old favourite. I first learned about him from a child's Ladybird book, which focused on the young servant girl who was so influential in the life of this important man. I probably wasn't much older than her when I read it, and certainly the welcome inference was that you're never too little to be part of God's story.

Naaman was a military man from beyond Israel's borders. As commander of the army to Ben-Hadad II, the notorious king of Aram, he was skilled, respected, distinguished and prominent among the officials and government of the day. Naaman was not only esteemed as a fighting man, but the king knew his commander was instrumental in achieving the military victories in which he was able to bask himself. King Ben-Hadad needed Naaman in order to validate himself and to keep his throne secure.

Unfortunately, for all his glittering career, a dark secret stalked Naaman: he had leprosy. This chronic and incurable skin disease was highly infectious; sufferers were ejected from their communities to live lonely, painful lives, hidden away from society. Although the term as used in the Old Testament covers a spectrum of afflictions, in its worst form, leprosy damaged nerve endings so the carrier couldn't feel pain. Inevitably they suffered from burns and wounds which, left untended, became infected, and fingers, toes and even limbs could be lost permanently. It was a disease that carried enormous shame;

lepers had to cover themselves and declare their presence by use of a bell to warn the healthy to keep away. The label of 'unclean' would live with them for the duration of their miserable lives.

For Naaman, it meant that same looming ignominy and the inevitable loss of everything he had enjoyed in his important position, as the insidious disease progressed and strengthened its hold on him. A desperate situation. For a man used to praise and deference from others, including his monarch, this would have been the bitterest of pills.

However, on one of the army raids into Israel, a girl was captured who then worked as a maid to Naaman's wife. Far from home, away from her parents and everything familiar, this remarkable young lady held on to her faith in God. Perhaps her faith was more in Elisha, but she hadn't forgotten that back in her home country there was a recognised prophet with a powerful ministry empowered by the living God, and which included the gift of healing. Perhaps she was prompted by the sadness of her mistress, but this girl bravely offered her information to a wife who knew her married life was heading for a rapid unravelling.

Seizing this glimmer of hope, Naaman went to the king, who was aware of his commander's secret. He relayed the happy news that there was still a possibility that his medical situation could be reversed; he might yet remain at the helm of the army and keep the king's military and political position secure.

With such a possibility, Ben-Hadad, not entirely unselfishly, offered to write a letter to King Jehoram in Israel, to pave the way for his sick commander to visit. In it, he included his expectation that the king of Israel would cure his commander. Such a thing was far beyond the monarch's power; he didn't react well, despite the gifts Naaman had brought. Jehoram saw the situation as a sneaky trick by his long-term enemy to provoke him into further conflict. He knew he had no power to heal anybody, commander or commoner. He was so distressed that he 'tore his robes' (2 Kings 5:7) and responded petulantly.

Somehow, word from the palace filtered through to Elisha, who sent word that the king should really know better, and reminded him that God was still very much at work. He told the king to send Naaman to Elisha himself.

It must have been a remarkable sight to see Naaman arriving at Elisha's modest house with horses, chariots and at least some of the lavish gifts that he had brought from home. Such an impressive entourage was a reflection of his standing, and Naaman seems to have expected a grand welcome and grovelling courtesy too. How disappointing and embarrassing, then, to find that the man he'd been sent to wouldn't even come out of his house to greet him. Naaman was left in the street with a mere messenger who brought a directive from Elisha to go and wash himself in the River Jordan seven times.

> Naaman went away angry and said, 'I thought that he would surely come out to me and stand and call on the name of the LORD his God, wave his hand over the spot and cure me of my leprosy. Are not Abana and Pharpar, the rivers of Damascus, better than all the waters of Israel? Couldn't I wash in them and be cleansed?' So he turned and went off in a rage.
> (2 Kings 5:11-12)

The commander was used to the finer things in life. He was accustomed to servants who did his bidding, people who honoured him, bowed, scraped and generally boosted his ego. He saw Elisha's treatment as an insult and a snub. His pride was severely wounded and, in spite of his skin disease which had brought him this far, all he could see was the affront to his position and his person. He stomped off in a fit of temper and sulked like a spoilt child.

What he had been asked to do was not difficult; but his expectations of what he felt due to him were not consistent with the ways of God. Naaman's peacock pride was still very much alive, despite his perilous state of health. He wanted a show;

some sort of grand gesture that would sort out his problem while still feeding his pride.

It was not to be.

Inside the house, Elisha must have been praying and listening for God's instructions; after all, it was probably a prompt from God that caused Elisha to invite Naaman in the first place. I wonder if he took a sneaky peek out of the window, or whether he heard the roar of displeasure form the Aramean, as he bided his time patiently indoors and waited to see whether the soldier would humble himself and obey God's directive.

It was a respectful servant, who clearly knew his master very well, who managed to make Naaman finally see sense. After all, he reasoned with him, if the man of God had told Naaman to do something grand, wouldn't he have done it? Of course he would! So why not do something simple? How hard could it be?

So Naaman calmed down and washed himself in the second-rate River Jordan seven times – the biblical number of completeness – and made the joyous discovery that he was completely healed. I'm so glad the story doesn't end there.

Elisha came out of his house after the event and met Naaman and his retinue of attendants and servants. Whatever had happened on the outside of Naaman's body, something radical had also happened on the inside. In front of everyone, he declared that there could be 'no God in all the world except in Israel' (v15). That was a risky thing to say, since it was almost certain that among his escort there would be informers who would report back to the king back in Aram, where a pagan god was worshipped.

While Elisha refused to take any gifts from his visitor, emphasising that doing business with God is never a trade, he was instead asked for something. Naaman requested four panniers of soil from the area to take home on a couple of mules, which he would use when he began a new prayer life with the God who had just healed him. It would be a physical reminder for him of the presence of the true and living God. With it, he could create a prayer place with a connection to

Israel, where this God seemed to live. He also asked that he might be forgiven for the times when he would be obliged to accompany King Ben-Hadad into the temple of Rimmon back home, as part of his duties. Although he had bowed his knees and surrendered his heart to the God of Israel, he knew that his obligations as commander would require certain acts of service that he no longer subscribed to. He was clearly aware that serving two deities was not an option, and Elisha's God had shown Himself to be the real one. It may have looked like compromise, but God gave Elisha an insight into Naaman's heart and he gave his blessing for both humble requests.

Naaman became an arrow fired back into a foreign land after God had dealt with his pride outside Elisha's house. We don't know how effective he was there,[54] but every time he knelt down to pray on the patch of earth he had brought home with him, he would have seen his restored skin, and known a new peace in his heart; he was humbled and grateful.

---

[54] You can read how Elisha's servant, Gehazi, hoodwinked Naaman on the way home in 2 Kings 5:20-27.

7. The Sanding of Forgiveness

Before the arrow is ready for the polishing that will keep it flexible and make it swift, it must go through one last process of refining. No longer simply a stick, this piece of wood has become something quite remarkable. It has endured painful batterings and planings, with the end in mind. Even during the apparently rough treatment, at no point has it received more pressure than it could bear. Its usefulness is beyond doubt; any archer would be glad to own such a weapon.

What is missing? What treatment still needs to be applied for maximum effectiveness?

This last stage is the use of high-grade, fine sandpaper along the entire length of the shaft. In medieval times, the arrowsmith used fish skin. This process removes any sap residue and the last vestiges of roughness. Spiritually speaking, it's a picture of forgiveness.

We've spoken about the wonderful, far-reaching forgiveness of God for all our wrongdoing; the liberating truth that there is no sin beyond His reach. We fully understand that this is only possible because of the power inherent in Jesus' blood, spilt for us.

Unforgiveness

Now it's time to look at how we give, or withhold, forgiveness to others.

Forgiveness is neither fashionable nor politically correct. In an age where most of the Western world is caught up in blame culture, and many are selfishly obsessed with their own rights rather than responsibilities, forgiveness is decidedly outmoded. I once heard it suggested that many psychiatric wards might be cleared of large numbers of patients if they only understood how to forgive others. I'm not sure whether there are any statistics to bear this out, but when we see the devastating results of not forgiving others, perhaps it's not such a wildly unreasonable thought.

Offences; fallings out; confrontations; misunderstandings; arguments; unfortunate, hurtful words which remain unresolved over many years, can all cause physical and emotional problems for people, regardless of their creed, culture or colour. Such grievances can become an emotional burden in our hearts that produces a physical ache or worse. If they are allowed to fester, or are taken out, repeatedly examined and regularly relived, these hurts and sorrows can turn into emotional cancers. Just as a child keeps pressing a bruise they've picked up in the course of physical play to see whether it still hurts, we can keep these emotional hurts alive.

All of us have picked up such bruises on our separate journeys through life. They are inevitable; none of us is immune.

How sad that many people spend their days in bitterness of heart over something that happened years ago but has never been resolved. In holding on to the past, unable to open their hands to the present, they are robbed of joy and hope, for both today and for the future. They are forever looking backwards; bound to some events of yesteryear, frozen in a moment of time and unaware that they have become their own prisoner.

The book of Proverbs says:

> A happy heart makes the face cheerful,
> but heartache crushes the spirit.
> (Proverbs 15:13)

It's true that there are some hurts that run so deep that you can actually see them in people's faces. The emotional part of us has a deep and clear effect on the physical body. What complex beings we humans are, and what tragedies we can carry around etched into our very beings!

Real forgiveness

The importance of forgiveness, though clearly stated by Jesus Himself when His disciples asked Him how they should pray, and repeated in thousands of churches and cathedrals around the globe week by week, has perhaps not been given the attention it deserves.

> This, then, is how you should pray:
> 'Our Father in heaven,
> hallowed be your name,
> your kingdom come,
> your will be done,
> on earth as it is in heaven.
> Give us today our daily bread.
> *And forgive us our debts [sins],*
> *As we also have forgiven our debtors [those who sin against us].*
> And lead us not into temptation,
> But deliver us from the evil one.'
> (Matthew 6:9-13, my emphasis)

Of course, this is the Lord's Prayer, taken from Jesus' words in the New Testament. You've probably prayed it yourself in some form or another. It's a standard ingredient of religious gatherings; its comfortingly familiar words are found in traditional Easter and Christmas services, at weddings and funerals. But look at the lines that I've emphasised in italics and see whether something unfamiliar strikes you.

Jesus tells His disciples that when they pray they should ask God to forgive them *as*, or *in the same way*, that they forgive others. That may prompt us to stop and think.

First, we are encouraged to ask God to forgive us – that's pretty straightforward. But next, there is an assumption that we will be forgiving other people.

We know we need forgiveness, because we recognise that we have fallen short of God's exacting standards. But here's the startling news: this prayer shows us that there is a correlation between how God forgives us and how we forgive others. That's very sobering.

Apparently, if I am reluctant to forgive others, or am stingy in my attitude of forgiveness towards others, then I am actually asking God to employ those same characteristics when forgiving me. If I can only forgive grudgingly, then that is how I am asking God to forgive me.

Think about that for a moment. It's a powerful truth, and a massive incentive to not allow unforgiveness any space in our lives to wreak its ghastly devastation.

Let's ask a different question.

On what basis does God forgive us in the first place? We have already unpacked this in previous chapters, but it bears repeating for the sake of clarity at this point. One New Testament writer put it like this: 'without the shedding of blood there is no forgiveness' (Hebrews 9:22).

There is no substance on earth that is sufficient to expunge, or cover, our sin, except blood. A blood sacrifice was necessary; blood is the only cleaning agent with enough power to eradicate the stain of sin. It's the blood of Jesus that holds that once-and-for-all-time power. So we are forgiven on the basis of the blood of Christ.

Forgiveness is about pardoning; it means we stop hostilities and resentment against someone. Again, the Bible spells it out clearly:

'Come now, let us settle the matter,'

says the LORD.
'Though your sins are like scarlet,
they shall be as white as snow;
though they are red as crimson,
they shall be like wool.'
(Isaiah 1:18)

The Old Testament prophet speaks here about forgiveness in the context of cleaning or cleansing.

David, the psalmist, used a different image:

For as high as the heavens are above the earth,
so great is his love for those who fear him;
as far as the east is from the west,
so far has he removed our transgressions [sins] from us.
(Psalm 103:11-12)

This is a graphic song about the removal of our sins, using literary, poetic language. David used terms of space and distance to convey the reality of how far those sins have been taken away from us.

Jeremiah picked up a different aspect of God's forgiveness when he prophesied to the people of Israel, bringing them God's own words: 'For I will forgive their wickedness and will remember their sins no more' (Jeremiah 31:34).

God chooses not to remember our sin any more; as I said earlier, that's not the same as absent-mindedly forgetting something. It's a deliberate decision, which means that our sin is dealt with. We're clean, and He will not bring those things up again; they're gone. Forever.

Forgiveness does not excuse sin; it does not rationalise sin; it does not justify sin. It is not simply forgetting about sin, or putting it behind us in the vague hope that we might be able to draw a line under it and walk away.

Sin needs to be dealt with, not explained away or hidden away; and it can't be spirited away.

Forgiveness doesn't try to make the offence, or misdemeanour, palatable or more acceptable. There would be no purpose in that.

True forgiveness brings enormous freedom, both to the one receiving and the one extending that forgiveness.

Withholding forgiveness

Here's a truth you're probably familiar with, quoted by minister's wife Gail MacDonald: 'When I refuse to forgive a person, I become his slave.'[55]

It's an ironic truth that withholding forgiveness usually fails to have any significant effect on the one who has caused us hurt. They may not even be aware that they have inflicted emotional, or actual, damage on us by their careless words or thoughtless action. The one who is primarily affected is us. If we choose to hold on to an attitude of upset, disappointment, wounded pride or betrayal, then the one who is tied up in knots is ourselves. That point of pain becomes cemented in our personal history. Rather than dealing with it, it remains hidden under a proverbial carpet, where it grows larger rather than smaller. Try though we might to give it a wide berth, eventually there will come a day when we trip over it. Then we will experience more pain, along with the brutal discovery that a disproportionate amount of our life has been governed by an unresolved conflict and a failure to forgive. We have become prisoners of our own making, serving a sentence of mental and emotional incarceration. Our liberty, our freedom in Christ has been stolen from us by our own stubborn foolishness.

If we think of that hurt as a weight or a burden that we end up carrying, rather than that metaphorical bump in the carpet,

---

[55] Anonymous; quoted by Gail MacDonald, *Keep Climbing* (Carol Stream, IL: Tyndale House Publishers, 1989), p74. Used with permission of Gail MacDonald.

we can understand how Gail MacDonald describes the choice we have:

> Consider one ... who is deeply hurt by the failure of another and chooses not to forgive. In so doing, she effectively nails herself to that event and time and makes her climb [her walk of faith] a difficult one. Another ... however, knows a similar betrayal and chooses to manage the pain and hurt by giving mercy and forgiving grace. She not only steadily moves beyond the event to further growth but gains a bit more strength and resilience to become an even more forgiving person in the future. One act of forgiveness usually begets another.[56]

That's not to say that extending forgiveness is easy. Don't underestimate the struggle that inevitably comes where pain is real and deep. In some cases that wound may have been buried, or carried, for many years. The emotional wound may need cleaning before it can be mended. This sort of forgiveness is not some light, spur-of-the-moment decision.

Oswald Chambers showed great perception when he said:

> We talk glibly about forgiving when we have never been injured; when we are injured we know that it is not possible, apart from God's grace, for one human being to forgive another.[57]

The path of forgiveness

We cannot dismiss the hurts of someone else as trivial; we cannot have their experience, and we have no right to judge them on that basis. Nevertheless, the path of forgiveness is the

---

[56] Ibid, p76. My emphasis.
[57] Cited at www.rockbridgechurch.net/gospel-anthology (accessed 12th September 2023).

only one that will lead any of us out of our prison and into the freedom that Jesus has for us.

This is true regardless of the offence, although we must understand that where the wound is deep, the process of arriving at a place where the wronged one is able to walk this path may take many years. Victims of sexual abuse cannot be expected to truly forgive unless they have known deep and thorough healing, physically, emotionally and spiritually – usually facilitated by a mature believer or counsellor who has years of experience and substantial training in this specific area. It is a long, gruelling process for all, but rushing this journey will be counterproductive and cause further layers of damage.

The act of forgiveness involves handing the person we are forgiving over to God. It means that rather than judging them ourselves, we allow God to be God and to deal with them as He wishes, and in His time. This is difficult when everything in us shouts out for justice that can be seen and which sees us vindicated. There are times when we want to be both judge and executioner.

Resisting that urge becomes even harder in those instances where the one who has given offence shows no signs of remorse or repentance themselves.

It's tempting to try to trade forgiveness: 'I'll forgive you if you say you're sorry.' That's a natural reaction; but to gain freedom and forgive in the same way that God forgives us, we can't put conditions on it. Forgiveness cannot be dependent on the reaction of the offender.

It's wiser, and so much more effective, to place the one who caused the hurt into God's capable hands; He will not make a mistake and does not have the fallibilities we carry.

Abraham recognised this early on in the Bible, when He pleaded with God for the lives of the righteous in the wicked cities of Sodom and Gomorrah. Having prayed that God would avert the judgement and destruction of those dreadful places, he declared, 'Will not the Judge of all the earth do right?' (Genesis 18:25). He was not really asking a question, but making a statement of faith in the One who is 'the Alpha and the Omega, the First and the Last, the Beginning and the End' (Revelation 22:13).

The choice of forgiveness

We have to conclude that forgiveness is a choice.

Forgiving others means we choose not to bring the matter up again to that person, to ourselves, to others or, indeed, to God. We have placed them entirely in His hands both for this life and the life to come. This is no small matter; but remember, this is how God forgives me and you. He does not forget like an ageing amnesiac. He chooses not to remember my sins any more, as if they were placed at opposite ends of the compass and were out of reach for ever.

Theologically, this means that when we go to Him and confess a sin that we've already been forgiven for on a previous occasion, God effectively says, 'I don't remember that.' It means that if we come and repent for something that we know we've messed up before, He treats it as if this time is the first time. He doesn't say, 'Oh no! Not you with this old chestnut again. Have you still not got this sorted out in your life? Why do you keep messing this up? What's wrong with you?' He doesn't rub our nose in the sins of the past, but mercifully and firmly leaves them there. It's another example of amazing grace.

Can we forgive others in the same way?

Our own strength and resources are not sufficient for extending forgiveness like this; we simply don't have the capacity for that. But, because God has lavished His forgiveness on us, we can't afford not to pass it on to others in the same way. We will need His power to do so.

God forgives His children in four clear ways: completely, thoroughly, frequently and unhesitatingly. I am delighted, overwhelmed and often rendered speechless by the sheer extravagance of His love, and the continual forgiveness that He showers on me. I am all the more thrilled when I consider what a poor bargain He got when He bought me at the extortionate price of the death of His only, much-loved Son. Yet He insists that I was worth it, and He thinks the same about you.

The challenge of forgiveness

I know only too well that the four-fold type of forgiveness He extends is going to be needed time and time again in my life. There are, as James 4:17 implies, sins of omission and sins of commission that I commit every day of my life, in thought and word and deed. Knowing that I can be made clean every day is astonishing.

I cannot afford to forgive others in any lesser way if I want to ask God to continue to forgive me completely, thoroughly, frequently and unhesitatingly; and I do.

It's not helpful for us to have unrealistic expectations of others. Redeemed sinners are not perfect saints; they will need my forgiveness from time to time, just as certainly as I need theirs.

Gail MacDonald again:

> I am convinced that we do not learn to forgive in the hour of crisis, we actually train for it. Is it strange to say that in our best moments we prepare for the potential worst ones? In this case, we study the meanings of forgiveness and how it is portrayed in Scripture. We watch and learn from others who are going through situations needing forgiveness. And we monitor our own spirits to observe our progress in times of small irritation or conflict. Are we instantly vindictive or easily drawn to give grace?
>
> Do we hold grudges easily? Is it difficult to disengage from hard feelings toward another who has offended us? Are there those with whom it would be difficult to sit down and pray because we harbor hostilities toward them? Asking such questions is imperative if we are to guard our hearts closely. For ... few things are more

crippling to the person who wants to climb spiritually
than the inability to forgive quickly and thoroughly.[58]

Withholding forgiveness opens the door to all sorts of other
ugly sentiments: resentment, bitterness, ingratitude, hostility,
negativity, cynicism, sourness and misery. None of these is a
reflection of Jesus; so when we fail to forgive, and choose to
harbour resentment in our hearts, we bring dishonour to the
name of our Father God, whom we claim to love.

The other problem we have in keeping an offence alive is
that, in doing so, we don't allow that person to change.

In our minds that person is cemented as 'the one who
wounded us'; we've trapped them mentally in a place where we
want them to remain until the offence is answered for to our
satisfaction. We no longer see them in any other way, and thus
we project an incarceration on to them.

This is not a reflection of God's heart for anyone.

When I forgive someone I release him to become what
God intends him to be. But if I refuse to forgive, I bind
him to the moment and act of offense.[59]

A woman who perhaps experienced the liberation that comes
from forgiveness more intensely than most was Corrie ten
Boom. Although she died more than forty years ago, her story
carries an authentic honesty which never fails to move me.

This courageous and indomitable Dutchwoman was
subjected to the horrors of the concentration camp at
Ravensbrück during the Second World War. Both her father
and her sister, Betsie, died after their imprisonment; her father
a couple of weeks after his arrest, and Betsie of starvation just
twelve days before Corrie was released. Corrie held fast to her
faith, just as Betsie had done, and survived despite unspeakable

---

[58] MacDonald, *Keep Climbing*, pp77-78. Used with permission of Gail
MacDonald.
[59] Ibid, p88.

cruelty and poor health. After the war was over, she began to speak all over the world about their experiences, and how even in the darkest times of despair God had sustained them and allowed them to be channels for His love to many women in the camp. Forgiveness was a challenge, but Corrie was never one to turn away from difficulties, however daunting they might be.

The high cost of such forgiveness was a painful reality, as she discovered on returning to Germany on one occasion.

Corrie was often invited to speak at church services, and that's where she encountered a former SS officer. The recognition was all the more painful because she remembered him as the Ravensbrück officer who had been in the processing centre of the concentration camp. Seeing him triggered all her memories of humiliation and suffering.

After the service, the smiling man came and expressed his thanks for her message. Enthusiastically, he shared his joy at knowing the reality of having his own sins forgiven by Jesus.

As he put out his hand to take hers, Corrie found herself recoiling, full of dark, angry thoughts. Yet she was simultaneously struck by the reality of God's enormous span of forgiveness while recognising that she had no capacity to extend that forgiveness to the man in front of her. Feeling no compassion or benevolence towards him, she prayed silently, fervently, asking God to give her His forgiveness for him since she had none of her own to share.

In her book, *The Hiding Place*, Corrie explains how, as she reached to respond with a handshake, she felt a supernatural warmth, like an electric current flow through her arm to the former SS guard. In that moment she caught a glimpse of God's love for one of His children which almost overcame her.

She realised that the command to love our enemies isn't given in a vacuum, but comes with the resource of God's own love and forgiveness from heaven itself.[60]

---

[60] Corrie Ten Boom, *The Hiding Place* (London: Hodder & Stoughton, 1971).

What would have happened had Corrie chosen not to forgive that day? We could so easily say that her resentment and anger were understandable after all that she had been through. Why should she forgive? Didn't she have a right to demand recompense, to get her own back in some way? Would we have been as humble or as willing to access God's grace and reach out towards our enemy as she was? I'm ashamed to find that for myself, I doubt it.

It has helped me enormously to remember that the thing I may struggle to forgive in someone else is, more than likely, something that God has already forgiven in me. In the light of that truth, I cannot in all integrity hold on to a hurt or a grudge or unforgiveness any longer. The only appropriate response is to release them to God.

The motives of our hearts, which lead us into sin, are universally shared. The greed, hatred, anger, envy, pride and selfishness that are present when someone sins against us have also been present in our own hearts at one time or another. I know that God has forgiven those ugly things in me. Therefore, it is inappropriate for me not to forgive them in someone else, even if these traits manifest themselves in ways I have never behaved myself. How can I withhold from others that which God has never withheld from me?

Conversely, the longer you leave someone else's offence unforgiven, the more difficult it is to face the situation again, to offer the cleansing forgiveness that releases all those involved. You don't need to be either a theologian or a psychiatrist to know that being quick to forgive brings great peace of mind, as does being quick to apologise.

The reality of forgiveness

In January 2003, my cousin Detective Constable Stephen Oake was killed by a suspected terrorist in a ricin raid on a house in Crumpsall Road, Manchester. In protecting his fellow officers, Steve forfeited his own life. The whole family went into shock.

For his immediate family there was also the added pressure of a media circus on their doorsteps, and the invasive witness of the general public to their own grief. Steve's family and wider family are believers, but this does not mean that we didn't all go through the natural emotions of horror, disgust, anger and a desire for retribution. The challenge to forgive Steve's killer was huge and each of us will have faced it differently, but the challenge remains. If I fail to forgive that man, I become a prisoner to that choice, and I open the door to unresolved anger and bitterness. I may rage against God and shout that 'It's not fair!' but I am still the one who's trapped. Like Corrie, we needed to extend God's forgiveness where our own resources were insufficient. I cannot be responsible for how anyone else handles this challenge, but I know I have needed to leave justice in God's hands and take responsibility before God for my own reaction.

The realisation that God will forgive me in the same way that I forgive others was startling in this context. How could I possibly forgive this man? But, in the light of all that God has done for me, how could I possibly not forgive him?

My uncle, Steve's dad and former chief constable of the Isle of Man, Robin Oake, expressed forgiveness for this suspected terrorist to TV and newspaper journalists at Steve's funeral and later on a Radio 4 Sunday service, in which he preached a powerful and eloquent message of forgiveness which simply dripped with the grace of God. The testimony of the family has been a challenge and an inspiration to people around the world and has consistently pointed to the goodness and faithfulness of God throughout. It has been nothing short of extraordinary. The freedom that forgiveness brings is manifest daily in their lives.[61]

[61] Robin Oake, *Father Forgive* (Milton Keynes: Authentic Media, 2008); Jenny Sanders, *Spiritual Feasting* (Rickmansworth: Instant Apostle, 2020).

Forgiving ourselves

It would be remiss if we didn't turn our attention to one more person to whom we probably need to extend forgiveness: ourselves.

It's great to embrace the forgiveness Jesus has brought us, with a thankful heart. We may even have wrestled through the difficulties of releasing forgiveness to those who have hurt us over the years, and come through victorious in that area. But there are many people who have never allowed themselves to enjoy the freedom that self-forgiveness would bring.

Perhaps you've heard people say, 'I can never forgive myself for the way I did such-and-such,' or, 'I will never forgive myself for what happened that day.' It's the heavy sound of regret that weighs down a heart and paralyses the best of men and women. We can hold ourselves prisoner while we let those thoughts have space in our heads and our hearts.

Living with regret and recrimination is not living in the abundant life that Jesus talks about in John 10:10. It's like trying to drive a car with the handbrake on. The journey is seriously impeded, and the result is a great deal of internal damage to the engine, as well as a lot of smoke which blocks the view.

As I review my life, there are several things I would have liked to do better, and a few I might have done completely differently. It would be such an advantage if we were able to live the past with the knowledge and experience of the present! Not only could we do better, but we would be better. Fortunately, I have very few regrets, but one in particular sticks with me.

It could easily have trapped me in a place where I persistently flagellated myself over my choices. In this case – regarding a letter that should never have been sent – I did that very effectively for nearly ten years. Eventually I realised that the only person suffering from the long-term consequences of my rash correspondence was myself. By continually chastening myself, I was making little headway except to weigh myself down even further with a belief in my own stupidity which then affected the way I did other things. I sought God and prayed for His forgiveness and then sat down with a large slice of humble pie to write another letter to the addressee of the original letter, asking them to forgive me. Although I never received a reply, by doing this I extended forgiveness to myself for something that had effectively kept me a prisoner for far too long. It did not bring back the wasted years, but it was a huge relief.

That may seem quite trivial to you, but the effect it had on me was significant.

You may find yourself with something far weightier than a letter as the source of regret in your life. Perhaps it involves a soured relationship that can't be restored because the person involved (maybe a parent or grandparent) has died. It may be that you are estranged from a partner or child, or that you look back on the parenting of your own children with regret over the mistakes you made. You may have compromised in a work situation and felt guilty ever since.

It's worth taking time to seek forgiveness, but don't discount the necessity of forgiving yourself. Allow God's grace to access every part of your heart so you can walk in the liberty He has for you. Why stay in prison when the door is wide open for you to walk in freedom?

Forgiving God

I wonder whether you've ever thought about this. Why would God need to be forgiven? After all, He's God – He's perfect in truth and holiness; He has never done anything wrong. Absolutely so, but there are times when we have quite possibly blamed God for something that happened in our life: a betrayal, a bereavement, a set of circumstances that caused us to suffer in some way – a disappointment, a redundancy, a financial crash, a health breakdown. It could be many things; but where we have laid the blame for that at God's door, rather than acknowledging it as the outcome of the choices of others, or simply the byproduct(s) of living in a world which has, for the most part, turned its back on God, we will find an obstacle in our relationship with Him.

It may simply be that God has disappointed us. We may not have put it in those words, but there may have been a time that was particularly important to us when God didn't come through as we'd hoped; He didn't meet our expectations and we've never come to terms with that. Perhaps we've harboured resentment against Him or, out of our hurt, spoken negatively about His faithfulness; we may even have become cynical about His goodness.

We can't live in His fullness and know the love, joy and peace for which we have been designed if we ignore these things. Admitting that we were wrong to make such a conclusion and letting go of the conviction that God was to blame will clear the way for renewed, clean and open intimacy again.

Following Jesus and loving God actually means frequently saying sorry; it means continually embracing forgiveness for ourselves, and releasing it to others as a way of life. This is crucial if we are to enjoy the abundant life He has promised us. We must humble ourselves, swallow our stubborn pride and understand that forgiveness is God's wonderful provision for keeping the way to Him open and clear.

Mastering this will mould and mature us so that we can walk in the works He has prepared for us, and allow Him to shape us into the image of His Son. It's all part of becoming a useful arrow in His hands.

Target Questions

➤ What are the characteristics of God's forgiveness towards us? Which of these are reflected in the way you forgive others?

➤ 'The act of forgiveness involves handing the person we are forgiving over to God. It means that rather than judging them ourselves we allow God to be God and deal with them as He wishes and in His time.' How do you feel about this statement?

➤ God has forgiven His children *completely*, *thoroughly*, *frequently* and *unhesitatingly*. What are the implications of this?

➤ What does this look like in your life? How can we train ourselves in forgiveness?

7a. Woman with a Jar of Perfume

The story of Jesus and the woman who lavished perfume on Him is told in Matthew 26:6-13, Mark 14:3-9 and Luke 7:36-50. In John 12:1-8 we read of a similar story in which perfume is poured on Jesus' head by Mary, the sister of Martha and Lazarus, at their home in Bethany. In this example, we're going to focus on the account by Dr Luke.

Jesus met this woman after he'd accepted an invitation to dinner at the home of Simon, the Pharisee. This in itself is quite interesting, since Jesus kept His most excoriating words for this group of religious elites. The Pharisees were often more concerned with preserving their holier-than-thou demeanour than with enjoying the life of God with genuine faith that would have expressed concern for anyone else, especially for the poor and marginalised. It's not clear why Jesus chose to go to this man's house; perhaps it was purely to put Himself in a place where she could easily find Him.

What is clear is that Simon was not a particularly good host. In first-century Palestine, it was common to greet your guests and then provide them with water to wash their dirty, dusty feet. Visitors might also have access to fragrant oil for their heads; after walking in the relentless sun, this freshened and fragranced their hair as well as acting as a type of insect repellent. Jesus was not offered any of these things, which suggests that whatever Simon's motives for inviting this popular rabbi to his house, he wasn't too bothered about making Him feel at home. By denying Jesus those common courtesies, he was actually dishonouring Jesus in front of the other guests before He'd even sat down.

In that culture, the meal table was not too far off the ground; diners reclined around it on a selection of cushions. This is where Jesus was when a woman with a terrible reputation dared to cross the threshold and come in.

It's not clear how she managed to gain access; perhaps she had watched and waited for some time, plucking up the courage to approach Jesus. Maybe she took advantage of a moment when the servants were occupied with bringing dishes in and out to slip in through the door; or perhaps the men were eating on an outside terrace to which she had access.

Luke simply tells us that she was 'a woman in that town who lived a sinful life' (Luke 7:37). The inference is that she was a notorious prostitute or sexually immoral in some way. Whatever the details, there was no hiding who she was; everybody knew about her. What a burden it must have been for her to have this label sticking to her wherever she went. There was nowhere she could go where whispers and gossip didn't follow her. People would not want to be seen with her or be associated with her; it must have been a very lonely life. I wonder what defensive defaults she had put in place to survive in a consistently brutal and ostracised life.

Why did she come and find Jesus at all? Had she been in a crowd somewhere and heard Him teach, or had she met someone whose life was changed because of him? Maybe she'd crossed paths with someone who'd been healed, or who knew Mary Magdalene and saw the dramatic difference in her life once Jesus had cast 'seven demons' out of her (Luke 8:2). Or perhaps she'd just heard on the grapevine about this extraordinary man who didn't shy away from interacting with the outcasts of society: the despised, the rejected, the least, the lost and the lonely. If that was really true, then the possibility of meeting Jesus for herself threw her a metaphorical rope of hope. Perhaps Jesus might have some comfort or help for her in her desperate situation from which she saw no escape. The glimmer of acceptance, even for the briefest of moments, may be what drove her to venture to Simon's house that night. It was a bold plan, but also an authentic cry for help.

She didn't turn up empty-handed. This lady had very little to offer Jesus, but she did have a special jar of perfume made from valuable alabaster – a type of gypsum, used in the crafting of ornaments and jewellery. It's neither as costly nor as strong as marble, but it lends itself to carving, and was probably sealed with wax to keep the contents fresh. Her jar was special, but what was inside it was worth much more. This perfume was probably made from nard, or spikenard, an essential oil mentioned in Song of Solomon 1:12 (KJV) in the context of an intimate, loving relationship.

Once in the house and in the presence of Jesus, this precious woman said not one word. Overwhelmed and overcome, she simply stood behind Him and let her tears fall. Just being in Jesus' presence unlocked a world of sorrow and repentance which needed to be expressed. Thanks to the table arrangement, those tears began to drip on Jesus' feet; so she knelt down and wiped them away with her uncovered hair. For a woman to appear in public without a head covering was shocking, and indicative of a loose woman at the time. This lady wasn't there to defend her reputation or to make a point about the social construct of the day; her focus was fully, purely on Jesus.

There, on her knees, she broke the narrow neck of her bottle to access the fragrance inside, and poured it lavishly on Jesus' feet.

Simon, the host, reacted indignantly to this and recoiled from the very presence of such a woman in his house. Although he never said it out loud, Jesus knew just what he was thinking, as Simon grumbled to himself that Jesus could not be much of a prophet if he didn't realise what kind of dreadful sinner was touching Him.

Jesus, full of love and grace, as ever, chose to catch his attention not with a sarcastic putdown, but with an intriguing story. In His rabbinic tale, two men had borrowed money: one a substantial sum, and the other just a tenth of that amount. When it was time to repay the debt, both found themselves in the unfortunate position of not being able to pay back what they owed. Rather than burden the men with their debt plus interest, or even an extension of the loan, the man who lent the men money cancelled the whole debt for both of them. So, Jesus asked, which of those men would be the most grateful?

It didn't take long for Simon to figure out that while both got off scot-free, the man who'd owed the most must have been proportionally more grateful to find himself released from any obligation to pay back the moneylender. Jesus agreed.

Then, throwing cultural mores aside, Jesus challenged Simon: 'Do you see this woman?' (Luke 7:44). In that moment, he forced Simon to acknowledge the presence of the woman in his house. Culturally, Simon would not have paid her any attention at all, even though he was clearly watching her out of the corner of his eye the whole time. Women were not allowed to be present in such a gathering of men. Jesus demanded that Simon look, see and consider her with fresh eyes. Then comes his wake-up call:

> I came into your house. You did not give me any water for my feet, but she wet my feet with her tears and wiped them with her hair. You did not give me a kiss, but this woman, from the time I entered, has not stopped kissing my feet. You did not put oil on my head, but she has poured perfume on my feet. Therefore, I tell you, her many sins have been forgiven – as her great love has shown. But whoever has been forgiven little loves little. (Luke 7:44-47)

Jesus' words must have stung Simon. I bet they would have had the servants whispering among themselves when they cleared the supper later. Luke doesn't record who the other guests were – other Pharisees, or friends he wanted to show his connections off to, perhaps – but they were unsettled by Jesus' reference to forgiveness of sins.

What we know for sure is that this damaged, broken lady was very much present, and Jesus' words of affirmation must have filled a void in her heart and soul. Jesus knew that her sins were not trivial, and that there were many of them but He had them covered. In that last line, he was obviously referring to Simon whose love was found wanting.

In case she missed it, between sobs and self-consciousness as the men spoke together, Jesus reiterated, 'Your sins are forgiven' (v48).

In four little words, her world was made new. Her devotion to Jesus had been demonstrated without speaking a single word; Jesus knew her heart, saw her pain and met her where she was. Mercy, grace and forgiveness set her free.

Jesus had one more instruction for her, citing her faith as the trigger for her forgiveness and the opportunity to start over with a clean sheet before God. He told her to 'go in peace' (v50). He spoke peace to her heart and mind, as He fired this grateful arrow into a new chapter of her life.

Not only did this encounter change the life of one messed-up, broken woman, but her story itself has been an arrow fired through the generations, reminding us all of the lavish nature of God's love and the forgiveness in which we find new life.

8. The Nock

The nock is the cleft, or notch, cut into the back end of an arrow; it's used to slot it onto the bowstring so that it doesn't slip. An archer nocks his arrow before firing, to position it correctly in relation to the bowstring.

These days, detachable nocks are made of plastic and can be bought in packs of a hundred at a time. In medieval times, however, a craftsman would make a cut in one end of the arrow after sanding the shaft and before the feathers were added. A sharp knife needed to be wielded carefully in order to create a cleft without splitting the entire shaft and ruining the arrow. A narrow file then carefully widened the space so that it could be lined with either leather or horn to reduce the friction between the arrow and the bowstring. This ensured a snug fit as well as a streamlined exit from the bow, and therefore a greater impact on the target.[62]

In a later chapter we'll see how the archer's bow is a picture of God's purposes, into which we are slotted ready for firing, while the bowstring is illustrative of the calling and timing of God. The nock has an intimate relationship with them both, which is crucial to the arrow's function and effectiveness.

---

[62] 'Making a Medieval Arrow', www.youtube.com/watch?v=r1WMcnA2 940 (accessed 21st April 2023).

Fitting with God

Although we were originally designed to fit perfectly in God's world and enjoy privileged intimacy with Him, it all unravelled when Adam and Eve chose to follow a path other than the one God had designed and created for them. Consequently, the close relationship they had with Him, and with one another, came to a shuddering halt. An apparently unbridgeable chasm opened up between them, ushering in the ugly arrival of guilt, shame, selfishness, subjugation, dominance, oppression, manipulation and the constant battle against nature in both raising crops and bringing forth children.

God's purposes were carelessly discarded; open relationship with Him was no longer possible, and they felt the need to hide both from Him and from one another. Pain, sorrow and death arrived in the beautiful new world, and the enemy laughed, delighted that he had managed to smear God's image in His creation; to sow seeds of doubt about both His goodness and the veracity of His words into the fabric of the earth, thus warping the DNA of humanity until history is finally wound up.

Thank God, He did not allow this to be the end of the story. He already had in mind the plan for our salvation: the way to mend that yawning gap between Himself and His world. Jesus bridged it by giving up the riches of heaven in obedience to His Father and by taking on the flesh of a human being with all its limitations in first-century, dusty Palestine. He paid the ultimate price to bring us back into a place of friendship and fellowship with our Maker. Jesus is the sacrifice that makes knowing God possible.

So the spiritual war is won, but we have an unspecified number of battles to endure before God brings everything on earth to a close. We live in the in-between place – somewhere between the now and the not yet – of history. Sin still runs rampant in the world. The devil and his demons continue to wreck as much havoc as possible while they still have space and permission to operate. They are running out of time.

Unveiling ourselves

One day all will be made new again. Jesus' close friend John saw a vision of 'a new heaven and a new earth' (Revelation 21:1) to be revealed in the future. When that becomes a reality, the enemy will be banished and destroyed forever.

Until then, we're told:

> The creation waits in eager expectation for the children of God to be revealed. For the creation was subjected to frustration, not by its own choice, but by the will of the one who subjected it, in hope that the creation itself will be liberated from its bondage to decay and brought into the freedom and glory of the children of God.
> (Romans 8:19-21)

Not just humanity, but everything that God has made is looking forward to that day when things are once more aligned under His mighty hand; when they are free from the wearying cycle of the seasons, from deterioration and death.

For us as spiritual arrows, to have a functioning nock we need to allow ourselves to be revealed to the world. That sounds dramatic, and in one sense perhaps it is.

It means embracing who God has made us to be. We've talked about shaking off the perceived and/or unrealistic expectations of ourselves and others, the need to be rid of sharp splinters of unforgiveness, and how God's grace changes us so radically. To be able to slot snugly into God's plans and purposes, we need to know both who we are and whose we are.

Not too long ago, a popular cinematic musical gained traction with cinema-goers in its depiction of a motley crew of strange people who were mostly outcasts in their contemporary society. Based very loosely on true events, they came together under the auspices of the American showman Phineas T Barnum, formed a formidable community who looked out for one another and became a successful, sensational circus troupe.

The rhythmic anthem they sang together in the film included lyrics about stepping out of the shadows and accepting themselves for who they were without fear or favour from the general public. Some of the minor characters portrayed were less than compassionately disposed towards them, and relished spreading suspicion and fear across the town about the strangers who were so different from themselves.

The message was that each uniquely created individual carried intrinsic and inherent worth. Their natures and their characters held value in and of themselves. The fact that they were so different from the majority – bearded ladies, giants, conjoined twins and albinos among them – altered that plain fact not one bit.

In a world where we are constantly harassed by the advertising industry to believe we lack physical items – whether it's smoother skin, finer coffee, better insurance, etc – the idea that we are enough in and of ourselves is appealing. We're exhausted and disillusioned from relentless messaging about new products; as soon as they're purchased, they're out of date, or out of fashion, or incompatible with the next iteration. To dispense with all of that and discover our inherent value is empowering and liberating, but it's not the whole story.

God pronounced His creation, once completed with both male and female, to be 'very good' (Genesis 1:31). Both genders are needed to fully express His nature and character. God is a community – Father, Son and Holy Spirit – and therefore needs a community to truly reflect Him, in both the biological family and the spiritual/church family. God does not make mistakes. The disintegration of Western culture, which seems intent on reinforcing adolescent confusion over changing bodies, flies in the face of what we know about who God is, and who He has made us to be. More than ever we need to know that God has made us and doesn't just like the result; He loves us with a fierce and passionate love.

Paul's words to the church in Rome remind us that all of creation is waiting for us to step up and take our place, to become who we were born to be.[63] No one else can be who we are. We must resist the temptation and the lie that being someone else would make us happier, wealthier, more popular or more successful. Only you can be you; and you will always be the best at that. Rejecting that wonderfully created uniqueness God has woven into us means also rejecting God.

That's the reason Lucifer was cast out of heaven.[64] Not content with being created as one of the angelic beings serving the Lord of Hosts, he fell into jealousy and wanted God's throne for himself. For generations he has focused his anger on all that God has made and consequently missed out on the birthright that would have been his, of being one of that glorious, heavenly multitude of celestial worshippers.

Popular influencers are spreading the message that each of us is enough in and of ourselves, but it's no good saying we are 'enough' if we live ignoring or rejecting God, or making the terrible mistake of thinking that we know better than He does. Without Jesus, we can never be enough because we can never conquer the parts of ourselves that are contrary to His plan. Thus, we will be far from enough without Him, because we'll be missing a crucial component for life.

We are spiritual beings, as well as physical and emotional ones; we are designed for relationship with Him. Jesus is the only One who has made that possible; when we embrace Him, we find the solid satisfaction and fulfilment that His abundant life brings. Thankfully, that is not dependent on the stock market, interest rates or whatever our boss might say in our annual review. He is bigger and more enduring than all of those things.

Only in Jesus can we be enough, because He is more than enough.

God is making us more like Jesus, day by day. One step forward, two steps backwards, three steps forward, one step

---

[63] Romans 8:19-21.
[64] Isaiah 14:12-14.

backwards. Our overall progress is onwards, upwards and forwards, in His strength and by His grace.

Wounds and scars

Here's another interesting thing about the nock: a shaft with a deliberate cut in one end looks less than perfect, but it's crucial for the effectiveness of the arrow.

We've explored how we carry knotty bits in our personalities which God softens and enhances as we walk with Him. Arrows made in the way we are talking about were not mass produced. A veteran archer might recognise the maker of his arrows by the way the fletchings were arranged, or the style and colour of the whipping cord by which those feathers were fixed. Regardless, there is an individuality about this kind of arrow which illustrates the point well.

None of us is perfect, but God uses us anyway. He sees value, worth, potential, His own reflection – if rather blurred – in us, and considers the price paid for us by His Son was worth it.

We need to repeat this to ourselves until we've really grasped it; to massage it into our souls and our psyche as we keep reminding ourselves of the profound truth and wonder of such a statement.

That cut, wound or imperfection allows us to slot perfectly into God's bowstring. Paul knew this for himself. In his second letter to the church at Corinth, he explained how a chronic physical condition had been a major trial for him. It seemed that God would not remove it, even though the apostle prayed fervently, three times, for just that. He felt God come alongside him and say, 'My grace is sufficient for you, for my power is made perfect in weakness' (2 Corinthians 12:9).

The place where Paul recognised he was not strong allowed space for God to come and fill it/him in power. It served as a restraint in so far as it removed the temptation for Paul to rely on his own qualifications, both physical and academic, in church planting and discipleship. He was unlikely to fall into the deadly trap that trips many modern Church 'celebrities', when the focus of ministry becomes themselves rather than their Saviour.

Paul was able to keep things in perspective and decided instead to:

> ... boast all the more gladly about my weaknesses, so that Christ's power may rest on me. That is why, for Christ's sake, I delight in weaknesses, in insults, in hardships, in persecutions, in difficulties. For when I am weak, then I am strong.
>
> (2 Corinthians 12:9-10)

There was something redemptive in Paul's suffering, as there will be in ours. God doesn't always remove our suffering, but He can come and fill it with His presence. Whatever wounds we carry – often, but not exclusively, emotional ones – and however they've been inflicted on us, it's imperative that we keep them clean. Just as untended physical wounds fester and become infected, so hurts, disappointments, betrayals and let-downs can turn all too soon into bitterness of heart unless they receive the appropriate attention. The enemy delights in scenarios that leave wounds, traumas and the like unresolved. They so quickly hinder our intimacy with Jesus; we must not allow them to drive a wedge between us, but find His comfort and hear His voice as He leads us through a path of healing, however long that may take.

We must be sure to keep our scars clean.

On a smaller scale, none of us is infallible; we've seen how all of us have weaknesses, foibles and flaws. Most of us are all too aware of them. Rather than disqualify us for effective endeavours within whichever context God has placed us, if we run towards God rather than away from Him, He can be glorified in us and through us. The fact that He wants to do life with us and walk alongside us each day says more about His Father heart for us than about our own skill or competency.

Remember what He did with five loaves and two fishes? Broken, blessed and multiplied, they provided nourishment for a vast crowd.[65] That's a powerful picture of how He can use us.

An unlikely bunch

Take a look at the twelve disciples. A mixture of rough, blue-collar workers who hadn't been picked out as likely students by any other rabbi, they included a despised tax collector who worked for the occupying power and was probably trusted by none of the rest; a zealous, almost certainly violent, freedom fighter and a boastful loudmouth who thought he was better than everyone else. Hardly promising material. Yes, there was a thieving traitor in there too, but even he was part of the ragtag Jesus-family who witnessed miracles and went on mission trips with the others, until he threw it all over for the sake of thirty pieces of silver. The disciples didn't realise he had a different heart from them; none of them guessed Judas was the traitor Jesus talked about. The remaining men, plus a group of women, were involved in turning the whole world upside down in a movement that continues today, as it seeks to put things right side up while God's kingdom keeps growing, just as He promised it would.[66] We are called to be part of this too.

There's no doubt that the God who spoke light into being with just a word can command angels to go to work on His behalf. Obedient, perfected, divine beings with supernatural power would carry out God's wishes far faster and more effectively than we ever will.

And yet, in His wisdom and kindness, He has chosen to have us work alongside Him, despite our weaknesses, our imperfections, our excuses, our stumbling and our relatively feeble faith. I imagine the angels must roll their eyes in exasperation from time to time.

---

65 Matthew 14:13-21.
66 Daniel 2:35, 44; Luke 1:33.

God is still showing His power in our weaknesses.

That little groove on the end of an arrow may seem insignificant, but everything else depends on it. It is the part of the arrow most in touch with the bowstring, and therefore, the archer. Though His fingers grip the shaft, the arrow will not fly far if it hasn't been nocked properly.

Kingdom culture

We 'fit' when we embrace God's kingdom culture, leaving our preferences, our traditions and our desires at the cross. Our national proclivities and predilections are subservient to those of the kingdom. We put our own culture aside and, in doing so, discover one much larger, more exciting and more fulfilling than our own. There is an equality in God's kingdom that breaks down the man-made walls of race, gender and social strata.

Paul explained to the church at Galatia that in God's eyes it's as if we are all 'wearing' Jesus:

> All of you who were baptised into Christ have clothed yourselves with Christ. There is neither Jew nor Gentile, neither slave nor free, nor is there male and female, for you are all one in Christ Jesus. If you belong to Christ, then you are Abraham's seed, and heirs according to the promise.
> (Galatians 3:27-29)

Paul is not saying that we lose our individuality (we've already established that's not the case), but he is saying that skin colour, salary, academic achievement, man/womanhood are irrelevant within a kingdom culture. Rather than dwelling on our cultural differences, we are part of a bigger, more inclusive, liberating culture in which we are focused on seeing God's kingdom come, together with Jesus-followers from every nation, tribe and tongue. We are new creations;[67] our old life, including our

---

[67] 2 Corinthians 5:17.

personal and national culture, is dead to us. We embrace God's kingdom culture which crosses every barrier and boundary. We will all be represented one day around God's throne in heaven;[68] all focused on our wonderful Saviour, caught up in the 'white-hot worship'[69] of the King of kings. It might be smart to start practising now!

Kingdom culture has the King at the centre. As we are being transformed, our culture moves from an individualistic one to a kingdom one. It shifts from one in which decision-making and conflict resolution are worked out according to our personal preference – that mixture of nature and nurture – to one that references Jesus first. He is the hub from which everything else radiates.

This takes time. You can begin the task today, but it may not have shifted to your default culture for several years. The famous Austrian–American management consultant Peter Drucker became known for his famous quote: 'Culture eats strategy for breakfast.'[70] It's a reference to the persistent nature of culture which is so embedded in individuals and organisations that it resists change without us even being conscious of it. All our good ideas are subsumed by the way that we do things, because we've been doing them that way for years. You can see it operating every January as the best of resolutions fall away when a wish for change disintegrates in the light of a personal culture that hasn't yet altered. Like the principle of putting off and putting on, we need to dismantle that personal culture if we're going to build a new one that is in sync with that of God's kingdom.

We no longer simply ask God to bless the things we've already decided. He is not to be an afterthought or a spiritual stamp of approval to add to the things we've put in place. We

---

[68] Revelation 7:9.

[69] www.desiringgod.org/articles/spiritual-awakening-and-the-knowledge-of-god (accessed 26th June 2023).

[70] www.managementcentre.co.uk/management-consultancy/culture-eats-strategy-for-breakfast (accessed 26th February).

mustn't separate the spiritual thread from the practical one. Our first question needs to become, 'What is Jesus saying?' and then, 'In the light of that, what does He want me to do?' They're not different things.

He is the source and the start of everything, just as He was at the birth of time. The community of Father, Son and Holy Spirit oversaw creation itself. He needs to be the starting point of all our endeavours in every sphere of life. Hearing from Him and following His promptings will keep us on track and protect us from distractions and a lot of mistakes which could damage both ourselves and other people.

Including the Holy Spirit

Where the nock is lined with strong, smooth leather or polished horn, we find yet another picture of the Holy Spirit. He is not an optional extra; neither is He just for big meetings or warm, fuzzy tingles. That is not flippant; but the fact is that a great deal of church activity would probably trundle on for many weeks even if the Holy Spirit left. That's tragic; it really shouldn't be so. We must keep listening for Him; the more we listen, the more we'll hear and the faster we'll recognise His voice.

It's so easy to fall into habits, traditions, programmes and rotas; services can often pretty much run themselves, and we know what to expect, regardless of the denomination to which we belong. Church was never supposed to be like that; it's meant to be a community of 'living stones' (1 Peter 2:5) – or people – not a series of meetings.

The day of Pentecost recorded in Acts 2:2-4 describes the powerful and highly disruptive arrival of the Holy Spirit, released from heaven after Jesus' ascension. Even though the disciples and other followers were sitting indoors, talking and praying together, suddenly He arrived like a mighty wind, enveloping them all. They saw miraculous flames dancing on one another which, like the ones Moses saw in the strange plant on Mount Horeb in Exodus 3, didn't burn them at all. As if that wasn't dramatic enough, the Holy Spirit then empowered them to speak in other languages they had never learned. That must have been quite a gathering; it certainly sounds a lot more dynamic than some I've been in over the years!

The real question is, regardless of whatever space is given to the Holy Spirit within a church programme, how much of our daily lives do we give Him? Are we following the commands of Jesus to believe, be baptised and keep in step and communion with God by welcoming and listening to the Holy Spirit as we pray in the name of Jesus?

Whatever else He is saying, there are some commands we don't need to wonder about. There are a number of imperatives in the New Testament that we can take on board, many of them given by Paul in instructions at the end of his letters to various churches. Here are a few, together with their respective references in case you want to look them up and explore them further:

➢ Watch out for people who try to cause divisions among the community of believers (Romans 16:17).

➢ Stay alert; be rooted securely in your faith; be bold too, and all in a spirit of genuine love (1 Corinthians 16:13-14).

➢ Love each other (Galatians 5:14).

➢ Keep in step with the Spirit (Galatians 5:16).

➢ Share the things that weigh you down, and help carry the weight others are burdened with (Galatians 6:2).

➢ Don't be worried or anxious (Philippians 4:6).

➢ Forgive each other (Colossians 3:13).

➢ Seek wisdom and use it appropriately (Colossians 4:5).

➢ Speak to one another with grace (Colossians 4:6).

➢ Rejoice in all circumstances (1 Thessalonians 5:16).

- ➢ Pray all the time (1 Thessalonians 5:17).

- ➢ Stay thankful for everything (1 Thessalonians 5:18).

- ➢ Keep away from evil (1 Thessalonians 5:22).

You could do a whole Bible study on this topic, and may well be surprised by how many exhortations are given to us in Scriptures which encourage us to keep walking closely with Jesus, to enjoy not only His company, but also the life He has given us.

To be living in the fullness of God we need to enjoy 'the grace of the Lord Jesus Christ, and the love of God, and the fellowship of the Holy Spirit' (2 Corinthians 13:14). To only have a relationship with one or two members of the Trinity means we aren't living in the fullness that God designed. It would be like driving a car on a motorway without ever shifting up beyond second gear: bad for the engine, the driver and other road users.

Without the Holy Spirit, we become cognitive followers of Jesus; adherents to a set of beliefs and values, but without the power to put them into practice. We may know the Bible inside out and back to front, but vibrant faith turns, all too quickly, to dry, legalistic religion; it's a shell – a dead thing – that drains and traps us. It brings life to neither ourselves nor the world around us.

We cannot, we must not, jettison the Holy Spirit.

First love and red-hot passion

We were not made just to acknowledge our relationship with God, but also to enjoy Him in intimacy. When Jesus' closest friend John was near the end of his life, living on the island of Patmos, he received a vision in which he was shown extraordinary things. Right at the start, he was told to write down what he saw, including seven letters for seven specific churches.[71] They make challenging reading as God both commends them and points out where some of them are missing Him.

The first letter to the church in Ephesus, so beloved by Paul, praised them for their hard work and perseverance, but chastened them for losing their first love for Him.[72] Their passion for nurturing their relationship with God had got lost somewhere among the many good things they were involved with.

Marriages and friendships experience this; it's all too easy to take one another for granted, or drift apart. Relationships, both horizontal and vertical, human and divine, need time, care and nurture in order to flourish. The giddy period when we fell in love needs to have time and space to grow into a mature, deep, selfless, sacrificial love. We learn about one another's weaknesses and strengths, the things that make us laugh and the things that irritate us. We discover more stories, thoughts, feelings, hopes and dreams over a period of years, which glue us more closely together, but it's costly in terms of time. We need to lay aside our own programmes and preferences to do it. Intimacy with our heavenly Father requires all of this and more. The level of trust is so much deeper with One who never lets us down, but if we neglect the relationship, we lose the joy and peace that are our birthright in Him.

Perhaps the saddest of the seven letters is the one to the church at Laodicea (in modern-day Turkey). In it, God rebukes them because their love for Him, though not cold and dead, is not passionately alive either. There's a nonchalance to it which grieves His heart. He expresses a desire that they be either one or the other, but 'because you are lukewarm – neither hot nor cold – I am about to spit you out of my mouth' (Revelation 3:16). In other words, 'Your complacency and lack of fervour

---

[71] Revelation 1:19-20.
[72] Revelation 2:2-4.

in knowing Me grieves Me to the point that it actually makes me sick.'

The Message translations updates the language for us:

> You're not cold, you're not hot – far better to be either cold or hot! You're stale. You're stagnant. You make me want to vomit.

It's graphic language. What it tells us is that God is jealous for His relationship with us to be authentic, close and vibrantly alive. It also tells us that He provides what is needed to make that a reality: gold (faith), white robes (forgiveness) and eye salve so we can see Him clearly (Revelation 3:18). And it tells us that He is knocking at the door of the church, eager to be invited in for intimate companionship and feasting (verse 20). Rather than spitting us out of His mouth, Jesus' desire is for us to be an accurate expression of His voice in the world; one that is an authentic representation of His heart – clear, compassionate and relevant. We cannot represent Him properly without that intimacy. This is what we were made for, just as an arrow is made to slot snugly into the bowstring.

Like the lining of the nock, the Holy Spirit helps us sit safely in God's hands and stay there. Close to the Father, we become more familiar with His voice and alert to hearing His softest whisper. We can pick out His voice, distinct from the other ones around us. We can also relax into His plans and purposes, assured that He will handle us with care.

Target Questions

➢ How can you truly embrace the person God has made you to be without making excuses for the things you know that God wants to change in you?

➢ In what way can you agree with Paul that God's strength can be made perfect in your weakness?

➢ What does kingdom culture look like? Why is culture so difficult to change?

➢ How can we rekindle our first love for Jesus?

8a. Moses

Moses was born into a turbulent time. The entire nation of Israel served under the cruel boot of Egypt's pharaohs, and had done so for almost four hundred years. Set to work on constructing some magnificent edifices – the remnants of which you can still see today – they were driven by the whip, and suffered terrible lives of servitude under the scorching sun in a culture that was soaked in superstition and worshipped multiple malevolent gods.

The Egyptians considered the Hebrew people a threat through their sheer force of numbers.[73] Consequently, when a king came to the throne who failed to consult the history of how and why these immigrants were there, he issued a decree that all male children should be thrown into the Nile and drowned. While the midwives dodged his wrath by claiming that Hebrew women were so strong that healthy births happened before they even got to the expectant mothers,[74] Moses' parents hid their newborn second son away, eventually committing him into God's hands by placing him in a waterproofed papyrus basket and setting him among the reeds of the great River Nile. You may be familiar with the story of how Pharaoh's daughter came down to bathe, found the child and effectively adopted him as her own son after his early years were spent back with his mother, thanks to the quick thinking of his big sister, Miriam.

---

[73] Exodus 1:9-14.
[74] Exodus 1:15-21.

Moses spent forty years in the palace, followed by forty years in the wilderness living with the family of a Midianite priest. He learned what it was to be both prince and priest.

At that point, the preparation God had worked in him was sufficient for Moses to receive his commission to lead the Israelites out of Egypt to freedom, and to the land promised to Abraham, Isaac and Jacob more than four hundred years before.

Moses' first meeting with God took place at Horeb, when he was drawn to the curious burning plant which didn't turn to ash, but kept aflame. Earlier in this book, we followed Elijah to the same place many years later, after he'd run from Queen Jezebel and desperately needed to meet with God after the rigours of the contest on top of Mount Carmel against the prophets of Baal. Moses' famous encounter with God was the reason why Horeb was considered special; an honoured place where a genuine seeker might connect with God.

God spoke to Moses out of that strange fiery shrub; His instructions were crystal clear,[75] and all Moses' excuses were overruled by the awesome statement, 'I AM WHO I AM' (Exodus 3:14). The capital letters express the seriousness, majesty and holiness of the living God. It's the first time the Bible calls God 'Yahweh' – a more weighty and distinctive name than previous references to Him as Elohim.

Their conversation is recorded in detail through thirty-six verses. It's one of the longest exchanges recorded outside the prophetic books, and marks the beginning of another forty years of Moses' increasingly close relationship with God, as he learned to be a prophet.

His task – to lead more than 1 million people through the desert – was surely one to make the stoutest heart quake. The logistics of travelling, camping, resourcing and communicating with such a large number of people are mind-boggling. No one person would be able to facilitate such a journey; it had to be done under the guidance of God and in submission to His

---

[75] Exodus 3:5-22; 4:1-17.

words. It was vital that Moses pressed hard into God to know what he needed to do. Seeking God on his knees, Moses consistently heard the voice of God as He faithfully led His people day by day.

Of course, when they set out, Moses had no idea that this would be the third forty-year section of his life. The direct distance between Cairo and Jerusalem is about 260 miles. Even allowing for frequent stops and stragglers, it shouldn't have taken longer than about a month so, although the prospect was daunting for Moses, perhaps knowing it would all be over in a month might just have made it more manageable; but that's not what happened.

God led this multitude by a 'pillar of fire' at night and a 'pillar of cloud' by day (Exodus 13:21). All the people saw how God delivered them from Pharaoh after ten excoriating plagues back in Egypt, and how the despot and his charioteers were swept away when they had pursued the escapees across the Red Sea. Nevertheless, their complaints and rebellion against God, their ingratitude, grumbling and yearning for the diet they missed when they were slaves,[76] meant that none of the adults would get to see the place their hearts and their forefathers had longed for. Generations had waited for fulfilment of the promise to have the land of Canaan as their own, and they forfeited it all when they stopped trusting the merciful God who had rescued them.

Moses continued to seek God on their behalf. Frequently, passages describe how he prayed fervently for protection, deliverance, water, food, healing and mercy. At one point, when pleading on their behalf for forgiveness, he even suggested that God's anger be turned on to himself and he be removed from heaven's book of life in their place.[77]

In another great encounter between Moses and God, this time on Mount Sinai, God manifested His presence through

---

[76] Numbers 11:4-6.
[77] Exodus 32:31-32.

thick cloud, thunder, lightning, fire and a trumpet blast.[78] He called Moses to come and join Him at the top, but no one else was allowed to approach. He was entrusted with the Ten Commandments; a freedom charter for a recently liberated people who were not used to being allowed to worship the true God: to be away from idols; to have a day off to focus on replenishing with their Creator; to own their property without fear of it being taken away, and without anxiety over whether someone might take their wife on a mere whim. It must have been such a relief to know that God was taking care of them under His banner, and ushering them into a liberating, life-giving culture.

A little later, God confirmed the covenant He had made with His people, on the same mountain. In a prefiguring of the transfiguration of Jesus, Moses, his brother Aaron, Aaron's two eldest priestly sons and seventy elders were given a glimpse of God in an extraordinary encounter. These seventy-four men 'saw the God of Israel … and they ate and drank' (Exodus 24:9-11).

This was an unprecedented event since no one was allowed to see God's face. In fact, the apostle John wrote in his Gospel, 'No one has ever seen God, but the one and only Son, who is himself God and is in the closest relationship with the Father, has made him known' (John 1:18).

Not only that, but ten chapters further on in Exodus, Moses received another set of stone tablets from God with the commandments written on them (the first set was broken when Moses came down the first time, discovered the people indulging in all sorts of pagan worship in front of a golden calf idol, and threw them down in righteous anger).[79] When he got to the bottom of the mountain after forty days with God, his whole face reflected the glory of God to such an extent that he began to wear a 'veil' over it, because his appearance frightened people. God's holiness literally shone from Moses; it was so

---

[78] Exodus 19:16, 18.
[79] Exodus 34:1-28.

'other' to the ordinary people that they found it deeply disturbing.

This then, became Moses' practice:

> Whenever he entered the LORD's presence to speak with him, he removed the veil until he came out. And when he came out and told the Israelites what he had been commanded, they saw that his face was radiant. Then Moses would put the veil back over his face until he went in to speak with the LORD.
> (Exodus 34:34-35)

It's hard to imagine the kind of intimacy Moses enjoyed with God. Elijah experienced the presence of God passing by,[80] but wasn't allowed to see His face. Previously, Moses had another powerful meeting with God after the golden calf incident, when he was so discouraged by the people that he wanted to give up the whole sorry crowd. In the Tent of Meeting, God came down in the pillar of cloud and encouraged him, with the promise that His presence would go with him.[81]

This is a tricky passage because in Exodus 33:11, it says: 'The LORD would speak to Moses face to face, as one speaks to a friend.' But, having pledged to be with Moses, to teach him and give him rest, Moses asked to see God's glory. It was an audacious request, and God's reply was affirmative, but:

> 'You cannot see my face, for no one may see me and live.'
> Then the LORD said, 'There is a place near me where you may stand on a rock. When my glory passes by, I will put you in a cleft in the rock and cover you with my hand until I have passed by. Then I will remove my hand and you will see my back; but my face must not be seen.
> (Exodus 33:20-23)

---

80 1 Kings 19:11.
81 Exodus 33:14.

Did God use His literal hand to protect Moses from the death-inducing reality of seeing the Holy God, Creator of the universe? Probably not, but He certainly shielded Moses from the dazzling, infinite, overwhelming awesomeness of God in three dimensions.

In the same way, the clarity Moses had in communicating with God from a place of enviable intimacy is a depiction of that closeness they had in their times together. God is spirit, so when the Bible talks about God holding us with His hand,[82] or putting things 'under his feet' (Ephesians 1:22), or meeting face to face, it's not necessarily literal, but a picture of His action and involvement with the world.

American author and pastor A W Tozer famously said that we 'have as much of God as we actually want'.[83] You might be tempted to disagree, but mark the difference between what we want and what we wish for. We might all wish to grow our relationship with God, to have the same kind of clarity that Moses enjoyed and an intimacy that leaves us markedly different, but do we want it enough to get down to serious business with God?

Are we prepared to change in order to pursue Him; to alter our habits to make more space for leaning into Him and pursuing intimacy with Him? Let's ask Him to help us set unhelpful things aside and choose to keep pressing in to know Him better.

---

[82] Isaiah 41:10.

[83] A W Tozer, cited at: www.cmalliance.org/devotionals/tozer/?id=155 8 (accessed 9th June 2023).

9. Polishing Oil

Our arrow has now been through every stage of crafting. It is unrecognisable from the rough branch it used to be. It is ready for its final transformation before it can be handed over to the blacksmith and fletcher for their contribution to the process.

Before the arrowhead is fitted at one end of the shaft and the tail feathers at the other, the wood simply needs to be polished.

Rich, oily polish will reduce the friction generated when an arrow travels through the air. It will enable the arrow to fly faster, further, more smoothly and more accurately. Not only that, but as the oil seeps into the deepest parts of the arrow, it ensures that the wood will not become dry. A dried-out arrow is a brittle arrow; easily damaged before it even reaches the quiver, let alone the bow, and more than likely to snap under the pressure of the archer's strong hands. A little flexibility is necessary in order for the arrow to withstand the pressure under which it will come, immediately prior to firing.

There are, of course, different types of polish. Not even the finest beeswax will suffice for this important job. The fletcher and the archer – God, in our allegory – will apply the best and purest oil of all: the oil of the Holy Spirit.

Holy Spirit polish

The Holy Spirit is the third person of the Trinity, made up of Father, Son and Holy Spirit. They live as one in perfect unity and mutual honour. One God; three distinct persons – not merely different forms – united in relationship with one another and in their love for the children of God.

Father, Son and Holy Spirit have worked together from the beginning of time. It was the Holy Spirit who was 'hovering over the waters' in Genesis 1:2 and who, together with the Church – the bride of Christ – longs for the return of Jesus the Son.[84] Until then, He is the One who lives within us, giving us the power and strength to live the life to which God has called us. He comforts us, spurs us on, encourages us, empowers us and reminds us of God's words over us and in us; He makes the Scriptures come to life, lifts our heads when we're weary, and fills us with the confidence of those who implicitly trust God. He gives us peace as well as a lasting joy which is never dependent on our circumstances.

This is an incredible truth; God can live, not simply among us as Jesus did in first-century Palestine, but within us in the form of the Holy Spirit, unrestricted by geography, since He is spirit rather than flesh.

This is why Jesus was able to reassure His apprehensive disciples before His ascension to heaven, and leave them with a promise: 'surely I am with you always, to the very end of the age' (Matthew 28:20).

The Holy Spirit can live, or dwell, with us on a permanent basis that was not possible before the ascension.

Paul wrote:

> Do you not know that your bodies are temples of the Holy Spirit, who is in you, whom you have received from

---

[84] Revelation 22:17.

God? You are not your own; you were bought at a price.
Therefore honour God with your bodies.
(1 Corinthians 6:19-20)

Although he was particularly referencing sexual sin to believers in a city rife with prostitution, Paul was nevertheless reminding the Corinthians that they had a responsibility to look after themselves physically, since God the Holy Spirit was living in them. In hosting the pure and holy Spirit of God, it would be highly inappropriate to neglect or abuse their bodies, in the same way that it would be inappropriate to let your house go to rack and ruin if royalty were coming to stay.

Our whole lives, including our physical bodies, are to acknowledge and honour God.

Quench your thirst

Jesus spoke about the Holy Spirit when He was in Jerusalem for the Feast of Tabernacles – a festival celebrating the faithfulness of God to the Israelite people during their forty-year camping trip in the wilderness with Moses, between leaving Egypt and entering the Promised Land:

> On the last and greatest day of the festival, Jesus stood and said in a loud voice, 'Let anyone who is thirsty come to me and drink. Whoever believes in me, as Scripture has said, rivers of living water will flow from within them.' By this he meant the Spirit, whom those who believed in him were later to receive. Up to that time the Spirit had not been given, since Jesus had not yet been glorified.
> (John 7:37-39)

The death of Jesus purchased the privilege of free access to both His Father in heaven and, after His ascension, to His Holy Spirit, who is frequently referred to in pictorial biblical language as both water and oil. This new access ushered in a whole new level of intimacy between God and humanity, unknown up until this time, symbolised by the tearing in two of the curtain in the temple which walled off the holiest place. This was ripped from 'top to bottom' (Matthew 27:51) – no human hands could have performed such a feat. God announced in a dramatic and visual way that access to Him was now open for everybody.

Old Testament encounters

In the Old Testament, the Spirit of God generally came on individuals at a specific time, and for a specific purpose. When Moses delegated authority to seventy men to help bear the burden of looking after the journeying Israelites, God 'took some of the power of the Spirit that was on him and put it on the seventy elders. When the Spirit rested on them, they prophesied – but did not do so again' (Numbers 11:25).

Similarly, during the time of the judges before the Israelite monarchy was established, Samson operated at specific times under the power of the Spirit, who gave him enormous strength against the Philistine enemy.[85] The same was true for Deborah and Gideon.[86]

Further on in Old Testament history, we've seen how Elijah challenged the prophets of Baal to a competition on top of Mount Carmel to see which deity (Baal or Yahweh) would answer by fire. Afterwards, he ran all the way down to Jezreel, beating King Ahab in his chariot, because the power of the Spirit gave him a supernatural turn of speed.[87]

Back when Moses led the Israelites out of Egypt, he was given instructions by God for the construction of a mobile place of worship: the tabernacle. The directives for this structure were specific and detailed, involving symbolism which all pointed

---

[85] Judges 14:6, 19; 15:14.
[86] Judges 4; 6.
[87] 1 Kings 18:46.

forward to the ultimate sacrifice which would one day be made by the promised Messiah.

A special recipe was followed to make an anointing oil for the priests who would serve there. This was used symbolically to distinguish things, or people, who were set aside for God and His service. The oil served as a symbol of holiness. Heavily fragranced, it contained myrrh, cinnamon, cane, cassia and olive oil, and was not to be used in the same way as any other perfume. The only men allowed to wear this exclusive blend were the Levite priests; the tribe of Israel set aside for priesthood. Making this oil for your own use was absolutely prohibited. Anyone who did so was to be cut off or excommunicated, as was anyone other than a priest who wore it.[88]

The seriousness of the offence was proportional to the importance of the anointing oil and, more importantly, it indicated something of the nature of God's holiness. He was not, and is not, to be trifled with. Samuel's mentor, Eli, had sons who played fast and loose with the things of God (as did the two eldest sons of Aaron), and were destroyed in direct consequence.

When Aaron and his sons were commissioned into the priesthood, Moses was told to anoint his brother's head with oil. As the oil dripped down Aaron's face, off his beard and onto the special garments he wore, Aaron would literally carry the holiness, presence and favour of God. Everywhere he went throughout the tabernacle, the unmistakable smell of the anointing oil would linger, reminding everyone within its walls of the holiness of God and the awesome nature of His manifested presence with them.

The only exception to this priests-only rule was the anointing for kingship. Samuel anointed both Saul and later David for sovereignty over Israel.

---

[88] Exodus 30:22-33.

The phrase 'anointed with oil' came to be a euphemism for 'the bestowal of divine favour'.[89] David used the phrase in his famous shepherd psalm: 'You anoint my head with oil; my cup overflows' (Psalm 23:5).

Again, when prophesying about the coming Messiah, he wrote:

> You love righteousness and hate wickedness;
> therefore God, your God, has set you above your companions
> by anointing you with the oil of joy.
> (Psalm 45:7)

Anointed with joy

As far as Jesus was concerned – who lived in 100 per cent communion and oneness with both the Father and the Holy Spirit – the anointing of the Spirit was a joyful, happy thing.

Anyone who claims to be a Christian living in the joy of the Lord but who consistently has the demeanour of someone living on a diet of lemons cannot, by definition, be full of the Spirit. Likewise, a super-spiritual exterior may belie what's happening on the inside of a person. Sooner or later, what is in our hearts will become evident to those who really get to know us.

Once Jesus had ascended to the Father, the Holy Spirit was sent, not for occasional visits or experiences to the people of God but to stay with them, to infuse them with power and boldness. So even though the physical Jesus was no longer present on earth, the subsequent presence of the Holy Spirit meant that He could be with everyone, everywhere, all of the time, rather than physically confined to a single geographic location. That's why Jesus said:

---

[89] Hillyer, *The Illustrated Bible Dictionary*, p69.

It is for your good that I am going away. Unless I go away, the Advocate will not come to you; but if I go, I will send him to you ... when he, the Spirit of truth, comes, he will guide you into all the truth.
(John 16:7, 13)

The Old Testament prophet Joel looked forward to this awesome event as he brought God's word to the people of Judah, hundreds of years before Pentecost:

And afterwards,
I will pour out my Spirit on all people.
Your sons and daughters will prophesy,
your old men will dream dreams,
your young men will see visions.
Even on my servants, both men and women,
I will pour out my Spirit in those days.
(Joel 2:28-29)

Peter quoted these exact words when he preached to a bemused crowd in Jerusalem on the day the Holy Spirit fell in dynamic power at Pentecost.[90] The promise was fulfilled.

Power encounters

Not so long before, the disciples had been huddled miserably in an upstairs room, behind locked doors, in fear of a visit from the authorities. Meeting with the risen Jesus was a truly life-changing experience for them. Jesus told them to wait in Jerusalem until the Holy Spirit came, but they weren't yet sure how to carry out Jesus' final instructions, to spread His message throughout the nations, teaching, discipling and baptising along the way.[91]

---

[90] Acts 2:14-36.
[91] Acts 1:4; Matthew 28:19-20.

Acts 2 records how the Holy Spirit broke into one of their regular prayer meetings with:

> A sound like the blowing of a violent wind ... They saw what seemed to be tongues of fire that separated and came to rest on each of them. All of them were filled with the Holy Spirit and began to speak in other tongues as the Spirit enabled them.
> (Acts 2:2-4)

Not only did this break up the meeting, but this event also marked a new beginning for all those present; it triggered the birthing of the early Church. Peter's subsequent preaching on the street saw him transformed from a frightened former fisherman into a dynamic, bold witness for Christ, in the face of hostility and opposition.

The Holy Spirit is a person whom we can know, not an abstract force.

The real deal

Church history shows how, during the early days of charismatic renewal in the UK, in the 1960s and 1970s, there was disagreement over the nature of the Holy Spirit and how His presence was facilitated in church meetings. Some Jesus-followers appeared to be trying to lord it over others by claiming to have had an encounter experience that elevated the authenticity of their faith. Others were made to feel like second-class Christians, giving rise to insecurities over their relationship with God. Some found the unusual manifestations of the Spirit awkward and discomforting.

There is no doubt that, as so often happens during moves of the Spirit, a mixture of things went on, some more attributable to the fallibility of people than to the work of the Holy Spirit. Everywhere that God moves in a genuine way, the enemy will try to counterfeit something. We can choose whether to press through for the reality, or jettison everything, throwing out the proverbial baby with the bathwater.

In the same way that nobody bothers forging £7 notes, the devil doesn't need to counterfeit something that isn't real anyway. However, he is very happy to try to trip us up by playing on our insecurities and fears, or by copying something real, if it dislodges us from our faith in God and the centrality of Christ.

Some of us still struggle with the thought of a greater degree of intimacy with an Almighty God – especially those of us from a British culture where emotions tend to be played down. Expressing emotions in any formal setting continues to feel inappropriate for a whole generation of people. While emotionalism can send us veering off course and away from the centrality of Jesus, a relationship without emotion is a dry and unsatisfying thing. We can easily see the danger that love for God may become a stale, intellectual assent, rather than a living passion. Fear has robbed many people of the joy of living their Christian life in the power of the Holy Spirit, and consequently it's as though they live their whole lives in black and white instead of glorious colour.

The Holy Spirit is the One who draws us to the Father, convicts us of our sin and brings us a revelation about who Jesus is and what He has done for us. Salvation is not the result of our own strategic thinking or the intellectual prowess involved in processing facts. We must have the Holy Spirit within us to be able to call God our Father: 'God sent the Spirit of his Son into our hearts, the Spirit who calls out, "*Abba*, Father"' (Galatians 4:6).

Since spiritual things cannot be understood simply by cognitive understanding, but require spiritual discernment,[92] it comes as no surprise to learn that debates and arguments seldom, if ever, persuade people to come into God's kingdom. None of us could see the truth until God opened our eyes to it, and to Himself. It is the Holy Spirit who works in people to

---

[92] 1 Corinthians 2:14.

bring them to a place of revelation, where everything falls into place.

The hymn writer John Newton (1725–1807) expressed this idea of moving from blindness to sight in his famous hymn, 'Amazing Grace'. His encounter with God came with a powerful revelation of his own helplessness and hopelessness before God. The Holy Spirit opened his eyes to his spiritual condition, and led him to the place of salvation.

If the Holy Spirit now lives in us, then it's up to us to ensure that we give Him a place that reflects that privilege. We'll want to look after our bodies, and not abuse them with behaviour or substances that would desecrate His dwelling place. They no longer belong to us; God paid a high price for us, and part of our worship response is to sacrificially put His desires and requirements before our own, even in regard to our physical bodies.

New Testament encounters

The New Testament chronicles a number of encounters with the Holy Spirit that coincide with conversion. In the book of Acts, which is an account of the birthing of churches in the early years after Jesus' resurrection and ascension, Peter went to the house of the Roman centurion Cornelius – an upright and God-fearing man. Peter explained the gospel to him, and to the members of the household. As he did so, the Holy Spirit fell on his hearers.

> The circumcised believers who had come with Peter were astonished that the gift of the Holy Spirit had been poured out even on Gentiles. For they heard them speaking in tongues and praising God.
> (Acts 10:45-46)

Paul, however, had a contrasting experience when he went to Ephesus, where he discovered there were already some believers. His questions were different:

[He] asked them, 'Did you receive the Holy Spirit when you believed?'

They answered, 'No, we have not even heard that there is a Holy Spirit.'

(Acts 19:2)

Paul baptised them and then put his hands on them and prayed for them. Subsequently, these believers also 'spoke in tongues and prophesied' (v6). Speaking in tongues was one of the manifestations of the Holy Spirit then, and still is for many believers today, regardless of denomination. They may use a spoken language that they haven't learned formally, or they may find themselves running out of words in their first language, and tipping over into a special prayer language which bypasses logic but edifies them as they pray.

The supernatural meets the natural

Speaking in tongues may sound odd, but a quick study will show that it was a normal part of transformed life in the New Testament Church. We certainly shouldn't be surprised that when the supernatural Holy Spirit meets the natural of our mortal bodies, there can be a reaction. I've seen people fall to the floor, shake apparently uncontrollably, laugh and weep when the Holy Spirit is present. I have seen others sit quietly as if they were soaking up God's presence, and later discovered that they have been seeing and/or hearing very specifically from Him. I don't have a scientific explanation for either, but if God chooses to meet with people in a particular way, then He doesn't need our permission to do so. He doesn't need to fit into our boxes of what is comfortable, or discreet. It's not up to us to decide whether such a reaction is real or counterfeit. There are probably instances where people copy what they have seen in others, but that is their responsibility. The important questions are, 'What is happening?' and, 'What happens next?'

I once met someone who showed me the gold fillings in their mouth which were discovered after a meeting where the Holy

Spirit came in power. They didn't claim to understand why God should do such a strange thing, and I don't have an explanation either. Perhaps God just wanted to show that He cares about details. What I do know is that I am not at liberty to decide that God wasn't in this curious event, however baffling it is to my limited understanding. A person's ongoing life will be evidence of whether or not they met with God. I have a finite mind and body, whereas He is infinite, and He owes me no explanation whatsoever; He cannot be boxed.

Some people will have had real encounters with God. He may have spoken to them very specifically. It's OK, and perfectly natural, to ask them; just don't be weird about it. There may be real change in their lives as a result, but a good question is, 'What is God saying to this person in this moment, and how can I help them to respond?' It is not legitimate to judge others in these encounters. We simply do not, and cannot, fully know what has transpired between any individual and God in its entirety. If encouragement is needed, let's give it. Engage, ask questions, encourage them to tune in to what God is saying or highlighting. If a mild rebuke is in order, it must come with grace and love, or not at all.

We may not be familiar with some of these apparently strange reactions to the Holy Spirit, but it doesn't mean that God is not in them. If we stay walking in step with Him, they won't distract us or pull us off course.

God has always used unconventional methods of meeting with people, whether it's Balaam's donkey, Joseph's dreams or the mysterious hand that wrote on the wall in the palace of King Belshazzar in Daniel's time.[93] God is God; He does not operate according to the confines of our limited understanding and human rationalism.

As God polishes us with the marvellously rich oil of His Spirit, we arrows become more sensitive to His voice and His

---

[93] Numbers 22:28; Genesis 37:5-11; Daniel 5:5.

touch. The Holy Spirit is an extravagant present to us from our generous Father, and He brings gifts with Him.

Gifts and fruits

You can read about some of these in Paul's first letter to the Corinthians. In chapter 12:8-10, he lists some of these gifts: wisdom, knowledge, faith, healing, miraculous powers, prophecy, discernment, speaking in tongues and interpreting tongues.

In the book of Romans, Paul refers to other gifts of the Spirit, including service, teaching, encouraging, giving, leading, mercy and administration.[94]

All of these wonderful presents are available to us as God's much-loved children. They are not given so we can show off, look important or draw attention to ourselves. They are all for the benefit of other people. Like the anointing for apostles, prophets, evangelists, pastors and teachers, all of these things are:

> ... to equip his people for works of service, so that the body of Christ may be built up until we all reach unity in the faith and in the knowledge of the Son of God and become mature, attaining to the whole measure of the fullness of Christ.
> (Ephesians 4:12-13)

None of these gifts is of any value in the long term if it is not motivated by love. In our Bibles, where the passages are divided into chapters and verses for ease of reference, the famous chapter 13 of 1 Corinthians is nestled between chapters 12 and 14, which discuss the outward demonstration of some of the

---

[94] Romans 12:6-8; see also 1 Corinthians 12:28, RSV, which mentions the gift of administration.

gifts. Crucially, chapter 13 focuses on the motive or driving force for effective use of these gifts: love.

If the gifts of the Spirit are to be handled, facilitated and used both wisely and correctly in a godly fashion then, above all, this must be done with love. The gifts are not an excuse for competitiveness, one-upmanship or showing off. They are to be used to serve the body of Christ; not for any selfish pursuit of glory, fame or popularity. They are not the sole property of any individual who would seek to lord it over anyone else; neither are they to be used in a controlling or manipulative way. Love, therefore, is the foundation and key to enjoying these God-given gifts.

The Bible also speaks about the fruit of the Spirit. Unlike gifts that are given, fruit grows over time; 'the fruit of the Spirit is love, joy, peace, patience, kindness, goodness, faithfulness, gentleness, self-control' (Galatians 5:22-23, RSV).

That's quite a list. All of them are characteristics of Jesus, and therefore a reflection of God. I would like all of those attributes to flourish in my life, but I know they don't grow overnight. Just as a tree doesn't produce fruit by concentrating all its effort into pushing them out on its branches, so too, I cannot squeeze them out by my own effort. Fruit is a natural byproduct of healthy growth. Like any healthy plant growth, they will need warmth, water, fertilising and pruning.

The grace of God at work in my life will provide all these things: the warmth of His unconditional love; the water of the Word; the fertiliser of life experiences walked with Him (including the mucky, manure-like bits), and careful pruning as God deals with my character at grass-roots level. These processes will clear the way for such attractive character fruits to grow.

Without God's Holy Spirit, the only fruit I can possibly produce will be stunted, shrivelled and sour. His oil must be allowed to saturate every area of my life.

A one-off encounter at conversion is not sufficient to keep us supple and responsive to what God wants. We need to meet with Him daily. When Paul exhorted the Ephesian Christians to 'be filled with the Spirit' (Ephesians 5:18), he was telling them to keep on being filled. He told another church that the Holy Spirit is like a downpayment on God's promises, which guarantees all the other wonderful things He's promised. God is absolutely not going to lose the 'deposit' (2 Corinthians 5:5) which He has put down, or invested, in us.

If we are full of Jesus, then He will be spilling out onto those around us every day. We'll need to keep on being refilled, so that tomorrow we can be as effective as we were today, or more so, as His influence in us grows and we become more attuned to His voice and promptings.

There needs to be a continual overflow of the Holy Spirit in my life, and I can't overflow unless I am filled. A childhood chorus we used to sing exhorted us to keep being filled with His oil so we could sing, praise and burn with Holy Spirit fire 24/7.

One of the great things about this is that if I am so full of Jesus, then I don't have room for anything else. I've heard this called 'the expulsive power of a new affection'. It means that the presence of Jesus is so great that any other affection is simply pushed out by the force of the arrival of a new one. If you try pouring liquid into a glass from a height, you'll see what I mean.

The oil of God's Holy Spirit penetrates deeply; we can be drenched in Him daily. All we have to do is ask and receive. That's real polishing, and God will make His arrows shine with a lustre that reflects Himself.

Target Questions

➤ What is the difference between the Old and New Testament descriptions of, and encounters with, the Holy Spirit?

➤ Your body is a temple of the Holy Spirit. What are the implications of this?

➤ What are the obstacles to staying filled with God's Spirit?

➤ How can we overcome those obstacles?

9a. The Disciples at Pentecost

The disciples had always been an unlikely and motley crew. A mixture of blue- and white-collar workers, each of them was specifically called by Jesus to come and follow Him. That meant learning from Him, living with Him and taking on His teachings.

The job of a rabbi was to unpack truths from the Hebrew Bible and Torah, in the same way that one might examine precious jewels. They would hold them up to the light of God and turn them over verbally to focus and reflect on the many facets of their meaning. Different rabbis would emphasise different things. Students who studied with a rabbi were called *talmidim*; their goal was not just to learn from their rabbi, but to become like him in every way.[95] They would frequently become rabbis themselves, and the process would begin again with a new generation. Rabbis and their disciples lived in close proximity for this season of intense learning, in much the same way that Jesus lived for the three years He travelled around with the twelve. Walking time and living together on the road provided space for discussions, questions and debates; to listen, question and respond was very much part and parcel of following any rabbi.

Jesus would have been seen as a senior rabbi in so far as he spoke with great authority, and drew out fresh interpretations

---

[95] www.thattheworldmayknow.com/rabbi-and-talmidim (accessed 16th June 2023).

from the teaching He referenced. While some Torah teachers trotted out the same rather tired interpretations of Hebrew history, Jesus asked questions which sometimes turned accepted thinking on its head. The crowds loved the authority and confidence He had, the religious elite were discomforted by Him, and the disciples got to ask all their questions once the crowds had slipped away.

The fact that Jesus chose His students indicates that He saw the potential they had for becoming like Him. Calling Judas Iscariot wasn't a mistake. Jesus indicated at the Last Supper that one of the group would betray him, but none of them said, 'It must be Judas; I've always known he was flaky.' Judas was very much a part of the action when the disciples were sent out, as recorded in Luke 9. These missions were an opportunity to practise what they had learned, and to step into the role we might call 'probationary rabbi'. Their joy on discovering that God worked on their behalf when they prayed for people was probably only superseded by Jesus' joy in them.[96] It's interesting, however, that no one came back and reported that everyone saw miracles except Judas.

While all twelve saw Jesus move in the power of the Spirit, in healing, deliverance and miraculous provision, and knew a measure of this themselves in the exploits recorded in Luke 9 they weren't living fully in the power of the Spirit until Pentecost. Jesus gave them the promise of the Spirit of truth who would come.[97]

Just a few days after Jesus was greeted by celebratory crowds as He rode into Jerusalem on a donkey, the disciples prepared their Passover meal in an upper room in a very different atmosphere. Jesus had spoken in the past about the fact that he must die and rise again,[98] but none of the group had understood what He was saying. However, after Jesus washed their feet and they shared bread and wine, Jesus talked about a broken body,

---

[96] Luke 10:17-21.

[97] John 14:16-17; 16:12-15; Acts 1:8.

[98] Matthew 17:22-23; Mark 9:31-32.

blood and betrayal. It was a sombre meal, during which Judas left to put into action his plan to turn Jesus over to the religious authorities.

After the meal, the whole group headed out across the Kidron Valley to a garden they frequented, where Jesus prayed. It was here that Judas brought a group of torch-wielding soldiers, and betrayed his rabbi with an ironic symbol of loyalty and affection: a simple kiss.[99] We've already seen how Peter acted under pressure, both here in Gethsemane and later in Caiaphas' courtyard. Now, with fear, confusion and evil unleashed, the entire collection of disciples scattered, hot-footing it out of the garden, abandoning Jesus, intent on nothing but saving their own skins.

The next time we see them together is hiding away in the same room where they had eaten that last special meal with Jesus. The doors were firmly locked out of fear that the Jewish leaders who had so recently crucified their master might now be setting their sights on anyone who was associated with Jesus. The prospect of arrest, imprisonment and possibly death for them as well kept them hidden away, anxious and fearful, their ears straining for every footstep or knock on the door.

This out-of-the-way place must have become their base because, despite Jesus showing His resurrected self to them, a week later they were still there, scared to leave and nursing their emotional wounds. When Jesus came to them again, Thomas was present, and Jesus allowed him to touch His fresh scars to reinforce the truth of the resurrection.[100]

It's always fascinated me that Jesus chose to keep His scars. The One who called life into existence, banished demons, healed lepers and raised two men and a little girl from the dead could surely have come through death Himself with perfectly restored skin. That He chose to keep the reminder of His sacrifice tells me that He chose a constant visual memorial to us

---

[99] Matthew 26:48-49.
[100] John 20:26-28.

for whom He died. It's the metaphorical reality of having our names written or 'engraved' on his hands (Isaiah 49:16).

Forty days after the resurrection, the disciples were still staying in that same upper room. Judas, overwhelmed by the events he had put into motion, had taken his own life.[101] The remaining eleven plus a group of women, including Jesus' mother Mary and her other sons, spent their time praying and referring back to the Scriptures, tracing the prophetic pointers that had been fulfilled through Jesus.

It was here that the Holy Spirit came in power on the day of Pentecost, fifty days after Jesus' resurrection. I've quoted these verses before, but it describes the event so vividly that it seems appropriate to do so again:

> Suddenly a sound like the blowing of a violent wind came from heaven and filled the whole house where they were sitting. They saw what seemed to be tongues of fire that separated and came to rest on each of them. All of them were filled with the Holy Spirit and began to speak in other tongues as the Spirit enabled them.
> (Acts 2:2-4)

What a dramatic milestone – one which really marks the birth of the early Church. For the disciples, life changed radically; from being hidden away, they went down onto the streets and immediately began to preach the good news of Jesus. Transformed from frightened men to courageous speakers, they saw about three thousand people flock into God's kingdom that Sunday. Peter connected this new outpouring of God's Spirit with the prophecy of Joel 2, in which God had promised that His Spirit would flow into His people in a dynamic way with profound consequences.

For the first time, God's Spirit was released to dwell within all people. The Holy Spirit can be with all of us, all of the time, unfettered by either our geography or our time zones. He is the

---

[101] Matthew 27:5.

empowerer, the interceder, the One who convicts, reveals, reminds and restores us; our companion, encourager and comforter.

The disciples were drenched in the Spirit that day; this was to be a daily reality, with continual and consistent refilling.[102]

Just as arrows need to be oiled so that they keep their flexibility and usefulness, so we need to be 'arrows' that avoid becoming dried out, brittle or prone to breakage. We too need to keep on being drenched in Holy Spirit oil.

The disciples were fired into the neighbouring communities and nations as they took the life-changing words and revelation of Jesus to people far and wide. Mark says they went 'everywhere', preaching and witnessing miracles as God 'confirmed his word by the signs that accompanied it' (Mark 16:20). Jesus entrusted them with the same authority in which He had operated:

> Go and make disciples of all nations, baptising them in the name of the Father and of the Son and of the Holy Spirit, and teaching them to obey everything I have commanded you. And surely I am with you always, to the very end of the age.
> (Matthew 28:19-20)

Most of the apostles left Jerusalem behind and headed out to spread the good news of Jesus as He'd instructed. Records differ, but all the disciples, except John, were martyred, though not before taking the gospel as far as India (Bartholomew), Greece/Turkey (Philip), Lebanon/Syria/Iran/Iraq (Thaddeus), Turkey (Matthias), Georgia/Bulgaria (Andrew), Iran (Matthew), Italy and Asia (Peter), Afghanistan (Thomas)...[103]

In other words, to the ends of the earth.

---

[102] Ephesians 5:18.

[103] raychoi.org/2012/06/01/what-happened-to-the-12-disciples-after-the-resurrection-and-ascension (accessed 26th February 2024).

These arrows flew into cultures and communities far from the comfort and familiarity of home. Others remained more local, but effective in the places where God placed them. They could not have made their mark so profoundly had they not known regular soaking and polishing with the powerful oil of God's Holy Spirit, who continued to burn within them.

10. Arrowsmiths and Fletchers

Our arrow needs just three more things before it can be placed in the quiver ready for action: an arrowhead and some tail feathers, all bound together with whipping cord. Without these, it's still a stick; while it could be fired from a bow, it wouldn't go far, or have any serious impact.

Historically, arrowheads were made from flint or metal – usually iron – in a number of shapes, depending on the target. Some were made to penetrate chainmail or plated armour; others were used for piercing flesh at close range (human or animal). All of them needed to be sharpened to a lethal point to be of use to the archer.

The arrowsmith had to balance the weight of the head correctly in proportion to the tail weight, to ensure a steady flight and smooth trajectory. The arrow then needed to be fired in such a way that it arrived on target at the optimum angle for maximum penetration.

To continue with the metaphor of God shaping us to be arrows in His hands, we can draw parallels in achieving and maintaining the sharpness we need. Tools are made sharp by the skilful application of three elements: oil, water and iron. These are all mentioned repeatedly in the Bible, in pictorial fashion.

Oil

Oil is the lubricating substance used on a sharpening stone to remove the metal filings from a blade. Heavy oils interfere with the sharpening process, but a light, mineral oil works well as the oil covers the whole edge of a blade in the angle of sharpening against the stone.

In the last chapter we looked at the oil of the Holy Spirit and reminded ourselves that having a relationship with Him is not a one-off experience, but an ongoing, daily encounter. We need to keep on being filled with the Spirit if we are to live in the fullness of Christ. It's this oil that gives us polish and power, as well as the softness of heart we need in order to respond to what our heavenly Father asks of us, and to keep us attuned to His voice.

The shaft of the arrow is polished with oil that seeps into every part of the wood to stop it becoming brittle, but the arrowhead itself also needs treatment with oil to help it stay sharp and have the edge it needs for effective impact.

Water

Water prevents the sharpening stone from clogging up and reduces the frictional heat caused by vigorous movement at the interface of the sharpening materials.

In Ephesians 5 Paul talked about the Word of God as though it were water. In the context of marriage, he exhorted husbands to love their wives in the same way that Christ loves His Church – sacrificially. One way of loving her was 'to make her holy, cleansing her by the washing with water through the word' (Ephesians 5:26) – a tall order for any man. Who could possibly love his wife with the same selfless love that Jesus has for His bride – the worldwide body of Christ?

Jesus is involved in the ongoing task of making His Church-bride holy, pure and beautiful. Husbands are urged to use the water of God's Word, the Bible, to help their spouses be all that God has called them to be. They are not to misuse God's Word to bludgeon, or to bully – that would be a terrible misuse of Scripture and an abuse of the marriage relationship – but as a gentle washing.

If we are to keep and maintain sharpness as Christians, male and female, we need to ensure that we are continually cleansed, rinsed and washed with the Word of God.

Finding a time to spend exclusively with God and His Word takes effort; it becomes less and less easy in increasingly busy lives. It's funny how we always seem to find time to do the things we really want to do: shower, eat, see our friends or watch our favourite series, but not necessarily the things we only wish to do.

Personal hygiene is part of our daily grooming; baths or showers keep our bodies clean and fresh, dissipating the dirt and sweat of the day. We emerge renewed, both physically and emotionally. This simple, regular discipline helps us look after the health and welfare of our physical bodies.

Sometimes we grab a quick shower; at other times we enjoy the extended time of a long, hot soak in the bath. Both will get us clean. It's the same spiritually: we can grab a quick couple of verses, read a pre-prepared Bible note in a devotional, or we can set aside time to meditate more deeply on God's Word, allowing it to soak into us as we tune in to what He may be saying to us or highlighting for us.

There are days when we grab food on the run, or opt to eat junk rather than choose a healthier alternative. Likewise, spiritually, there are days when we nibble on God's Word rather than feast on it and other days when we grab someone else's insights on God's Word rather than take the time to dig into it ourselves. That's OK, but at the same time, it can be a bit like eating semi-digested food.

When we don't have time to eat properly, we tend to get headaches and become lethargic or crotchety; we don't function properly. If we miss a meal through circumstance, rather than deliberately fasting, none of us really operates at our best; we don't think as clearly, we tend not to make good decisions and we lose our edge. Our sharpness becomes blunted quite quickly, just as it does if we over-indulge in a big meal. Spiritual sharpness is no different.

The apostle Paul made it clear that since our bodies are hosts to the Holy Spirit, we should ensure they are in the best state possible – a suitable dwelling for Him. Why would we show any less care and attention to our spiritual bodies than we do for our physical ones? We need to regularly and consistently feed, clothe and clean our inner person as well as our outer person. The most effective way of doing that would be to do it daily.

Spiritual babies need spiritual food that's easy to digest, while believers who are more mature need to get their teeth into meatier stuff. The writer to the Hebrews says:

> In fact, though by this time you ought to be teachers, you need someone to teach you the elementary truths of God's word all over again. You need milk, not solid food! Anyone who lives on milk, being still an infant, is not acquainted with the teaching about righteousness. But solid food is for the mature, who by constant use have trained themselves to distinguish good from evil.
>
> Therefore let us move beyond the elementary teachings about Christ and be taken forward to maturity.
> (Hebrews 5:12–6:1)

These verses tell us that a believer can train themselves by getting to grips with God's Word, and enjoy spiritual nutrition which will cause them to grow healthily.

I remember when I was encouraging my (then) seven-year-old daughter to read the Bible for herself and explore the exciting things in it. She looked at me as though talking to a slightly simple person and said, 'But Mummy, I've read it.' She was thinking of her Bible in the same way as one of the books on the school reading scheme. Read it, tick the box, get another one; job done. You never reread a book in that context; it's all about going on to the next book and attaining the next level. The Bible is not the same.

We'd be dishonest if we didn't admit that there are times when our reading can seem dull – usually when we've neglected to ensure that we are well oiled with the Holy Spirit. When we're out of joint with Jesus or are distracted by the other concerns in our lives, Bible reading can seem like a chore. Nevertheless, it's well worth pursuing. Defensively claiming that we don't want to become legalistic in our reading can be little more than a thinly veiled excuse for the fact that we don't want to make the effort; we really can't be bothered, but we're too embarrassed to say so out loud. We feel we ought to enjoy it, but sometimes we just don't. On other occasions it can feel like nothing is going in, or sticking.

I've often felt as though most of what I read is going in through my eyes and leaking out fast; but I know that refreshing my memory with truth and allowing God's Word to wash over my mind brings life, even when I don't feel as though I am retaining a great deal. It's like a soldier doing drill; it may not have much impact at the time, but when the moment comes, they're always glad they mastered it.

These seasons pass in time. Being honest with God about my struggles helps me to push through into a new place of freshness. I'm reminded that the Bible says He is always far more anxious to meet with me than I will ever be to meet with Him: 'Come near to God and he will come near to you' (James 4:8). That's a promise for which I'm deeply grateful.

It's not a question of trying to persuade God to talk to us, or us twisting His arm to get His attention. We're the pinnacle of His creation, His pride and joy. The prophet Zephaniah tells us that God sings over us with 'great delight' (Zephaniah 3:17). That must be quite a song! Perhaps we'll get to hear it one day.

It's us who struggle to get into the presence of God, not vice versa. All the human effort in the world will not take us there. We need humility and clean hearts to meet with Him. Jesus told the crowd in the Beatitudes, part of His Sermon on the Mount, that those who are 'pure in heart ... will see God' (Matthew 5:8). That's compelling.

When we're struggling to meet with God, it can be helpful to take some time to allow Him to put His finger on anything that might be hindering our relationship with Him. We might be as surprised as the lady I once heard about who had planned a couple of days away, specifically to seek God. She was a little put out to discover that God began to pinpoint some things in her own heart that were not quite right. Initially, she was quite affronted – even irritated with God – telling Him she'd put this time aside to know Him better, not to spend time on herself. That's when she realised that in order to see God more clearly and know Him more deeply, she had to start by sorting out what was lurking in her own heart and put it right with Him.

If your time of reading the Bible has become a little stale or dry, here are some ideas that might help you. Pick one or two and give them a try:

1. Use a different translation of the Bible for a while; hearing familiar words in a fresh way can be helpful.

2. Buy or borrow a study guide or commentary to unpack what you're reading.

3. Try reading a Bible with cross references in the middle column of each page and enjoy a treasure hunt, or paper chase, through the Bible.

4. Find a willing friend and agree to read the same passages for a few days; make some notes and then book a coffee date to get together and compare your findings.

5. Make your 'quiet time' a louder time. Include some worship to stir your soul and help focus on God and what He may have to say.

6. If you do a lot of driving, why not use that time and space in God's presence? Just don't close your eyes if you're praying, please!

7. If you struggle to retain Scripture verses, find some worship songs with lyrics lifted straight out of the Bible. Memorising whole chunks can be quite a challenge, but singing them repeatedly may be a better way of massaging them into your heart.

Iron

The third sharpening tool that the arrowhead needs is iron – or it used to be. These days a different material might be used, but our medieval blacksmith is more likely to have created a lethal edge on their arrowhead by using another iron tool with a different texture. Two iron items of the same texture wouldn't do the job. Even so, the blacksmith had to take care that he was truly forging the blade and not dulling it by crashing them together carelessly, or even ruining it completely.

In this context, iron is the biblical metaphor for one another, as observed by wise King Solomon:

> As iron sharpens iron,
> so one person sharpens another.
> (Proverbs 27:17)

We ourselves are a resource for each other to ensure that we stay sharp. Getting on with each other in the family of God, just as in any family, can be a challenge. Earlier, in Chapter 5, we looked at some of the issues that can crop up, when we explored the unrealistic expectations we can have of one another.

If we fall into competitiveness with each other within our Jesus communities, we completely miss the point – missing Him and each other – as well as end up inflicting damage on one another. Then we're more like iron crushing iron than sharpening it. Serious wounds may be the unfortunate consequence.

Jesus must have known this, and perhaps that's why He was so keen to emphasise to His disciples the need to love one another.

> As the Father has loved me, so have I loved you. Now remain in my love. If you keep my commands, you will remain in my love, just as I have kept my Father's commands and remain in his love. I have told you this so that my joy may be in you and that your joy may be complete. My command is this: love each other as I have loved you. Greater love has no one than this: to lay down one's life for one's friends. You are my friends if you do what I command.
> (John 15:9-14)

Jesus was the embodiment of the type of love He wants us to show to one another. Not a selfish, what-can-I-get-out-of-it love, but one that truly seeks the best for others. He also knew what a powerful weapon love is: victorious over all the destructive forces of hate, cynicism, resentment and anger in our conflicted world.

Like so much of His teaching, Jesus pushed against the cultural norms. Where a person would naturally strike back at another, either literally or verbally, He encouraged people to break the cycle of aggression with a soft word, and to see the power of forgiveness at work to overcome ongoing wickedness. He told His disciples that this type of love would mark them out in the world as people who truly followed Him. It's still true for us.

Love should be the motivation and foundation for all that we do in God's family. If it isn't there, then we've missed something fundamental; it's the foundation for everything else we do because it's the essence of Jesus. Paul reminded the church in the famous 1 Corinthians 13 passage, so beloved of wedding services, that even though we may be highly gifted in many areas, without love we really don't gain anything at all and diminish ourselves.

Everything we can possibly do, or aspire to, is a waste of time unless it's undergirded by this self-sacrificing, seeking-the-best-for-the-other type of love. It's not based on what we think anyone deserves; it's the way Jesus loves us.

Jesus' closest friend, the disciple John, wrote three short letters which each include instruction on the subject of love. We could call them a reality check on how we live our lives.

For instance:

> Whoever claims to love God yet hates a brother or sister is a liar. For whoever does not love their brother and sister, whom they have seen, cannot love God, whom they have not seen.
> (1 John 4:20)

He's very direct, isn't he? No hiding or pretending; no saying one thing to look the part but doing something quite different on the inside. Love for one another means that we want the best for each other. We'll be thrilled when someone prospers, regardless of our own circumstances. We won't resent it when someone else gets a promotion, or a new car, or a wonderful holiday. We won't gloat when others encounter hardships or fail interviews. We'll cry with the people who are hurting and celebrate with those who reach their goals. These are marks of true family.

This is where the sharpening happens: from that foundation of grace and love.

John's words remind me of school sports days, when we cheered for our children's team, regardless of who was representing them. We were less interested in the raw talent – or lack of it – on the field, and more concerned about encouraging each child to give their all. We waved, shouted, cheered and yelled without restraint. Perhaps your sports days were more refined affairs than ours used to be, but by the end of the afternoon we felt as though we'd been fully involved. This was the spirit that says, 'We're in this together and we'll support one another all the way, through thick and thin, no matter what.' What an impact that attitude would have if it were to be authentically reflected in our communities and beyond.

The sharpening friend

Finding people with whom you can have a sharpening relationship is an enormous privilege. They will be the people you know who have walked with God for many years, and who have been faithful to Him in trying times. They will be people who exude the presence of Christ; people who don't just talk about Jesus, but who clearly walk with Him, whether they prosper or not. Like all of us, they will have known hurts, disappointments and struggles, but have found God to be faithful through those times. They don't dress things up to sound spiritual – they neither disguise their struggles nor wallow in them – yet there is a steely determination about them that says they are in this for the long haul. They're some of the most honest, real people around. We admire them; we want to be like them.

These are not fair-weather Christians, who look as though everything is wonderful while their circumstances are going well but who buckle when the pressure is on. These are the warriors who are bruised, but not broken; scarred, but not mortally wounded; disappointed, but not bitter; let down, but resisting cynicism with every fibre of their being. They continue to declare the goodness and faithfulness of God when the odds are stacked against them, and in the face of loss and heartache. They may not be able to explain all the mysteries of how God works, but they know beyond doubt that He is good, He is faithful, He is kind and He is present, because they truly know Him.

These sharpening individuals know what it's like to let God use His gold-refining process on them. When heated up, it's the impurities that come to the surface of melted gold which must be scooped off. This refining process is repeated; the more frequently it happens, the purer the gold left behind. Those who have felt the heat of spiritual battle will have also known the indignity, and sometimes the surprise, of discovering the 'gunk' that was inside them come to the surface; but they will have humbled themselves before God so that He could skim it off and improve the quality of the treasure within.

These soldiers are completely aligned to God's will; authentic and sold out for Him, whatever the cost. Their passion for God is infectious, and something resonates in your own heart when you are with them. Just as sparks can fly when iron strikes iron, so they can ignite a fire of passion for the things of God in the heart of another. Who knows where that fire may spread...

We are not looking for gurus, or someone who has got it all together. Primarily, we are looking for a true friend who is full of integrity. A sharpening friend is the friend who continually points us back to Jesus in every area of our life. We don't need a super-spiritual, preachy or condescending individual; this is the friend who is bold enough and loving enough to tell us when our attitude stinks.

The sharpening friend listens and loves, but does not sit down and join us in unrighteous self-pity. This friend is a safe place to vent, but then they will draw us back to the route that David evidently trod in so many of his psalms, pointing out that our emotions are what we feel, but what do we really know?

They will ask difficult questions like, 'Which truth will help you get back on track?' 'Are your feelings consistent with what God has said to you?' 'What's the biblical principle here?'

The true friend will not back off from rebuking us gently if we are out of step with God or behave in a manner contrary to Scripture, but they will always do so with tenderness and compassion, because they genuinely want to see us grow, flourish and become all that God has in mind for us. Not only that, but they will keep walking beside us through the journey.

The sharpening friend gets under our skin while loving us to pieces. They understand that 1 Corinthians 13 is so much more than a nice Bible reading for a wedding.

Love never gives up.
Love cares more for others than for self.
Love doesn't want what it doesn't have.
Love doesn't strut,
Doesn't have a swelled head,
Doesn't force itself on others,
Isn't always 'me first,'
Doesn't fly off the handle,
Doesn't keep score of the sins of others,
Doesn't revel when others grovel,
Takes pleasure in the flowering of truth,
Puts up with anything,
Trusts God always,
Always looks for the best,
Never looks back,
But keeps going to the end.
Love never dies.
(1 Corinthians 13:4-8, *The Message*)

We all covet friends who can love like this.

Sharpening is not a one-way street; 'iron sharpens iron'.

Who can you sharpen? Who can sharpen you?

If we want to grow in our faith, we can ask God to give us relationships like this, and then see who He brings into our lives. There are probably people around you already who could be part of the sharpening process in your life.

The spiritual and secular worlds have made major moves towards mentoring, which is really just another word for discipling. It doesn't happen in a formal meeting, but as we do life together. We are whole people – each area of our life affects the others – and much of our learning comes from seeing and following the example of others. Reading a textbook can be interesting, but it's not the most reliable transformational tool.

When we share life with those who are pressing in to know Jesus better, we may well find that their passion is infectious. We can learn so much by asking questions, sharing doubts, wrestling through tricky bits of Scripture with someone who knows it better than we do, and watching how fellow believers navigate their heartaches, setbacks and sorrows with integrity, choosing to keep their eyes on Jesus through them all.

Historically, church communities have tended to follow a teaching model from the educational world rather than drawing from the world of the family. We usually run our Sunday mornings in a format that has been taken from the classroom or the lecture theatre. That's not how Jesus discipled His followers. Although He went to the synagogue, the real teaching times happened as they walked along the road, sat round the fire or shared a meal together.

In almost every church building we sit in rows facing one person on a platform, who explains and expounds a topic or passage. It may be brilliant; often the result of hours of study, research and writing; but what are we trying to achieve? Education or transformation? There's a place for both, of course, and new forms of church are flourishing all over the world – some by necessity, where meeting together in a building is prohibited. Nevertheless, the life of God is bubbling up and people are discovering the wonderful, liberating truths of God's Word and embracing the joy of a life with Him as they realise that they are loved, chosen and forgiven, and joyfully submit to His lordship.

Jesus modelled the rabbinic style of teaching, which involved a lot of back and forth questioning and debating to get to the truth in a way that drew people down a path of discovery, rather than serving out the answers on a plate. This style of discipleship guided people to their conclusions and helped them to own the truths they then sought to apply to their lives.

There are mentoring relationships and there are peer relationships; if we nurture both of these, we'll discover the power of mutual sharpening.

As we walk with Jesus and with one another, we build a history together. It is such a thrill to be able to look back with somebody and remember how God has answered our prayers, how He has broken through in situations, how He has taught us life-shaping truths. These memories cement our relationships and bring greater depth to our friendships. Praying together brings us closer to God and closer to one another. The Bible regularly bursts into life as we study it together. God speaks to us prophetically through others as well. It's always good to record and note down particular things that God has put His finger on; over time it's like creating a map of the journey God is taking us on. Although it's true that we might have been reluctant to set out in the first place if we'd have known some of the places God was going to take us, our experience can be an encouragement and example to others on their journeys. Their route and experience will be different, but some of the landmarks on the way may well be similar.

One of the great advantages of getting older is that the number of stories we have of God's goodness and faithfulness increase. We have more experiences to draw on, more acquired wisdom, and more to be grateful for.

Fletching feathers

Once our arrowhead is securely fixed and sharpened, attention must turn to fitting the tail feathers, the 'fletch'. They are fletched with three fins constructed from feathers, and a fourth part which is the whipping cord. You will see that there is a clear overlap with some of the elements that were required for sharpening, which emphasises their importance to the construction of the whole arrow.

To work on the fletching, the arrow needs to be fixed in a jig, or a vice, so that it doesn't move. God holds us tightly, carefully, in His hands. No one can dislodge us from there,[104] it's a place of refuge, security and safety.

These days, the fletch can be made of a variety of materials reflecting the scientific progression of arrow-making, and the

---

[104] John 10:29; Isaiah 41:10, 13.

world of plastics and carbon fibre. However, goose feathers are still the material of choice for traditional fletchers.

In medieval times, poor people could pay their taxes in goose feathers, which were submitted to the royal armoury for fletching the huge numbers of arrows which were made for use in the English wars, mostly in France. Royalty and the nobility would be prepared to pay even higher prices for arrows fletched with fancier feathers – swan or peacock – which they used for their sport.[105]

Feathers are natural, flexible, can cut into the wind as the arrow flies, have a natural curvature, as well as a degree of inbuilt weather-proofing, and still serve to ensure a smooth flight, good balance and the all-important factor of keeping the arrow on course.

In the past, the feathers were glued using a rabbit glue,[106] and tied or whipped onto the shaft with a strong linen thread.[107] They were then treated with a concoction designed to keep feather mites at bay.

The Word

The first feather stands for the Word of God, which keeps us on track. Fletchers used a grey goose feather for this first vane, which the archer would position so that it faced the sky; it needed to be positioned perpendicularly to the nock, and was called the 'cock feather'. This enabled the archer to nock his arrow quickly – crucial in a battle situation, when speed was of the essence. Trained archers were able to fire a dozen arrows a minute, but records show that the really skilled men could fire double that number. At the famous 1415 Battle of Agincourt,

[105] 'Making a Medieval Arrow', www.youtube.com/watch?v=r1WMcnA 2940 (accessed 21st April 2023).
[106] www.aprilmunday.wordpress.com/2020/03/15/medieval-bowyers-fletchers-stringers-and-arrowsmiths (accessed 11th May 2023).
[107] 'Making a Medieval Arrow', YouTube.

up to 50,000 arrows a minute could have been fired by approximately 5,000 archers in positions on each side of the battlefield.[108] With the enemy approaching, archers had a limited amount of time to make their arrows count. Even from 250 yards away, an arrow could cause serious injuries; at a hundred yards it could pierce armour and potentially kill a man.[109]

We have examined the importance of God's Word throughout the arrow's life; its reappearance here simply underlines that. Like the 'cock feather', God's Word acts as a plumb line; it helps us to align ourselves with His truths and position us for whatever circumstances throw at us. It is our reference point for ensuring that we are growing and building well – those in construction call it building 'true'.

The Holy Spirit

The second feather stands for the Holy Spirit, with whom we've spent much time in earlier chapters. He is our comforter, our helper, our power and resource; He intercedes for us with our heavenly Father, gives us a variety of gifts and is the source of growth in Jesus-like character which we refer to as His fruits. In our own strength we can do nothing, but God's strength has room to flow when we acknowledge and submit our weaknesses to Him. Our own lack of resources is no impediment to Him. While we engage with Him – and we are certainly not passive – it's His power that comes to the fore. When we are fuelled with the Holy Spirit, we have the power to live a life that reflects and points to Jesus Christ.

---

[108] kingjohnshouse.org.uk/the-longbow-and-its-impact-on-the-battle-of-agincourt/#:~:text=A%20long%20bow%2Dman%20could,knight%20there%20were%20four%20archers (accessed 26th February 2024).
[109] www.johnmooremuseum.org/medieval-archery-the-longbow (accessed 26th February 2024).

One another

The third feather is each other. As for sharpening the arrowhead, we've seen how we need one another, both for sharpening and for shaping. We cannot serve God on our own. Time and time again, the Bible indicates that we are part of a family, not just a random collection of lone individuals. Our modern European culture emphasises the individual over and above the community, so this is a change of paradigm for us. Even God lives in the community of Father, Son and Holy Spirit, yet they are 'One'. He is the ultimate model of healthy, functioning, mutually honouring community. If we are to truly reflect Him, then we need to belong to one too.

Suffering

The fourth element, which ties the whole back end of the arrow together, is the whipping. This cord stands for suffering, and we'll be exploring that in Chapter 11.

Target Questions

➢ What are some of the ways you have discovered that keep your time with God fresh?

➢ Who are you sharpening right now? Who is sharpening you?

➢ The three feathers in our allegory represent God's Word, the Holy Spirit and one another. Are there places you need to make adjustments to make more time for God, the community of believers, or to share your problems with others?

➢ How can you keep trusting in difficult times?

10a. Priscilla and Aquila, Apollos, Timothy and Titus

As we explored the work of the arrowsmith, we noted how the Word of God, the Holy Spirit and the community of believers all work together to sharpen us in the same way that the old-fashioned arrowhead was sharpened. The fletcher's skill lay in adding three flight feathers which symbolise the same three things, held together firmly by whipping: a cord of suffering which we will explore in the next chapter.

All of these ingredients are clear in the life of Paul and those he discipled. Each element cropped up multiple times in his spiritual walk. They contributed to his experience of God's faithfulness and his own maturity, which is what enabled him to encourage and disciple others who were younger in the faith. Embracing Paul's words and example, they sought out others to whom they could pass those things on.

Paul's letters are a legacy of much of that. Our own legacy is most likely to be what we leave as a deposit in other people. Far more valuable than a building that can be demolished or closed, or a cold, stone monument, we have the joy of passing on the eternal truths of God's Word to others, to share our pilgrimages and be part of seeing precious souls move and grow into the living hope of Jesus, guaranteeing their eternal destiny, and passing the good news on to others. In this way, one arrow can trigger another arrow, which can trigger another arrow and so on until Jesus comes again. What a privilege to be part of that sequence of discipling.

Paul was not making himself out to be a spiritual guru. He asked believers not to follow him as such, but to follow his example of running hard after Jesus: 'Whatever you have learned or received or heard from me, or seen in me – put it into practice' (Philippians 4:9). To have done otherwise would have been to set himself up as a cult leader, not an apostle, mentor, fellow follower, teacher or friend.

Priscilla and Aquila were two believers who benefited from this type of cascading discipleship pattern.

Aquila was a Jew from Pontus,[110] in modern-day Turkey, who had migrated to Italy where he probably met his wife, since she has a Roman name. Together, they were expelled from Rome around AD49 when the emperor Claudius sent all the Jews into exile after riots in the city between the Messianic Jews and the Jews who denied that Jesus was the promised Christ caused unrest.[111] Priscilla and Aquila fled to Corinth, in Greece, which was a Latin-speaking city. This is where they met Paul, not long after he arrived from Athens.

The Bible doesn't record their conversion story or whether they were already believers when they arrived in Corinth. They may have made the journey to Jerusalem for Passover in the past, or even have heard Peter preaching on the street at Pentecost. There is evidence that Peter himself went to Corinth, so they could have sat under his teaching there; or perhaps it was Paul himself who was able to lead them to faith.

Having left Italy with very little, they earned a living in their new city through tentmaking. Corinth was a commercial hub, strategically positioned with the sea on both the east and west sides, and home to the worshippers of Aphrodite, Apollos and

---

[110] Acts 18:2.

[111] www.biola.edu/blogs/good-book-blog/2012/something-about-the-book-of-romans-that-will-help-you-really-get-it (accessed 30th August 2023).

Melicertes.[112] Demand for tents, sails and equipment for the prestigious Isthmian games (second only to the Olympics) would have seen their skills in great demand.

Paul's visit to them seems to have turned into a long-term lodging. As a tentmaker himself, he worked alongside them to earn an income, which took pressure off the churches to provide for him. Working together doesn't work in every marriage, but after the trauma of their expulsion, it seems to have pushed Priscilla and Aquila closer together rather than further apart. The Bible always puts their names together as one, and Priscilla is usually named first. Whatever your view of female leadership, it's abundantly clear that both were leaders who enjoyed a great marriage, and were instrumental in helping Paul in his ministry. They even risked their lives for him in some unspecified way.[113] To him they became great friends as well as fellow workers in both their tentmaking and in their disciple-making.

Working with Paul would have given ample, and natural, opportunities for talking about Jesus, faith, doctrine and the application of God's Word. Paul's high level of education would have been called upon to shed light on the Old Testament Scriptures, pulling together the relevant Messianic prophecies and initiating discussions on how this all held together. Since Paul lived with them too, I imagine there were many late-night conversations exploring all sorts of topics. Living life together is one of the best and most natural environments for joining hearts, sharing values and working out kingdom living. We've valued gleaning from others ourselves in this way, as well as having people live with us for a season.

While in Corinth, Paul went to the weekly synagogue meetings on the Sabbath to reason and debate with attendees, trying to help them see and understand who Jesus was. Doubtless, his new companions went along too and drank in all

---

[112] www.letterstobarbara.com/ancient-corinth-visit-apollo-temple-facts (accessed 30th August 2023).
[113] Romans 16:3-4.

the wisdom they could, gleaning from Paul's exposition and following the debates with understanding.

When Timothy and Silas arrived in the city from Macedonia, Paul set his tentmaking aside for the sake of giving time to preaching and teaching. It was another opportunity for them to learn from him.

In Acts 18 we read that sometime later, when Paul left Corinth for Syria, he took Priscilla and Aquila with him as far as Ephesus – another important and influential city, positioned where trade routes crossed, and known as '"the mother city" of Asia'.[114] Here, the deity of choice was Artemis, or Diana, goddess of fertility; her cult was spread over the entire region. Paul again visited the synagogue and had conversations with the Jews there before he sailed on, strategically leaving Priscilla and Aquila to make a bridgehead for the Christian faith. They were kind, hospitable people, and welcomed a new church community into their own home.

Later on, another Jewish preacher arrived in the city. Apollos knew the Hebrew Scriptures well and taught powerfully about salvation, both in and out of the synagogue. Priscilla and Aquila heard him speak and saw that he was a genuine man of God; they admired his passion, his knowledge and his sincerity. They also realised that there were gaps in his understanding: he knew about water baptism, but not the baptism and filling of the Holy Spirit.

Using their gifts of hospitality and teaching, they 'invited him to their home' (v26) where they shared their insights and understanding, much of which may have been learned from Paul. Apollos listened well, understood and embraced their words, and so grew in his effectiveness for spreading the gospel. Here there was an effective sharpening of one another with all three elements familiar to our arrow: the water of the Word, the oil of the Holy Spirit and the experience and wisdom of believers with other believers; a growing and empowering

---

[114] http://resources.takingground.org.uk/ephesus-in-the-first-century/ (accessed 22nd June 2023).

relationship for all of them. They also modelled the natural cascade of discipleship chains as another link was added.

Apollos later felt a divine nudge to travel to a different area. The believers in Ephesus wrote a letter of recommendation to those already following Jesus at his destination point, and it's more than likely that Priscilla and Aquila were part of that sending team.

> When he arrived, he was a great help to those who by grace had believed. For he vigorously refuted his Jewish opponents in public debate, proving from the Scriptures that Jesus was the Messiah.
> (Acts 18:27-28)

Apollos began to function in much the same way as Paul had done, thanks to the influence of Priscilla and Aquila. So much so that Paul had to rebuke the church in Corinth for breaking into competitive factions claiming to follow either himself or Peter or Apollos. He had to remind them that everyone is to follow Jesus first, and not get caught up in personality cults, or be distracted by favourites.[115]

Paul knew the realities of that fourth ingredient for the arrow: suffering, which we'll be exploring next. You can read his list of adventures, exploits and trials in 2 Corinthians 11:23-33.

Paul came back to Ephesus on his third missionary journey and set up daily discussions in a local lecture hall. The disciples who were with him were able to watch, listen and learn as he passed on his knowledge and experience; Timothy was one of them. In his second letter to Timothy, Paul instructed him to:

> Be strong in the grace that is in Christ Jesus. And the things you have heard me say in the presence of many witnesses entrust to reliable people who will also be

---

[115] 1 Corinthians 1:10-12.

> qualified to teach others. Join with me in suffering, like
> a good soldier of Christ Jesus.
> (2 Timothy 2:1-3)

Paul had a great fondness for this youngster, whom he had known for a number of years. He knew his mother, Eunice, as well as his grandmother, Lois, who had both been godly women and Jesus lovers.[116] Two generations had already passed on the baton of faith – each firing the 'arrow' they had responsibility for into the future. Timothy would be the third if he embraced the things he had learned, and continued to lean into God through the Holy Spirit. Paul served as a mentor, discipler and encourager, modelling the values of what life with Jesus looked like and setting a solid example for Timothy to follow.

Paul called Timothy 'my true son in the faith' and 'my dear son' (1 Timothy 1:2; 2 Timothy 1:2), terms of affirmation and affection. Timothy went on to lead the church community in the challenging city of Ephesus. Paul wrote him two letters, in which he reminded Timothy of the important principle of passing on truths and sharpening one another, referring to their own long-standing relationship:

> You … know all about my teaching, my way of life, my
> purpose, faith, patience, love, endurance, persecutions,
> sufferings – what kinds of things happened to me in
> Antioch, Iconium and Lystra, the persecutions I
> endured. Yet the Lord rescued me from all of them. In
> fact, everyone who wants to live a godly life in Christ
> Jesus will be persecuted, while evildoers and impostors
> will go from bad to worse, deceiving and being deceived.
> But as for you, continue in what you have learned and
> have become convinced of, because you know those
> from whom you learned it, and how from infancy you

---

[116] 2 Timothy 1:5.

have known the Holy Scriptures, which are able to make you wise for salvation through faith in Christ Jesus. (2 Timothy 3:10-15)

Paul was still able to give guidance and advice to Timothy, who needed to square up to the particular opposition facing the family of believers in a city devoted to worship of a pagan goddess.

Paul also reminded him that while he was pursuing God's call on his young life, he should not allow people to look down on him because of his age, but, like himself, 'set an example' and remember that godly men had commissioned him for the tasks before him (1 Timothy 4:12-14). He was no boastful upstart, but a man pursuing a clear calling on his life.

From Paul's greetings at the end of his second letter to Timothy, it's clear that Aquila and Priscilla were still in Ephesus, working in the city and continuing to see God's kingdom extended there. It's almost certain that they, too, were inputting into Timothy's life as spiritual parental figures.

Titus was another son in the faith to Paul, into whom he poured himself, investing time and wisdom for raising him into leadership and effectiveness for leadership on the island of Crete. The pattern of discipleship was repeated, enabling and empowering Titus to pour himself into others. Thus, a multiplication of Jesus-followers was replicated all over the Mediterranean. More arrows firing into the predominant culture with a message of hope.

Meanwhile, back in Italy, Claudius died in October AD54, and a new emperor, Nero, came to power; he reversed the former decree regarding the Jews, so perhaps this was the reason that Priscilla and Aquila went back to Rome. We know that they did so, because they are included in Paul's greetings to the church there in his letter of that name.[117] Once again they opened their home for a local community of believers, so were

---

[117] Romans 16:3.

instrumental in passing on their love and experience of following Jesus.

With Nero in charge, we can only imagine how their story ended. The great fire that destroyed Rome in AD64, and which many historians believe was started by Nero himself in a bid to clear the area of the city he wanted to redevelop, was blamed on the Christians who were seen as a new Jewish sect. Using them as scapegoats, a great persecution against them broke out, and many ended up killed in the arena, burned or in prison.

What is certain is that those arrows were fired forward into new generations, who themselves submitted to the hand of the Master arrow-maker ready to take flight themselves into a variety of places, cultures and contexts, all seeking to see God's kingdom come.

11. The Whipping Cord

Our arrow is almost ready to be stored in the quiver. Its final requirement is the whipping cord, which is tied securely below the first feather vanes and then carefully wound around the arrow in several loops, slotting snugly between the vanes without damaging them, before being tied off at the top.

In our metaphor, the whipping represents suffering. Frankly, I'd like to leave this one on the workshop floor and forget all about it but, if I do that, I would miss a crucial part of God's design. This blueprint requires a fourth vital ingredient which will wrap around all the rest, binding the feathers tightly to the shaft. It provides grip and stability to the arrow as it flies.

Since all arrows need this cord in order to be effective, we will inevitably know seasons of suffering too.

Here in the Western part of the world, we spend a great deal of our time ensuring that our lives are as comfortable as possible. We enjoy round-the-clock access to heat, power, running water, indoor plumbing and the internet. We travel in cars with power steering, an inbuilt entertainment system and touch-of-a-button air-conditioning. Our kitchens are equipped with all manner of time-saving gadgets, and we have a certain expectation of a good standard of healthcare and education up to secondary level, which is all free at the point of delivery. We are mostly at liberty to express our thoughts and opinions in both word and print without threats to our personal safety, although evidence suggests this is changing.[118] Some would say that we have so many privileges in comparison with those living in other nations that we have no reason to grumble and no cause to complain. We do not suffer.

And yet, we know that isn't true. Suffering comes in all shapes and forms. We all have our griefs and our traumas, some more dramatic than others, but suffering is not a competition; there is no sliding scale of what counts as true suffering. A public humiliation for a child may cause as many mental scars as a violent encounter for a teenager or adult. A history of abuse can result in serious post-traumatic stress disorder for the victim, just as much as a military posting in a warzone or involvement in a major traffic accident. These things can follow and plague us for years.

We have very little idea of the journeys most of our contemporaries have travelled, or what crises they may have faced and, since we have all become very good at hiding our deepest selves from one another, we seldom get to see what's going on underneath, in hearts and minds. If we knew all that, the chances are that we would have more understanding and, hopefully, demonstrate a great deal more compassion and grace to each other.

Suffering

Contrary to popular misconception, Jesus does not invite us to a life of leisure and comfort; it is not a problem-free life of saccharine-enhanced indolence. To navigate it, we need 'less shallowness; more hallowedness'.[119] What that means is that we need to have prepared ourselves when things are relatively easy so that as and when things get tough, we have a measure of preparedness. This is the reason that soldiers do their drills in

---

[118] See Christian Concern: www.christianconcern.com/cases and Voice for Justice UK: cidac.co.uk (both accessed 11th September 2023).
[119] Attributed to A W Tozer.

peacetime over and over again. By digging deep, by repeating their manoeuvres and preparing themselves mentally, they are able to stand their ground when they are placed into conflict against a very real and present danger.

Indeed, Jesus invites us to follow Him only on His non-negotiable terms:

> Whoever wants to be my disciple must deny themselves and take up their cross and follow me. For whoever wants to save their life will lose it, but whoever loses their life for me will find it.
> (Matthew 16:24-25)

It sounds like the sort of phrase we might expect to find in the terms and conditions part of a contract. No one should be surprised when becoming a Christian doesn't instantly cause all their problems to evaporate in a puff of magic dust.

Following Jesus is costly; He told us quite plainly that we need to die to ourselves, and dying is an all-encompassing experience.

In other words, every part of our lives will be affected if we choose to follow Jesus. We cannot separate the secular and the spiritual as if living God's way is merely a hobby or a weekend pastime. We are in God's army as well as His family, where discipline and duty have their place as well as affirmation and forgiveness.

Following Jesus will almost certainly cost us in terms of popularity with our peers; it may cost us because of the sacrifices we are asked to make with our time, our space, our standard of living, our aspirations, as well as with our money. There will definitely be demanding sacrifices regarding our character as we give all of ourselves to Him – body, mind and heart. We can no longer pretend that negative character traits are simply part of our personality; they must be left at the foot of the cross as we press in to be more like Jesus.

All of these sacrifices are insignificant in the light of the sacrifice of Jesus, of course, but our culture has a tendency to squeeze out this important truth.

My rights

We live in an era where human rights are prioritised, and we can agree with the United Nations that these include 'the right to life and liberty, freedom from slavery and torture, freedom of opinion and expression, the right to work and education … without discrimination'.[120] This body lays out thirty articles which it deems to be the rights of every person. But Jesus gives us a different viewpoint, because when He talks about dying to ourselves, He is talking about laying down our personal rights, just as He did. This is personal; it includes the right to be angry, the right to hold a grudge, the right to take offence, the right to vindication or self-justification, just as much as the right to be happy, to own possessions, to live in safety or be healthy. It's vastly different from the way most of the world lives.

Our rights are no longer our own, because we belong to God. We laid them down when we gave Him Captaincy of our life. He now has the right to rule; we have given that to Him and, unlike the rulers of this world, He will use that right for our good, so we can flourish in Him as we were made to do. Surrendering to Him means just that: we give Him everything; absolutely everything. His kindness and patience will hold us to that as He embarks on the challenging task of making us like His Son: relying fully on Him, being in tune with Him and walking in step with Him all the days of our life, wherever that may take us.

Being a Christian is not for wimps. Following Jesus is not an emotional crutch for people who can't cope with the real world; it does not provide insulation from the trials that are common

---

[120] www.un.org/en/global-issues/human-rights (accessed 24th August 2023).

to all of us, and it is certainly not a spiritual anaesthetic against the rough and tumble of life in the twenty-first century.

Jesus could not have been clearer: 'In this world you will have trouble. But take heart! I have overcome the world' (John 16:33).

What is suffering?

Suffering takes many shapes and forms. In the West, we know very little of the sort of suffering experienced by our fellow Christians elsewhere, who experience first-hand the realities of being imprisoned for their faith, beatings and torture – even for simply possessing a Bible.

While there are political prisoners and people imprisoned on false charges in many places around the globe, it's Christians who are currently the most persecuted people group in the world. The International Society for Human Rights has reported that of all the acts of religious discrimination carried out in the world today, 80 per cent of them are perpetrated against Christians.[121]

Statistics tell us that 'more than 360 million Christians worldwide experience high levels of persecution and discrimination for their faith – that's a staggering 1 in 7 believers'.[122] North Korean Christians are subject to the worst persecution and suffering for their faith of any believers in the world today.[123] If one person is found to be following Jesus, then three generations of the family are routinely put into prison or labour camps, in order to root out the perceived canker.

[121] Quoted in Feba UK's *Voice* Magazine, Issue 2, 2023, p 12, and now considered a conservative estimate. Further information can be found here: https://commonslibrary.parliament.uk/research-briefings/cdp-2020-0019; www.theguardian.com/world/2015/oct/13/christianity-under-global-threat-persecution-says-report; and www.ucs.nd.edu/ (all accessed 7th September 2023).

[122] www.opendoorsuk.org/persecution (accessed 6th September 2023).

[123] Ibid.

Those from Muslim cultures who convert to Christianity can frequently suffer the loss of family and/or spouse, since they are routinely turned out of the home. They may also experience loss of employment – and therefore income – as well as loss of dignity and rights in the community. They may even suffer loss of life since, in some cases, it becomes a question of cultural honour; a Muslim convert can be considered to have brought shame on the rest of their community.

For those of us who feel we suffer injustice when the traffic lights don't favour us on the way to work, or who are the butt of office jokes from time to time, it can all seem far away and a little surreal. We are embarrassed to admit that we find these insignificant things difficult in the light of such sobering statistics. Our suffering will probably not take the form of such systematic persecution, although it is becoming increasingly difficult to espouse and verbalise Christian values in the workplace, whether that's the office, the school, or the hospital, as 'woke' and 'cancel culture' spread.[124]

However, quite apart from that, most of us have encountered painful bereavement, shattering betrayal, depressing unemployment, crushing disappointments, broken relationships, life-threatening health scares and/or chronic illnesses at one time or another. We've suffered traumas of multiple kinds, including accidents, or sexual, physical and/or emotional abuse, to which we will have responded in equally varied ways, all of which affect our mental health and our daily responses to the situations around us.

Why does God allow suffering?

This is a question people have been asking for generations. It's one that philosophers and theologians far cleverer than myself have wrestled with and attempted to answer; it remains one of

---

[124] See Christian Concern for further details. www.christianconcern.com (accessed 24th August 2023).

the most frequently asked questions by people exploring faith. While there are many things we do not know and cannot understand, there are others that are clear.

First, we need to understand that we live in a world where sin spoilt the original blueprint of perfection in the earliest moments of history. Sin came through Adam and was dealt with through Jesus. However, we all still live with the repercussions of what happened in the first garden.

The root of suffering

It took me a long time to understand the severity of the consequences of the choice that was made when Adam and Eve ate that forbidden fruit from the tree of the knowledge of good and evil.[125] I grew up in a family where knowledge and academic achievement were applauded; I thought knowledge was always a good thing, to be pursued with diligence. Surely, I reasoned, knowing the difference between good and evil would be sensible; why would God have forbidden it? How could they know what was good if they didn't know what was evil?

What I failed to understand then was that because God had designed humanity for a clear, clean, open relationship with Him, when they chose something else it was an act of treason against their Creator. He was to be their touchstone regarding what was good or evil, so their choice was a clear and open rebellion against God; they were deliberately turning their back on Him. Rather than trust Him to guide and speak to them, they chose to take things into their own hands and bypass Him. That's where the sin truly lay.

This was not a desire for truth, but a response to the seed of doubt sown by Satan that God was holding something back from them; that they were destined for a second-best life if they didn't eat that fruit. It was a despicable and destructive lie.

---

[125] Genesis 2:17; 3:4-7.

So I finally saw that even good is not truly good if God is not its source. The world is full of wonderful, intriguing and enticing things, thoughts and activities, which can look far more like good than evil, but if they don't originate in God Himself, they may lure us away from trust and faith in Him but, more importantly, they almost certainly bypass Him. That's not what we were made for. By the same token, things that are truly good may have their source in God even where He is not acknowledged.

Crippling, legalistic religion that is always focusing on what is either right or wrong has its roots in this way of thinking; it fails to embrace the life and death principles that come from the heart, and which Jesus espoused and illustrated so well in the following encounter.

In John 8:2-11 we read that a crowd brought a woman caught in adultery to Him; they wanted to know whether Jesus would carry out the instruction in the law of Moses which said she should be stoned. (The fact that two people must have been involved in the adultery had been blatantly ignored.) Jesus told them that whichever of them had never sinned, or broken God's law, was the one who should begin the stone-throwing. One by one they left. By the letter of the law, Jesus – the only one truly without sin – should have picked up a rock and carried out that judgement. But He didn't. He wasn't working from that right–wrong protocol. However, He didn't let her off or tell her it didn't matter, either. Once the angry crowd had melted away, He reassured her that He wasn't there to condemn her, but He did tell her she must break with her sinful lifestyle. He gave her life twice over.

God's heart has always yearned for intimacy with His creation. That precious relationship was discarded and trodden underfoot by the foolishness of defying His instructions for flourishing, and choosing something other than Him instead.

With sin unleashed into the no-longer-perfect world, deception, disease, jealousy, lies, anger, hatred, violence, abuse, grief, bereavement and a whole raft of selfish and ungodly things came in too, including suffering. Sin affected everything: body, mind, spirit and the earth itself, which became subject to weeds and thorns, making looking after it a chore rather than a pleasure.

Our suffering

If God's people lived in total isolation from difficulties, trials and suffering, we would have very little to say to the world around us. If we were to live wrapped in divine cotton wool, insulated from anything bad ever happening to us, we would live detached from reality, without empathy or understanding for those not yet in God's family. Why, then, would anyone take us seriously or think that we might have something to contribute in their circumstances?

None of us was designed to live in isolation, and suffering is a strong factor in bringing us closer to one another. News bulletins reporting natural disasters frequently feature communities coming together to share their grief and support one another. Collective suffering becomes the glue that keeps them together. Indeed, sometimes it's only those who have shared the same suffering who we feel can truly understand us, whether that's the loss of a child, a life-threatening health condition or a terrorist atrocity. No explanation is required, no reliving a traumatic situation; the shared experience unites the sufferers.

So our experiences can draw us towards one another, rather than divide and isolate us; such episodes can serve to unify us in an extraordinary way – a common factor on our separate journeys. We find people who truly understand us.

Jesus' suffering

Jesus left the riches of heaven to live within the constraints of a human body for thirty-three years. In that way, He identified with all of humanity. He was not just the Son of God, but also the Son of Man. He knew the realities of hunger and thirst, the experience of growing up in a family with less-than-perfect siblings, and of living in a country where the Roman government was not just unsympathetic, but brutal. Not only that, but Jesus was not immune from the trials, tribulations and temptations that we also experience.[126]

He knew bereavement and betrayal; physical, emotional and spiritual pain; and the terrible separation from His Father when He took on the burden of our own sins, as well as every sickness, grief and anguish known to humanity, on the cross. The physical suffering of crucifixion is beyond us: the nails tearing through flesh, the ripping of muscles, the agony of every bone being pulled out of joint, the slow suffocation as bodyweight forced air from the lungs. Adding the mental torture of carrying our sins, and the taunts of demons and evil spirits, all while cruelly exposed – naked in front of a crowd of tormentors – cannot be fully grasped. It's too much for us to even begin to imagine.

Yet that is why He understands us so well and knows us so well. Jesus has gone further and deeper into suffering than we ever will. When we experience even a small slice of suffering, we have a glimpse of what He has known, a taste of what He endured, a share in His own sufferings. So even when we know pain, we haven't necessarily stopped knowing Him unless we choose to walk away; we may even know Him better than before.

We must be on our guard to ensure that in those times we turn towards Him, not away from Him, even if we don't hear His voice or feel His presence.

---

[126] Hebrews 4:15.

Suffering at the hands of others

Why is suffering necessary for the construction of our arrow? It's not because God is capricious – He isn't. Neither is it because He takes pleasure in our discomfort – He doesn't.

Sufferings that are the consequence of abuse are not our fault. This is a highly important truth which itself may be the start of setting people free from lies and gaslighting, if they have been subject to coercive and manipulative control behaviours by abusers. Our brains are amazing, complex organs which store and revisit information and experiences in all sorts of convoluted ways. Trained therapists and counsellors can help untangle some of our thoughts, traumas and reactions. As a result, sometimes we can begin to make more sense of them; with skilled assistance, we can access tools to help us process our experiences, which can help bring us to a place of peace.

Very probably, we will still have questions that can't be answered. Our brains want logic, our hearts desire justice and suffering defies both.

Whatever we have gone through, this much is sure: bringing it to Jesus is the best next step. There is no wound too debilitating, no shame too deep and no life too broken for God to bring His light, life and healing to it. Nothing is too difficult for Him. He is the God of miracles; there is still power in His name, and through the blood of Jesus there can be restoration. God is well able to bring healing and wholeness to our minds as well as to our bodies. It may come gradually, or it may come in a moment, but it is more than possible. Suffering can be redemptive when He is invited into it.

Empathy

Suffering opens the door for empathy. Jesus knows our weaknesses, and that makes Him approachable. We know that He has experienced the same things as us, so He understands the challenges we face and what it is like to navigate them. His compassion can bring us comfort; that compassion flowing through us can bring comfort to others.

I am always more inclined to listen to someone who understands my problem, not because they perceive the words I'm saying, but because they have experienced something similar. I trust the mountain guide who has walked the route, anticipates the pitfalls, knows the dangers, is aware of the safe path, is alert to the dangerous places and is willing to share their valuable knowledge and insights with me. Likewise, the person who has found their own safe passage through the things that threaten to overwhelm me or that cause me pain can meet me in a place where our hearts connect with one another. Their own pain, if traversed with their eyes fixed on Jesus and their hands grasping the hand of God, will serve to give me wisdom, encouragement, advice, inspiration and, above all, hope.

We will have a natural shared bridge over which Jesus, and His promises, can travel unhindered. I won't feel 'preached at', and they will have the opportunity to reiterate the reasons for their trust in our faithful God. Both of us will come away stronger. My pain may be temporarily eased because now I see it in a new light or because I am reassured that despite what I am feeling, this is a valley to walk through, not one in which to camp out forevermore.

Hope is a commodity in grievously short supply. Certainly our politicians, world leaders and social commentators offer us very little. Yet without it, there is only hopelessness and despair. Our God is a God of hope; He comes alongside us and walks us out of darkness into His light, into a place where His life flows.

Listen to Paul in a written blessing to the church in Rome:

> May the God of hope fill you with all joy and peace as you trust in him, so that you may overflow with hope by the power of the Holy Spirit.
> (Romans 15:13)

When we choose to trust Him, we can access hope and discover that there is also an abundance of peace and joy; so much so that we can be not only filled, but also overflow with hope through the Holy Spirit. If we're overflowing with hope, we can metaphorically spill Jesus all over the people around us, throwing them a lifeline as they walk their own paths. What a wonderful gift to bring to others.

Trust can be nurtured so that our spiritual roots are deep, anchoring us against days of trouble. Perseverance only comes by persevering. We can wish for endurance and the spirit that keeps on keeping on, but that won't build anything into us. We nurture it by speaking God's truth to our souls, choosing to believe that His words and His character are unchanging, and pushing through moment by moment with our eyes fixed not on ourselves, our problem or our pain, but on Him.

Walking with us through and in suffering

God may not fix all our problems, but He promises to walk closely with us through them all. We have hope not just for this life, but for life beyond death. Our hope is not a flimsy, insubstantial thing, like the hope that it doesn't rain on our planned picnic; it's far more robust than that. Our hope is that which is 'divinely guaranteed' (Hebrews 11:1, AMP) and will stand the buffeting of any and every storm that rages against it, because God cannot be shaken from His throne.

Those who don't yet know Jesus will take note of how we walk through our seasons of suffering. If we abandon our faith, then they will assume that it is irrelevant and not something they would ever want to consider. Why would they? But if we genuinely, authentically walk through these trials with integrity, rather than with a superficial spirituality, then we will serve as a powerful signpost to the reality of God through good times and bad.

When our friends face their own times of suffering, rather than metaphorically shouting advice to them from a distance, we can come alongside them, crossing the ready-made bridge of empathy. Our shared heartache serves to strengthen us both.

Jesus comes to fill our suffering with His presence, power and peace. I love hearing stories of healing miracles and escape from trials and difficulties, but I know that it's in the crucible of suffering and the warzone of personal pain that the realities of God and His words can come to life. We can choose to push Him away and try to manage those challenges on our own while blaming God for bringing them our way, or we can invite Him to come and suffuse them with His peace that is like no other.

A personal story

In January 2020, I was diagnosed with breast cancer. To say it was a surprise is an understatement. I had been recalled from a routine mammogram and assumed that this was some sort of technical glitch. There was a disconcerting swiftness to how quickly I was ushered from the appointment room into a consultancy room where I was examined more thoroughly. As I lay on the medical bed looking at the screen on which the scan was projected, I could see a sinister lump very clearly.

As my kind consultant announced that she would do the biopsy immediately, I experienced two strange sensations. First, I registered that this was real, even though I felt strangely detached from the screen, as though I was watching a science documentary. I saw the inserted needle penetrate the lump, and found myself thinking that this was not how I expected to leave the world. Rather than fear, I felt an overwhelming gratitude for all the people in my life – my husband, my children, my extended family – the places we've been, the friends we've enjoyed, the fellow labourers around the world whom I've been privileged to know and who have walked the Jesus path for many years. If I were to die in the months ahead as a result of what they were clearly going to tell me was some sort of cancer, then I quietly asked God to help me to do it well. Second, I felt the peace that others have talked about, but which in that moment wrapped me up completely in a cocoon of extraordinary calm.

At this point, I realised that there were now several other people in the room who hadn't been there before, presumably to act as medical wicket-keepers – to leap into action depending on how I reacted. In fact, I found myself checking they were OK, and sympathising with their challenges of talking to patients about cancer so many times a day, every day. It was remarkable; it was supernatural; it could only have been God supplying His kindness and peace in the midst of the crisis.

That peace stayed with me through a return trip to South Africa, carrying a bag loaded with medicines designed to make the tumour shrink. When lockdown came and we had to be repatriated from Cape Town, His presence was palpable. Through surgery, recovery and radiotherapy, He was there. I lay in the complicated machine in a Bristol hospital for my final treatment and, bizarrely, remembered not one word of Scripture. It was very odd; but the nurses could hear me through the two-way speaker as I softly sang a simple Jesus song. It was all I could remember in that moment, but it brought me peace.

Change

Suffering provides a space for God to change us. It strikes at our very core, and that's exactly where real change takes place. In James' letter of the New Testament, he put it this way:

> Consider it pure joy, my brothers and sisters, whenever you face trials of many kinds, because you know that the testing of your faith produces perseverance. Let perseverance finish its work so that you may be mature and complete, not lacking anything.
> (James 1:2-4)

James wasn't being glib or facetious; he wasn't suggesting that we embrace difficult things in a warped, masochistic way;

neither did he attempt to specifically define what those trials might be. He understood that it's never the circumstances of our lives that define who we are, but our response to those circumstances.

Suffering can either drive us from God or into His loving arms. When we choose the latter – knowing that He is never the instigator of our situation – when we actively, desperately seek His face and listen for His voice, we will discover that His Spirit softens us. Somehow our own spirits tend to shed any brittle protective shell we may have constructed, and we mellow beneath His hands. Suffering is a process of tenderising our hearts towards God and towards others; another shaping which brings glory to Him and readies us for reaching out to others in their dark times.

Tough seasons of suffering give us the opportunity to stand on the promises of God, to dare to believe that He will do what He says He will do, and to allow God to mould us into His likeness more and more as we submit to His hands, even when they feel rough. They are an opportunity to depend on God far more than we do when everything is going well.

Where the rubber hits the road

Such times open the door for authenticating our faith and discovering where that faith really lies. It's the place where we choose to either feast on the dishes that life serves us or to push them away in disgust and refuse to engage, in which case we will miss out on the invitation to enjoy clear, close intimacy with Him.[127]

God is absolutely interested in our circumstances, but He is far more interested in how we react to those circumstances. He is concerned primarily with our character. How He sees fit to teach us, train us, shape us and mould us is entirely up to Him, and He owes us no explanation.

---

[127] Jenny Sanders, *Spiritual Feasting* (Instant Apostle 2020).

There is no doubt that the longer we walk with Him, the more obstacles we will have to negotiate and the more trials we will face. This is part of building up our spiritual muscle; how else will we develop the spiritual grit to stand firm in a world where our cultures are turning back to so much darkness? Endurance and perseverance are marks of maturity. Tender hearts respond more readily to His voice. Suffering gives our faith an authenticity that no 'fluffy bunny' life of ease can provide. Mature faith has to encounter difficulties, or it isn't really faith at all.

Whatever form they present themselves in, and however long they go on for, God will either remove these sufferings (always our preferred choice, of course) or walk with us to navigate them – whether that's a way around the problem or straight through the storm. Even when He entrusts the most difficult of circumstances to us in the form of illness, disability, unemployment or bereavement, He remains our safe place, our strongest advocate, companion and friend.

When Jesus was praying in the Garden of Gethsemane, He asked His Father to remove the 'cup' before Him. If that were not possible, He prayed that God's will, rather than His own, would be done. At that point, 'An angel from heaven appeared to him and strengthened him. And being in anguish, he prayed more earnestly, and his sweat was like drops of blood falling to the ground' (Luke 22:43-44). Jesus had an actual angel come to support and encourage Him; but see how the celestial being didn't make everything melt away. In fact, Luke points out that Jesus was in acute distress, physically, emotionally and spiritually. In the darkest moment, His prayers became more earnest, not less, after the angel arrived.

We may never have an angelic visitation, but I believe that God does trust us with certain experiences so that we draw closer to Him. Even in the most difficult places, He promises to walk with us and, though it may not always feel like it, that is a precious privilege.

The apostle Paul said:

> I want to know Christ – yes, to know the power of his resurrection and participation in his sufferings, becoming like him in his death, and so, somehow, attaining to the resurrection from the dead.
> (Philippians 3:10-11)

Paul wasn't asking for crucifixion; his deepest desire was to know Jesus – His Lord, Saviour and friend – better and more intimately. He recognised the privilege of submitting fully to the Father's will in obedience, so that even in the times of difficulty, he would know God's voice and His closeness, just as Jesus did.

There are moments when we too will probably pray in a new way. Not transactional prayers, bargaining with God for healing or removal of our particular challenge, but prayers that draw us closer to Him, that give us a new insight into who He is and which strengthen us with fortitude and courage to stand firm in Him throughout the trial; an opportunity to surrender to His will.

We don't revel in the suffering itself – that would be perverse – and we certainly don't pray for it – that would be weird – but we delight in His presence and align ourselves with Him as we trust Him in it all. Neither do we resign ourselves to suffering by taking the stance of a pseudo-martyr. There is no authenticity on that path because it puts us at the centre of our world again, rather than allowing God to take His rightful place. It causes us to veer away from God's intent, and leads only to resentment and bitterness.

Control

One of the most difficult things about seasons of suffering is how out of control we feel. When things happen to us that we can do nothing to avert, we can find ourselves tipped into anxiety and panic. We are used to being in control of our circumstances, of making decisions that lead us into more pleasant places and enjoyable times. When that control and autonomy are taken away from us, we find ourselves exposed and vulnerable in the most disconcerting ways.

The truth is that we can actually control very little in our lives: the weather, our health, job security, other people. Acknowledging that may help us come to a place of peace and of greater trust as we lean into the all-sufficiency of God instead of so frequently trusting our own opinions, assessment and/or skills.

We have yet another opportunity to choose. Will we press into God and trust that He sees it all and knows the bigger picture, or will we retreat into self-absorption and then overcompensate in the areas which we can control? The former will bring us life but might be uncomfortable; the latter will lead us into black holes of depression and isolation.

Every time we come out the other side of these things – and even in the middle of them, when we can see no ending and no way out – He will be who He says He is and do what He has always said He will do. That holds true even if our circumstances seem irreversible.

In this way, we prove His faithfulness over and over and over again, building that spiritual tenacity and adding to our confidence in His eternal presence, promises and power.

Warriors

Changing the analogy, just for a moment, we could say that we arrows become the warriors. Both Scripture and literature of multiple genres provide numerous references to the life of faith being a battle, requiring trained and disciplined soldiers to engage and overcome the trials of life. It would be a waste of time training any military conscript if the end goal did not involve engagement in a conflict of some sort. A phrase I have carried through many years of following Jesus is, 'Never trust a soldier without scars.' The scars we carry mark us out as warriors who have seen battle. Who would you rather have next to you in your bleakest times of difficulty and suffering – the experienced spiritual soldier who has been in the thick of it, or the newbie conscript who barely knows which way up their spiritual weapons should be carried?

When we look back and see how God has walked with us and demonstrated His grace and faithfulness, our faith is stirred and fed; we are increasingly well equipped to face all that the uncertain future will bring.

Back to our arrow. When the original stick was torn from the tree at the start of its development into an arrow, it could not make conditions with the craftsman; there was no room to negotiate terms. This was a complete surrender, a setting aside of rights and demands.

Choosing to trust

If God changes our circumstances without changing our character, neither we nor the world around us will be any better off. However, as God changes us, we can cooperate with Him in seeing the world changed; people around us can be reached with the power of His love, one by one, regardless of their circumstances.

We may not understand the enigma of suffering, but we can choose to trust, and invite God to meet us in it and fill it with His comforting presence.

As we lean into Him during difficult times, as we make cold-blooded decisions to trust Him regardless of what we see or feel, we become more tightly bound to Him in a relationship of growing intimacy. Head knowledge alone is of no value to us in the dark tunnels and shadowy valleys; it's a living, growing, vibrant relationship with Him that will keep us on a firm path.

None of us knows how well we will stand in the face of suffering until it comes to us. Will we hold out, or will we fold? We love reading and hearing about those who have endured terrible things and come out the other side, but there are also many stories of those who crumbled. Some recovered; some didn't. And what about those whose suffering has no end this side of heaven? Only a genuine, deep, robust relationship with God will be able to sustain a person.

In such moments, we must not rely on our feelings to determine truth, despite what the world may say. There is always an objective truth bigger than the circumstances we face; He is the Truth[128] – Jesus Himself – and in Him there is love, joy and peace beyond the self-fulfilment the world espouses.

Paul, who went through multiple episodes of suffering, including a mysterious thorn which was never removed despite his many prayers,[129] concluded:

> Therefore we do not lose heart. Though outwardly we are wasting away, yet inwardly we are being renewed day by day. For our light and momentary troubles are achieving for us an eternal glory that far outweighs them all. So we fix our eyes not on what is seen, but on what is unseen, since what is seen is temporary, but what is unseen is eternal.
> (2 Corinthians 4:16-18)

Cultivating an eternal perspective will give us the resolve and the courage to keep walking our path, knowing Jesus walks with us and God keeps us safe in His hands.

That whipping cord binds the fletcher's feathers to the shaft of the arrow. There's a vivid picture of proximity, strength and intimacy there. It binds the whole thing together, making it stronger and more robust. Some cords are plain linen and some carry a striped pattern. It would be true to say that even our suffering is shot through with a clear pattern of God's unending, fierce yet tender love for us. It's still very much there, even in seasons of dark pain and difficulty; when the walls are pushing in on us and the heavens seem like brass, He is present. His love is so much stronger, purer and more consistent than ours. It 'never fails' (1 Corinthians 13:8).

---

[128] John 14:6.
[129] 2 Corinthians 12:7b-9.

If we continually ask why such things have come our way, we may find that we hear nothing at all. The truth is that few explanations would be adequate even if they were to be offered. Perhaps it helps to remember that God's ultimate goal is to make us more like Jesus, and the whipping cord of suffering is bound tightly around the feathers as part of producing a quality weapon. Suffering is not there in isolation: the water of His Word, the oil of His Spirit and the sharpening of one another are also with us.

Will we trust who He is and what He says at all times, even in circumstances of suffering? It's a choice. It may not be an easy one, but it's one we must make, perhaps many times. He will meet us in our weakness; it's the perfect arena in which His strength can be shown. He will faithfully, abundantly and consistently provide us with as much strength, courage and grace as we need moment by moment, though we may need to press in with determination to find it. God graciously gives us multiple opportunities to renew that choice to trust, to nail our colours firmly to the mast and to lean into Him again.

When the answer to this question is a resounding 'Yes', we arrows are poised for action.

With a sharpened arrowhead and a full complement of pristine tail feathers bound together with tough whipping cord, this polished arrow is ready to fulfil its destiny, ready to take its place in the quiver, ready to fly at the will of the Master Archer.

Target Questions

➤ With whom have you shared a common experience of suffering? What did this look like, and did you find anything redemptive in it?

➤ Think about your own pilgrimage so far. Where has God led you that you would rather He had not? How has that impacted your relationship with Him?

➤ Consider the experience of other believers you know who have been entrusted with a difficult or painful path. How has God been manifested in their lives as a result?

➤ Can there be any privilege in suffering? What might that be?

11a. Job

Job's sufferings are legendary; so much so that he is the standard that believers and non-believers alike refer to in times of crisis and disaster. He has become for us the symbol and epitome of suffering.

Job lived in the land of Uz, a region somewhere around modern-day Jordan, Syria, or north-west Saudi Arabia. Judging by his length of life, some commentators think that he was probably a contemporary of Abraham, though there's no record of their paths ever crossing.

The biblical book that tells his alarming story begins by stating very clearly that Job was a good man: 'blameless and upright' (Job 1:1). The trials that came his way were unrelated to his character or his lifestyle; they were not a consequence of some wicked sin, secret or otherwise. I think it helps us to remember that when we reflect on our own situations.

His is a curious story, in which Satan himself somehow had access to God and, after 'roaming ... the earth' (v7), came before Him to accuse Job. While God pointed to Job as a shining example of someone who held Him in high respect and was vigilant in keeping away from evil, Satan claimed that was only because Job lived such a comfortable, easy life. God had blessed him in so many ways, he argued, that Job had no reason to doubt God. The implication was that Job's faith was flimsy; he was merely a fair-weather follower who had never known any troubles impinge on his lifestyle that might have caused his faith to falter. If all that he possessed were to be taken away, the devil claimed that it would be a very different story: Job would soon be shaking his fist in God's face and turning away from Him in anger.

So, for reasons that are never revealed to Job, God allowed Satan to take from him all his accumulated possessions, his servants and offspring. In a single day, he lost all of his livestock – 11,500 oxen, camels, sheep and donkeys – to a combination of freak weather patterns and bands of marauding Sabeans and Chaldeans, who slaughtered all the servants except the ones who brought the terrible news back to Job. Just as this horrifying litany of disasters was being unfolded in front of Job, another messenger arrived with the tragic news that all ten of his children had been simultaneously wiped out when the house they were in collapsed.

This was a trauma of epic proportions. Losing possessions can be tough, losing your livelihood is devastating, but to lose your children as well – all at once, and all on the same day – was a shattering blow.

We can almost imagine the ghastly pause before an inevitable outpouring of grief and rage, at which Satan would have clapped his hands in delight. It was not to be. Instead, Job expressed his deep sorrow by tearing his clothes and shaving his head, after which he dropped to the ground and worshipped God.

It was an extraordinary reaction. His words revealed his understanding that, having brought nothing into the world, he would take nothing out either. All that he had came from God in the first place and, for inexplicable reasons, God had chosen to take them away again. He is God; that is His right. Job's trust in God didn't falter. He praised the Lord and steadfastly refused to blame God for any of the dreadful things that had befallen him that day.

We might think that Job's cup of acute suffering was complete at this point, but Satan came to God again. This time he claimed that Job was only posturing as righteous because he himself had escaped. The devil insisted that while Job's own life wasn't threatened, there could be no certainty that his faith would hold up should that alter. If Job were to be afflicted in some physical way, it was suggested, then the real Job would be revealed as a duplicitous, faithless individual who would soon shift to cursing, rather than praising, God.

Once again, God gave permission for the arch enemy to bring some malady on Job, with the proviso that he must not kill him; Job's life was inviolate.

So, while Job was still grieving for his dead children and the destruction of everything he'd worked for, his entire body broke out in a hideous weeping skin disease, generating an itch and pain that could only be relieved by scraping pieces of broken pottery over his skin as he sat on the ground among ashes. What a pitiful sight he must have been.

As if that wasn't enough, his bitter wife – presumably clumsily dealing with her own grief – mocked him for maintaining his integrity and urged him, 'Curse God and die!' (Job 2:9). Yet Job still refused to do any such thing.

Rather than draw them closer, this trauma drove a wedge between them. His wife was repulsed by his appearance and exasperated by his insistence on honouring God. Mrs Job doesn't appear in the rest of the account, although the end of the book indicates she stayed with her shadow of a husband, as was culturally necessary, although her attitude may have increased his torment. There is no mention of kindness, mutual support or affection, which adds another layer of suffering to the story.

Three of Job's friends arrived to sympathise, but they were so overwhelmed by the scale of his losses, and the fact that they could barely recognise him, that they too tore their clothes in the culturally appropriate way, wept, put dust on their heads and sat with him in silence for a full week.

Perhaps it would have been better if they'd stayed quiet, because the next thirty chapters record the conversation between the four of them in which Job's friends, by turn, came up with various reasons why these calamities had come upon him. They may have been well meaning, but they were also badly mistaken in their poor theological interpretations of what was going on. One said that Job must have been trusting in his own works to gain God's approval, and now he was being judged; another claimed that clearly Job had sinned in some way to bring this on himself; and the third accused Job of the sin of pride which had now brought about his downfall.[130]

Job put up with their nonsense, though he called them, 'miserable comforters' (Job 16:2) – 'Job's comforters' is a phrase we're familiar with, referring to those who are of no comfort at all. When he did respond to them, he used irony in some of his replies, told them they must be specific in their accusations if there was really any truth in them, and to stop using broad generalisations that didn't apply to him. He refuted their theories about his condition by laying out examples of how the wicked prosper while the righteous suffer.[131]

Scattered through the conversation are Job's references to his trust in God. Throughout his ordeal, he kept his eyes fixed on Him and focused on his own hope of life beyond death, which he felt might be preferable to the excruciating pain he was enduring. That assurance provided a flicker of hope throughout Job's suffering.[132]

While he explored the desolation and abandonment he felt, Job never allowed those feelings to displace the things that he knew about God, who he continued to believe was watching out for him.

> But he knows the way that I take;
> when he has tested me, I shall come forth as gold.
> My feet have closely followed his steps;
> I have kept to his way without turning aside.
> I have not departed from the commands of his lips;
> I have treasured the words of his mouth more than my
> daily bread.
> (Job 23:10-12)

---

[130] Job 4:1-6; 8:3-6; 11:13-15; 11:1-6.
[131] Job 12:1-3; 26:2-4.
[132] Job 6:8-10; 13:15-16; 14:13-17.

Job saw his suffering as a trial, or test, and repeatedly expressed a desire to find God and state his case before Him, as a righteous man. This proved to be a sticking point. Job's integrity had become an idol in his life.

It's only when a fourth friend, Elihu, joined the others that he really hit a nerve, and prepared the way for Job to repent of focusing on his own integrity rather than on the righteousness of God. This companion picked up something in Job's spirit that was just a bit 'off', and he was the only friend who didn't get rebuked by God. He put his finger on a hard kernel of pride that lay deep below Job's exterior. Elihu wanted Job to be vindicated but, in fact, Job who had been so righteous was then so busy justifying himself before God that he rashly ended up suggesting that God was not just.[133]

Job was holding on to his integrity more firmly than he was holding on to God. The relationship was out of joint.

Elihu waxed lyrical about the magnificence of God and the wonders of His creation; he pointed out God's power and urged Job to lift his eyes from his problems – real as they were – and focus on God through his suffering.

It was Elihu's words that paved the way for the dramatic ending of both the book and the story of Job, as God Himself broke through the river of words with a dramatic storm. He told Job to steel himself and prepare to be asked some questions which he would have to answer.

Over the course of four chapters, God took Job on a metaphorical world tour of His activities and displays of His unquestionable might: from the glorious heavens to the pounding oceans; from the far mountains to the wide savannahs. He challenged Job to correct Him if he could; but Job, suddenly feeling small and insignificant, could only wisely answer:

---

[133] Job 34:5.

> I am unworthy – how can I reply to you?
> I put my hand over my mouth.
> (Job 40:4)

God's presentation included a series of searing rhetorical questions, pointing out that everything on earth belonged to Him, and Him alone, before Job plucked up courage to speak.

The one thing that God never did was give an explanation to Job for any of the horrendous things that had happened to him. The 'Why?' question which forms so easily on our lips was never addressed. This surely strongly suggests that it's not the right question, even in the bleakest and darkest valleys of life. There are other, more important issues at stake.

Job's last recorded words are telling:

> I know that you can do all things;
> no purpose of yours can be thwarted.
> You asked, 'Who is this that obscures my plans without knowledge?'
> Surely I spoke of things I did not understand,
> things too wonderful for me to know.
> You said, 'Listen now, and I will speak;
> I will question you,
> and you shall answer me.'
> My ears had heard of you
> but now my eyes have seen you.
> Therefore I despise myself
> and repent in dust and ashes.
> (Job 42:2-6)

Through Job's terrible ordeal, he moved; he changed; he grew in God. Where previously he cognitively knew about God and had heard a lot of things about Him, at the end he said he had actually seen God. At the point of greatest need, deepest hurt and exposed vulnerability, he had an encounter that blew all his previous experiences out of the water. His integrity, commendable as it was, was nothing compared with the revelation of actually having a relationship with his awesome Creator.

The wonder of it caused Job to repent, to lay aside the integrity he had clung to for so long and submit to the wise hand of God, while admitting that his understanding would always be limited. How could a finite mind ever hope to grasp the vastness and extent of an infinite one?

Job ends with a fresh and more accurate perspective on the world, and on God's dealings with humanity.

His season of suffering and trauma was followed by a period of incredible bounty during which he received an even greater blessing from God than before. Over the ensuing 140 years of his life, Job owned twice as much livestock as he had done previously, and had another ten children. No one is suggesting that these were a replacement, but they must have brought some solace and healing to both Job and his bitter wife. They certainly made some impact, since his three daughters were – quite against cultural norms – given an inheritance just like their brothers.

While Job's health and wealth were restored, and he came into a season of unparalleled blessing during which he honoured the nature and dealings of God, the conclusion of his account reveals that his faith was far more important than his circumstances.

John Piper points out:

> Job's pain is not the pain of the executioner's whip but the pain of the surgeon's scalpel. The removal of the disease of pride is the most loving thing God could do, no matter what the cost.[134]

Throughout his trials, he never blamed God, but it was only when Job had a revelation of who God was and is that his heart was truly changed. Job humbled himself and submitted to God's

[134] www.desiringgod.org/messages/job-the-revelation-of-god-in-suffering (accessed 24 July 2023).

sovereignty. It took unspeakable suffering to get him there, but the journey was also one of evidential grace, in which the hand of God is clearly seen. His suffering was, indeed, redemptive.

12. The Bow and the Archer

So what lies ahead for this arrow?

The allegory is clear. We are the prepared and polished arrows; we are ready to be used in battle.

Only two elements are now required: the bow and the archer. Without these, the arrow can be as beautiful and as extraordinary as it is possible to be, but it will serve no real purpose beyond the decorative. It may be admired as an example of craftsmanship, but it will never truly fulfil its destiny if it is never fired.

Who is the archer?

The skilled archer, of course, is also the master craftsman. God, our heavenly Father, will shoot us when appropriate from His bow.

That bow is a picture of the framework of His purposes, into which we are slotted ready for firing; the bowstring is the calling and timing of God. When the string is pulled back into position with the important nock allowing the arrow to be tucked snugly into place, then the archer can fire at will, knowing He will make His mark accurately.

The three work together in perfect union for maximum effect, and so the arrow finally becomes all that it was born to be:

He made my mouth like a sharpened sword,
in the shadow of his hand he hid me;
he made me into a polished arrow
and concealed me in his quiver.
(Isaiah 49:2)

Instructions for arrows

Before we are let loose to fly, there are four things we arrows need to know.

1. Arrows do not show off or carry inherent talent. It is the skill of the marksman, who selects the appropriate arrow from the quiver, that is admired. The expertise he shows in battle, or in competition, speaks for itself. If he chooses to admire his arrows, it is with the delight of the craftsman over what has been created, rather than for their own sake.

God is no exception. Though He delights in us, sings over us, has set His love on us and favours us,[135] it would be inappropriate for us to seek glory for ourselves. We are what we are because of His grace, not because of our merit.

The useful arrow brings glory to the one who fires it; never to itself.

Jesus told a story to His disciples in which the attitude of servants to their masters was explained:

So you also, when you have done everything you were told to do, should say, 'We are unworthy servants; we have only done our duty.'
(Luke 17:10)

Despite the fact that none of us can claim to have done absolutely everything God has ever asked of us, He has graciously elevated us from the position of servant to that of a

---

[135] Zephaniah 3:17; Psalm 91:14, KJV; Psalm 84:11.

son or daughter. More than acquaintances, He counts us not as servants, but as offspring and friends.[136] Our responsibility is to draw attention to our Saviour, not to ourselves.

An arrow cannot boast in its own ability; it has none. There is no room for pride or self-promotion in our hearts, regardless of how God chooses to use us. That is His prerogative.

The Westminster Catechism states that the chief end of man is to 'glorify God, and to enjoy him for ever'.[137] Bringing glory to God is our eternal destiny. Heaven will not be a task-driven, agenda-attentive, clock-watching, project-completing place. Neither will it be an eternal church service, nor consist of unending celestial boredom – harp-playing or otherwise – but a paradise of abundant worship-filled life that will make everything that has gone before seem no more substantial than a shadow. God will be magnificently glorified for all time in ways we cannot begin to imagine.

2. An arrow needs to be ready when the Master's hand reaches for it. In that moment of need, the arrow cannot shrink back. It cannot suddenly offer reasons why it would rather be excused from this particular mission. It is not appropriate to express reluctance, or offer excuses about leaving the safety and cosy security of the comfortable quiver. It does not cower in the shadows, hugging the familiar leather walls and hoping it won't be noticed.

What has God asked of you, in the past, the present and the future? I have no idea, beyond the universal call to follow Him; but I can guarantee that He will equip you and walk with you in whatever it is. It may be a task that requires great boldness, courage and inner strength, all of which the Holy Spirit can provide. It may be a job in a very public arena, or perhaps a challenge in a quiet backwater that no one will ever hear about this side of eternity. It may be that your name is to be

---

[136] John 15:15.

[137] www.apuritansmind.com/westminster-standards/shorter-catechism (accessed 24th August 2023).

remembered throughout history, but it's more likely that your name will be forgotten, even if it was ever known, by succeeding generations.

Success for arrows lies not in grandness, popularity and international renown. True success lies in obedience.

The prophet Isaiah spoke on another occasion about the coming Messiah. In our Bibles it's recorded under the added heading: The year of the Lord's favour. It begins like this:

> The Spirit of the Sovereign LORD is on me,
> because the LORD has anointed me
> to proclaim good news to the poor.
> He has sent me to bind up the broken-hearted,
> to proclaim freedom for the captives
> and release from darkness for the prisoners,
> to proclaim the year of the LORD's favour.
> (Isaiah 61:1-2)

Like the polished arrow prophecy from Isaiah 49, this is a predictive word about Jesus, but it also carries another layer of truth about all those in God's family. The pattern is clear – God gives an anointing for the job for which He has commissioned us. In other words, He will prepare and equip us for the task He has in mind for us. For every appointing, there is also an anointing.

Whatever plan God has for you, and however daunting it may be, you can be sure that it will be less of a leap in the dark and more of a step into the light.

3. It may be that far from holding back, some arrows might seek to jostle for position. They want to be the first to be chosen, the first to be fired, the first to make an impact; the supremely important one that everybody sees and talks about; the one that is used, apparently, at the expense of all the others. Perhaps you have met people on your journey who show such tendencies – perhaps you are one of them? This kind of arrow has little understanding about the timing of God and frequently tries to push into things prematurely.

Better to be the arrow that waits patiently in the cool and darkness of the quiver, however ignominious and routine it might feel; better to trust the intuition and wisdom of the archer who will fire when ready. Different colour whipping cords indicate different arrowheads, The archer will choose the appropriate arrow for the task He has in mind.

When the moment comes and the arrow is drawn out of the holding place and placed in the bow, the arrow must continue to submit to the strong hands of the archer. In order to shoot, the archer must nock the arrow and pull the bowstring backwards. Trusting the archer is imperative.

4. Before the bowstring is released and the arrow is launched, the archer uses his enormous strength to pull the string back to his ear. The longbowmen of yesteryear trained for years to develop the necessary strength to wield their English bows. This manoeuvre causes the locked arrow to be temporarily pulled in the reverse direction from the target. The arrow may feel as though it's going backwards, when what is really happening is preparation for great impetus when the bowstring is released and the arrow hurtles forwards.

There are times in our pilgrimage with God that we experience that same sensation. We were sure he was calling us in one direction, yet we seem to be further away than ever, or on a completely different trajectory. Again, trust in His timing and His promises is key.

If the arrow were to fight against the bow at this point, it would be impossible for the bowman to take the clean shot he planned. The arrow could well miss the target altogether. Imagine: all that hard work, all that preparation, wasted. Not only that, but such a blunder could jeopardise an entire battle, opening the door for defeat where victory should have been certain.

Fighting the bow

Are there moments when you have fought against the bow? I know I have. There are times when I haven't liked where God seemed to be sending me. I have kicked against it, squirmed and blustered. Even when I have known God was in control, He has not always taken me in a direction that has been my natural preference. I've felt that I was going backwards rather than forwards. God certainly has no qualms about challenging our personal comfort zones. Trusting that He sees the big picture will help us stay in a place of peace in confusing seasons.

Looking back, I can see several times when this happened in my life:

➢ The career I thought I was going to have in television, and which was within my sights, proved not to be where He wanted me. My pride was dented.

➢ Again, when God called us to the town of Andover in Hampshire, UK, I knew it was the right thing to do, but the attitude in which I went at the time was not one of unbridled joy. I was reluctant, and amid the arrival of a new baby and postnatal depression, I resisted the demands of further change.

➢ When unkind and untrue things were said about us, by people I thought should be cheering us on, I pulled against the 'bow'; it was not a place I wanted to be. It felt too painful, too demanding, too unjust and too difficult to bear.

➢ During the period when we responded to a clear call from God, confirmed by the teams we work with, to spend more time in South Africa, we put everything in storage and left without having a home to go to. I found the transition time far more turbulent than I had anticipated and struggled with feeling quite isolated.

➢ I was diagnosed with breast cancer at the start of the pandemic; my first reaction was to question the archer.

In retrospect, I can see that God knew exactly what He was doing in each of these instances.

➢ By changing my career track, He not only protected me from a great deal, but also brought me into something much more worthwhile, in terms of having an impact in the world.

➢ I was so incredibly blessed during the twenty years we lived in Andover that it's hard to believe I was reluctant to go in the beginning. I wouldn't have missed it for anything; I learned so much about Him, and about friendship, prayer, unity and enjoying Him. It was a precious time and I feel enormously privileged to have been there.

➢ As far as our reputation is concerned, I have learned that even that is safe in God's hands. He may vindicate us if He wants to, but even if He doesn't, I am only responsible for my own reaction to gossip, rumour and the like. That's a decision of the will, to be made one day at a time.

➢ God opened doors in Cape Town which led to us spending several years living in a beautiful apartment near the ocean from where we could see Robben Island. Our times in South Africa have proved a rich seam of leaning into God and being amazed at His leading and provision, as well as providing time and space for writing for me. We've made new friends, discovered others with the same desire to see God's kingdom come, and had opportunities to explore a wonderful country.

➢ Even during my cancer journey, I found a supernatural peace in God which I could not possibly have manufactured. It was marked by an extraordinary time of intimacy with Jesus, which brought Psalm 23:5 to life in a fresh way.

I am never a victim, because God orders my steps. I know beyond doubt the importance of Proverbs 4:23: 'Above all else, guard your heart, for everything you do flows from it.' This is an active process, a discipline of both mind and heart that is not without its difficulties. It is the only way for any of us to seek the good of those who, for whatever reason, wish us ill, and the way to find God's peace as we tuck into His bow.

We will all encounter circumstances on our spiritual journeys which will bring to the surface what's truly in our hearts. They will reveal how much of our belief has truly become established in our lives, what is only cognitive and what is truly being lived out in real life.

The target

I suspect that from time to time even the most insignificant arrow finds that the chosen target doesn't look quite like it expected or imagined. When you're bundled up with a bunch of other arrows, it will probably feel terribly ordinary. There can be something beautiful even in that.

We do not need to have headline-catching lives to have God's hand on us. Working in His kingdom is usually very ordinary. Daily routines are not glamorous or remarkable, and yet they provide the environment for living out His truths, and give space for creating life-giving habits and disciplines. We don't have to prove anything to the One who knows us through and through. Our own importance has been abandoned with everything else we left at the foot of the cross. The fact that we are chosen, loved and adopted[138] into God's family gives us significance beyond anything that the world can offer us.

---

[138] Galatians 4:4-7.

Indeed, the arrow that imagined a glorious firing into a bullseye target in front of an admiring crowd may find instead that it is used randomly, landing ignominiously, hidden among brambles. Perhaps its job was to be fired as a signal, rather than to receive thunderous applause, after all. Maybe the arrow will be used to kill a metaphorically rabid bear or wolf, to halt a trail of spiritual destruction by the enemy in some unknown backwater of the world.

We may never understand the significance of what we do.

Many arrows will never know why they were chosen or used for a particular purpose; their responsibility is simply to be ready, willing, available, obedient and submitted.

As far as the archer is concerned, his priority is to keep the arrowheads on every arrow in his possession sharp, and the fletchings dry and crisp. He must especially keep his bowstring dry.

This is not a one-off operation, but a care and maintenance routine that needs attention each day. Arrows get jostled and damaged by simple wear and tear in the quiver, and need ongoing care. However good our community, we will crash into one another from time to time; remember the exhortation to keep any scars clean.

We will never grow out of these things; we will always need to remain teachable and pliable in the hands of our Master.

Useful arrows

Historically, making arrows was a time-consuming and costly business; it's no surprise that, where possible, arrows would be used more than once. Retrieving them from the field of battle was an important job. The ones collected from the Battle of Crécy in August 1346 were sent back to England, where it took ten men six days to strip, clean and refletch them ready for the army to reuse. Edward III had overseen storage of 130,000 sheaves of arrows and 7,700 longbows in the Tower of London, in readiness for this campaign. At twenty-four arrows per sheaf, that's a whopping 3,120,000 arrows in all.[139] One arrow in its lifetime may have been used in multiple battles as long as it remained supple and could be refletched, either with new feathers or by steaming the damaged vanes back to pristine condition.

Other arrows might have just one spectacular flight to a target; some might be destroyed in the process if they were set alight, but their impact would be all the greater. Church history is filled with saints, missionaries and martyrs who gave their lives for the sake of the gospel in places where God's Spirit raised a harvest of souls won for Him.

Into the future

It would be remiss of me not to include the thought that there is a sense in which we ourselves fire arrows into the future. We looked at this in terms of discipleship chains in Chapter 10a, and King Solomon was celebrating children when he wrote:

> Children are a heritage from the LORD,
> offspring a reward from him.
> Like arrows in the hands of a warrior
> are children born in one's youth.
> Blessed is the man
> whose quiver is full of them.
> (Psalm 127:3-5)

It's a different picture, but the same principle as we saw lived out by Paul as he invested into younger believers so they could become mature and effective in the days ahead. Children, both natural and spiritual, are to be fired into the future. They are our legacy, and will go further than we will in terms of both years and, we trust, fruitfulness. Rather than make the same mistakes

---

[139] www.youtube.com/watch?v=gesJRwOTRi0 (accessed 21st April 2023).

we did, we long to see them grow strong and firm in their faith; determined, sacrificial and radical warriors who will make severe dents in the enemy's attempts to destroy genuine Jesus-followers, through all his devious schemes. They too need to be equipped to influence and change the prevailing godless culture, certain not just of doctrine but of the reality of the abundant life of Jesus, lived out with integrity and authenticity.

We are tired of hearing about leaders falling; of financial misdemeanours and sexual misconduct; of spiritual, physical and emotional abuse by those in positions of ecclesiastical power. The kingdom of God has always been about serving, preferring others; not a top-down but a bottom-up kind of operation in which hierarchies are rejected in favour of a family model; where everyone is encouraged to grow, mature and begin their own family or community. Unless we nurture genuine relationships where trust works more than one way, we will find ourselves with a poor imitation of what Jesus had in mind.

The early Church had multiple challenges. They too lived in a time of cultural upheaval, political intrigue and governmental brutality and persecution. They were a vulnerable minority who turned the world upside down. History records how true revivals brought the life of God to communities and nations where hopelessness and moral decay were so embedded it seemed there was no way back to anything else. It's a lie the enemy likes to perpetuate, but it is just that – a lie.

If your children are young: teach them the things of God; introduce them to Jesus early on and set them on a path of purpose equipped with His promises and His Holy Spirit.

If your children are teenagers: keep praying God's promises over them and keep the lines of communication open. Whatever it takes, make sure they can see the authenticity of your faith under your roof, every day.

If your children have left home and appear to have left Jesus, don't give up on praying for them. The prodigals still come home; their story isn't finished, and Jesus hasn't stopped looking for them. The Father watches out with open arms, ready to welcome them home again.[140]

If you don't have children, ask God about the people in your fellowship community. Who can you mentor? Spiritual mothers and fathers are so valuable, yet in short supply. Discipleship is most effective not when studying a book, but when a younger believer sees the fruit of a life lived with God in someone else and is able to walk alongside them for a season, asking questions, discussing doubts, fears, insight; the things that captivate and bother them. We've seen how Paul worked out the principle of chains of discipleship with Priscilla and Aquila, Timothy and Titus. It's a pattern that hasn't dated in more than 1,900 years. These apprentice Jesus-followers will be fired into places you couldn't possibly anticipate.

What a privilege to be part of God's strategy for winning a lost world.

Target Questions

➤ What are the obstacles you face that hold you back from your calling? How can you navigate them?

➤ How would you define true success? How does the Bible define success?

➤ What are the difficulties we encounter when waiting for God to move or speak?

➤ What is the best way to wait?

---

[140] See Luke 15:11-32.

12a. Examples from the Old Testament

God is the archer, and His bow represents His purposes from which He fires His arrows. That purpose is to see His kingdom come on earth, His Son glorified and multitudes come into a living, vibrant, authentic relationship with Him while becoming all that He intended us to be.

Each arrow is prepared for a task: some for a single moment, others to be used repeatedly; all to accomplish something of worth as enemies are thwarted, their strongholds destroyed and God's kingdom rule extended.

The Bible is full of such examples. Here we'll take a quick selective overview of each kind of arrow. First, let's look at some of those whom we might think of as single-impact arrows.

Noah was the ninth generation from Adam through the line of Seth.[141] He was a righteous man at a time when wickedness had become commonplace in the earth, and God was grieved. 'The LORD regretted that he had made human beings on the earth, and his heart was deeply troubled' (Genesis 6:6). God considered wiping out the entire human race, but held back because He saw that Noah's heart was different.

We all know about Noah's ark; this was the purpose for his life: to preserve a remnant of what God had created – animals,

---

[141] Genesis 5.

birds and reptiles, as well as his own family – ready for a fresh start. Despite his age, Noah did everything just as God instructed until, at six hundred years old, the torrential rain and floodwaters came.

He may have been a single-use arrow, but he was a crucial one. His obedience ensured that God's purposes continued to be worked out in the world. The plan of redemption was still unfolding.

Deborah was a prophetess as well as one of Israel's judges.[142] She would sit under a tree, known as the Palm of Deborah, and make godly decisions about disputes that were brought to her by the Israelites.

God instructed her to call for the military commander Barak to lead ten thousand men into battle and victory against the Canaanite armies. His reluctance to fight without her by his side meant that the glory of the conquest would not go to him, but to a woman.

Jael was the woman about whom Deborah and Barak sang in the ensuing song of celebration once the enemy had been vanquished. This resourceful woman lured Sisera, the commander of the opposing army, into her tent, where she gave him milk and lulled him to sleep before killing him by driving a tent peg through his head. It's a gruesome story, but Jael's fame spread far and wide. She was an arrow in the hand of God to bring about defeat for an army that had harassed the Israelites for so long.

Deborah's wisdom and godliness in this matter ushered in forty years of peace for the people of God. She made herself available and obedient to God's call to engage in the battle, and flew straight and true.

Samson was another in the line of judges over Israel. Famous for his long hair and incredible strength, his story is sad and complicated: a child of promise whose coming was announced to his mother by an angel; he was dedicated to God before

---

142 Judges 4–5.

birth.[143] Samson foolishly married a Philistine woman who was later given to another man. His anger over this spilt out in an arson attack for which the Philistines avenged themselves by burning both his wife and his father-in-law. He entangled himself with Delilah, the prostitute; she was working for the Philistines who wanted to know the secret of his strength. God's purposes were only fulfilled after Samson was blinded and spent time in prison. Sometime later, he was brought out to be mocked as a warped entertainment act at a pagan festival. God allowed Samson's strength to return one more time when, in a final spectacular feat, he destroyed the supporting pillars and brought down the entire temple, crushing thousands of Philistines and forfeiting his own life.

This arrow burned out even as it hit the mark for which God destined it.

Queen Esther won her position as consort to the powerful Persian king, Xerxes, in a bizarre beauty contest. God used her in the royal household to thwart the plans of the evil Haman, who had positioned himself to destroy the entire Jewish nation. She was sorely tempted to hold back from using her place of influence, knowing that visiting the king, who had not asked for her in a month, might cost her her life.[144] Esther's cousin, Mordecai, knew this too, but also believed that God had strategically placed Esther in the palace for this exact moment in history:

> If you remain silent at this time, relief and deliverance for the Jews will arise from another place, but you and your father's family will perish. And who knows but that you have come to your royal position for such a time as this?
> (Esther 4:14)

---

[143] Judges 13.
[144] Esther 4:10.

Esther set herself and her maids to pray and fast for three days before she took her life in her hands, trusted God and went to see King Xerxes. If she had not done so, an entire people group, including herself, could have been wiped out, and the whole plan of salvation would have been ruined; the line of Jesus potentially destroyed, unless God had brought about rescue from elsewhere.[145]

The obedience of Esther scored a direct hit on the target God intended: to deliver His people in accordance with the unfulfilled promises over them, including the birth of the Messiah.

Other single-use arrows might be Shadrach, Meshach and Abednego – contemporaries of Daniel who boldly stood up for the supremacy of God in the face of King Nebuchadnezzar's edict requiring his subjects to worship a golden statue of himself. Their refusal to give in to his blasphemous hubris led to the horrifying punishment of being thrown alive into a blazing furnace from which God miraculously rescued them.[146]

You could say that these arrows were literally on fire, yet they neither burned up nor smelled of smoke on their release. The most powerful man in the world at the time could only stand amazed and admit that no god was like their God.

Moses spent forty years in an opulent, pagan Egyptian palace and forty years looking after sheep in the harsh and rigorous conditions of the desert before God fired him back into Egypt. Only then was he ready to lead the Israelites out of captivity and on to the land God had promised them years before, in Abraham's time. He was used over and over again to bring God's words to Pharaoh and then to represent God to the people of promise for forty arduous years.

Elisha, the protégé of Elijah, was an Old Testament prophet whom God repeatedly used to bring His words to Israel. He saw God move in supernatural ways on many occasions. By the power of God, Elisha made water drinkable, raised a child to

---

[145] Esther 4:14,
[146] Daniel 3.

life, provided for a widow, fed a hundred people from twenty loaves of bread and saw the influential commander of a foreign army healed. You can read about these and other instances in 2 Kings.

Jeremiah, known as 'the weeping prophet', had a ministry covering forty years during which time he brought God's words of warning and rebuke to His people. He urged them to repent and turn back to God to avoid God's discipline. He took prophetic actions to reinforce and illustrate his spoken words using a linen belt, a clay pot and a homemade yoke.[147]

Tragically, the people refused to listen to him or heed the warnings about God's coming judgement. Their persistence in turning their back on God led to the ultimate downfall of the nation, their capture and seventy years spent in exile far from home.

In this book, we've seen how Paul, in the New Testament, was fired as an arrow into places and people groups to bring the good news of Jesus with power and authority. During three missionary journeys, as well as years spent in prison, his learning shed light on the Scriptures for new believers and old. His example caused a cascade effect as he discipled people who discipled others, creating a chain reaction that impacted much of the known world, the ripples of which still impact us today.

In every case these arrows, and all those whose stories you can read for yourself (for example, Joseph, Gideon, Abigail, Nehemiah, Daniel, Jonah), never chose the target for themselves. That was God's department. In every case the long and painful preparation was never wasted.

---

[147] Jeremiah 13:1-11; 18:1-10; 19; 27–28.

Conclusion

Every allegory falls down eventually, and this one is no exception.

Chronology

Having explored the arrow-making process in a series of chapters, the process looks chronological. For arrowsmiths who still craft their weapons the old-fashioned way, it is; but it is not typically the same in the lives of followers of Jesus.

God doesn't work exclusively on one aspect of our character until we reach a specified point. There's no tick chart to check us off that only allows us to progress to the next aspect of refining once we've completed the previous one. It's not like those school reading schemes my daughter so enjoyed, where completion means promotion to the next level.

When we commit our life to God, He will deal with us in some, or all, of these areas over the course of our lifetime, often more than once. It's a refining process.

Neither does God wait until we have reached some level of spirituality before we can be useful in the kingdom and enjoy living life with Him. We've seen how God works through brokenness and through weakness, even among the most gifted of His children. It's good to remember that we were designed for relationship with Him before anything else. Living in peace and walking in step with Him while enjoying who He's made us to be is paramount. There may be times in our lives when everything else is stripped away but this. Rather than flounder, we can still stand strong, secure in both who we are and who He is.

What we do trails far behind that, and only then comes authentically from the security of knowing we are loved, chosen and adopted into God's family. Whether we feel we have an ordinary or an exciting life, the important thing is to have that abundant life that we were made for. God is not interested in our great exploits or grand gestures. We can never impress Him by such things. He is still looking for those who listen, submit and obey with the joy He has planned for us through the fulfilment of covenant promises by Jesus and the Holy Spirit.

In Chapter 5a, we met Samuel, who learned to hear from God when he was still a small boy. In Chapter 6a, we saw how a captured little girl brought news of God at work in Israel to Naaman's wife in Syria. Walking with Jesus involves growing, developing and maturing in our knowledge, understanding, wisdom and application of spiritual things, but even better, in our closeness with, and enjoyment of, Him. Basking in His love and radiating the nature and character of Jesus with integrity is itself a giant advertisement for God's kingdom life.

Even if we live to a grand old age, we will still be apprentices in many ways; always learning, and always listening, as we submit to our friend, Master and King. None of us may ever know how significant or otherwise any of our words and deeds might be in the economy of God's kingdom: these things are in His very capable hands. Our responsibility is to give Him full rein (and reign) in every area of life.

The degree to which God has access to the recesses of our hearts is largely up to us. In the book of Revelation, the disciple John records the words of Jesus to the church in Laodicea. Jesus says:

> Here I am! I stand at the door and knock. If anyone hears my voice and opens the door, I will come in and eat with that person, and they with me.
> (Revelation 3:20)

This verse is often quoted out of context. It is actually written to those who are already Christians, not to unbelievers, but the implication is clear: these believers had not allowed Jesus completely free access into their lives and into their church community. Hence Jesus stood outside, waiting and seeking to be granted entry, and access to all areas.

If anyone is holding back in the relationship, it will not be Him. There is no reluctance on His part to pursue intimacy with us.

We are on a continual journey of learning and growing while walking with Jesus. I doubt that we can ever truly say that we have completely learned something, since circumstances never duplicate themselves and events still take us unawares. However, if we're in tune with the Holy Spirit we will recognise what He is saying to us and we can remain confident that God will continue to be 'our refuge and strength, an ever-present help in trouble' (Psalm 46:1).

Our history and our experience of walking with God help us to understand that the principles we have explored here will be applicable throughout our lives. Whatever the culture, geography or relationships surrounding our individual circumstances, God is shaping us and changing us – slowly, slowly, bit by bit – to be more like Jesus.

While the allegory disintegrates, the arrow quietly holds lessons for the wise man or woman of faith. Let's treasure each of them, assured that they repeatedly point to the plans and purposes God has for us.

The arrow tells us primarily of God's overwhelming love and His detailed care for us. It shows us how to make ourselves available to Him, to submit to Him, to joyfully sacrifice whatever He asks of us, and to confidently walk into the perfect destiny He has for us.

It reminds us that being 'conformed to the image of his Son' (Romans 8:29) can be an uncomfortable process, but one which is infinitely precious and worthwhile, undertaken with tender loving-kindness and soaked in the softening elements of unfailing, unconditional, divine grace and love.

We are assured, too, that we are safe in the hands of the supreme Archer; one whose skill is unparalleled, whose hands are strong and safe, and who is well aware of what's happening on the battlefield.

He employs us as He wills, without panic or uncertainty. We have purpose in His workshop, in His quiver, and when He selects us for firing into the world around us.

We are made for impact, effectiveness and to see His kingdom come into our culture and our contexts. His hands are steady and His aim is sure.

Psalm 7:13 says, 'He has prepared his deadly weapons; he makes ready his flaming arrows.' That's what we've been exploring together. Crafted and shaped according to His purpose, ready and willing to go wherever He sends us, full of faith, with fire in our hearts – fire of passion as well as in the power of the Holy Spirit. Will you be such an arrow?

There is great purpose and satisfaction in simply being an arrow when we belong, not to any old foot soldier with a bow, but to the King of kings.

He has prepared his deadly weapons;
he makes ready his flaming arrows.
Psalm 7:13